EVEN BETTER IF

BUILDING BETTER BUSINESSES, BETTER LEADERS AND BETTER SELVES

RACHEL THORNTON | LINDSAY KOHLER | CHARLIE SAMPSON

R^ethink

First published in Great Britain in 2021 by Rethink Press
(www.rethinkpress.com)

Contents

Introduction

Welcome. We're glad you're here. Before we get started, let us be clear about the journey you're about to go on.

We're not going to tell you this is the only business book that you'll ever need, and we're certainly not going to suggest we are effectively replacing those weighty, best-selling tomes on your office bookcase. That would be silly and boastful, even for us. We hugely respect, admire and have learned from many of these books.

This is not a 'business book' kind of business book. We often find with business books that the useful bit could have been written in twenty pages… but is hidden somewhere among 300. This book isn't like that. It is a practical distillation of decades of experience working with some of the best, most innovative, disruptive, successful (and unsuccessful) organizations, teams and individuals in the world. It is jam-packed with clear ideas, suggestions, proprietary thinking, models and exercises – with stories and examples from some of the biggest brands and ground-breaking, everyday-hero thinkers around today.

Much of what is accepted about succeeding in leadership, in business and in life is simpler than some would have you believe. Why? Firstly, because if we all accept that so much is impossible to do well and expensive and time-consuming to learn, it lets us off the hook for not even trying. Secondly, because there are multiple billion-dollar industries borne out of the misconception that we, the great unwashed amateurs, can't do it without the help of a horde of management consultants who charge a fortune.

We say that's nonsense.

Who are we? We're a communication expert and entrepreneur; an executive coach and leadership expert; and a behavioural scientist. Between us, we create the sweet spot you need to get to. Grounded in the science of why we do what we do, we'll tell you how to get there, and how to take others with you on your journey.

It's not about perfection. That doesn't exist. It's about incremental improvement, about being and getting even better.

If you are a leader, you work with a leader or you aspire to be a leader, this book is for you. If you are responsible for improving and moving your business towards its goals, this book is for you. If you are a human being with a curiosity for self-improvement and a desire to perform better, this book is for you.

We assume you're already good at many things. We assume you're keen to be even better. That's what *Even Better If* is about. Our coaching-style approach encourages you to ask: 'What could I be even better at if I just did something differently?' This book gives you the 'if' – the secret sauce. If you do even one thing from one of these nine chapters differently, you'll be *even better*.

PART ONE
BETTER BUSINESSES

I began communicating professionally first as a business journalist and then in B2B public relations before finding my heartland and calling leading internal communication (IC) and engagement in-house. For twelve years I worked for incredible organizations, including M&S Money, First Direct and Norwich Union.

In 2005 I co-founded scarlettabbott with a burning ambition to 'do it better': communication, building and motivating teams, and leading and operating a successful business with integrity, grit and a sense of humour. I had seen plenty of that in-house, but I firmly believe you can continually learn, evolve and do better.

When considering not just what we wanted this book to achieve overall, but what my three-chapter section on building better business should cover, with over twenty-seven years of experience I found myself going back into the mental archives of my career. What had I seen done best and worst – the good, the bad and the downright ugly of my decades in communication, engagement and leadership? Most importantly, from that lifetime of learning, what did I conclude was the difference that made the difference?

I analysed what the best businesses I know (of the many thousands of leading global brands, disruptive start-ups and impassioned not-for-profits I've worked with) all value and strive to do even better. What was their difference? As an entrepreneur and leader, what, too, was my own?

I'm not suggesting that the resulting three chapters are the silver bullet. Every organization is unique and driven by different cultural traits, strengths and weaknesses. What I am suggesting is that strength, understanding and capability in the areas covered will make your business even better, regardless of who you are and what you do.

Part One explores fresh insights, innovative and practical ideas and the behavioural science behind:

- **Purpose:** What it means to truly be purposeful and how to run your business with purpose, how to surface your purpose in your own organization and how purpose strengthens your employee value proposition.

- **Change:** Debunking change myths, developing the understanding that change is highly emotional and just what emotions it elicits, pushing aside barriers to change, and tips on how to design and deliver change programmes that work.

- **Diversity and Inclusion (D&I):** Why it matters (to every business), the truths and myths of D&I, some useful exercises to try out yourself and tips to make your D&I efforts even better.

A huge thank you to the amazing communication, change, HR and D&I pros and leaders that gave of their time, wisdom, experience and insights in helping me with these chapters. There is a truly stellar community out there and I'm proud to be part of it.

— Rachel

ONE
Purpose

'The purpose of the business is to make money for the owners.'

Some of you may have heard that from employees over the years, but how many of you have heard it uttered by a founder or owner? Money, to some extent, gets us out of bed in the morning. It's what enables us to take care of our basic, fundamental needs, but if money is the primary driving purpose of a business, that business won't be around for the long haul.

In this chapter, we will explore:

- Why purpose is not an 'add-on'

- What it means to be a purposeful company

- The four key individual purpose considerations to factor into broader purpose plans

- How purpose supports the employee value proposition (EVP)

- A step-by-step guide to surfacing your company's purpose, including our *Surfacing Your Purpose* questionnaire

- Six tips to run a truly purposeful business

Purpose is not an 'add-on'

Rachel Thornton, co-founder of scarlettabbott, provides an account of building her own business that shines a light on just how important purpose is, and even more importantly, how it must feel shared.

'I honestly hadn't considered the need for a clearly articulated purpose of our own. When we were small and growing at pace, our purpose was my personal purpose, mine and my business partner's – it pumped through our veins (along with stress, triumph, pressure and adrenaline) as we rode the rocket-ship that was our first seven or eight years in business together. Drive, optimism, focus, belief in ourselves and our team was purpose enough (for us) in those heady days.

'It wasn't purpose enough for a larger team, though. When a valued member of my senior crew tentatively floated the idea that what we lacked was a "purpose", something tangible to bind together our fast-moving, incredibly talented, fiercely competitive and highly ambitious tribe of communicators, I have to admit that I hadn't realised anything was lacking. I was a little affronted, to be honest; but I'm nothing if not open to smart people making smart suggestions, so I wholeheartedly agreed to explore it. As it turned out, that individual was considering a career move after several happy years with us. In hindsight, I wonder if that need for purpose was an expression of a personal yearning at a career crossroad, which made me muse: when you're not engaged, energized and clear in your own purpose, do you seek it elsewhere? Might you need something more, something shared and stated at work, when your own "personal purpose antenna' is on the blink?"

> Simply put, **purpose** is the core reason you exist. It informs your company values, which in turn determine your ambitions and guide your business decisions.

Purpose, in large part, is what makes companies different from one another. It forms the fabric of the organization and helps bring an organization together. From a business perspective, purpose can be a powerful driver of any desired turnaround. UK telecom giant BT underwent a purpose transformation project in 2019. When we asked Helen Willetts, Director of Internal Communications at BT, why the time was ripe to undertake such a project, she got straight to the heart of it:

> 'One reason is that anyone who has been following BT's story knows that it's been transforming at pace over recent years. That can take its toll on employees, especially when it might have felt like not much changed at BT for many, many years. Then suddenly, there's a real injection of pace into changing things. This year was a particularly big one for us as we looked to set out a new ten-year ambition and bold plans to bring that to life. We're digitizing and becoming more of a technology company and that runs right through the plans we've got. It was an important strategic, commercial and cultural moment for us to bring the organization together, and for us, we felt that had to be anchored in re-imagining why we exist.'[1]

What is a purposeful company?

Purposeful companies know something non-purposeful companies don't. They know, and can articulate, why they exist. They know what their role is in relation to their people, their customers and to their place in the world.

Your purpose statement is not just words on a page for the sake of having a purpose statement. Purpose provides organizations and colleagues with a shared structure. It is a shorthand language and rule book within and upon which to make decisions, behave and be. Think of purpose as a filter through which your business sees the world and orientates its place in it. Within that safe and co-created structure, employees can adopt more autonomy, enjoy increased ownership and take accountability for their decisions – all of which have been proved to promote flexibility of thought.[2]

Purposeful companies do the opposite of striving to make money for a select few (the owners or shareholders). Purposeful companies have multiple winners. They have colleagues with secure employment, challenging and stimulating work, personal growth and prospects, and bonds of friendship and support. They have clients or customers who can rely on best-in-class products and services when they need them most. In turn, there are the millions of employees globally whose working lives are made better, clearer, more motivating and more rewarding as a result of the activations and interventions that leaders, HR and internal comms (IC) teams design and deliver in the name of being purposeful.

Finally, there are the people in the wider community that benefit from a company's sense of shared purpose. These are the suppliers and partners relied upon to do business, the voluntary and charitable activities businesses undertake in the spirit of being truly purposeful, and even the local shops and restaurants teams purposefully frequent to build connections, relax and recharge. Being purposeful is a game that results in many winners.

Individual purpose matters, too

Companies that do not consider individual purpose as a powerful part of the overall employee value proposition (EVP) are at risk of falling behind the competition. Traditionally, security, benefits, bonus structures and payslips may have been a large part of what initially lured employees in, but those times are changing. While the traditional EVP elements are still important, the EVP is shifting to emphasize more programmes, benefits, perks and philosophies that allow for individuals to meet their specific needs and explore their own purpose. Thornton reflected on her individual purpose and how that drove her own wants and expectations from her work:

> 'Within myself, I identified the purpose factors that drove me at work: a yearning for autonomy, the opportunity to compete and do it better than others in the field, a passion for helping and developing others, a deep sense of responsibility to clients and my team, and the need for personal stretch and to learn new things every day. The thrill of working together towards a common goal, the deep pleasure drawn from human connection,

and the relationships and friendships I built
with clients, partners and colleagues. These
were the component parts of my joy in work:
my drive to do more than just show up, to
make a difference. That's what all employers
are seeking from as many of their people
as possible – that they show up to make a
difference.'

She did what potential and existing employees
are doing in increasing numbers. She took a good,
hard look at what she wanted out of work. Not just
the standard stuff we think of, such as interesting
work, nice colleagues, good pay and a company
that isn't overtly evil – but she considered the non-
standard stuff as well, such as what drives her,
motivates her and brings her the greatest pleasure
at work. She also looked at the impact she has on
the wider world and how her contribution helps
others.

It is within this expanded frame of what employees want that you should evaluate your company's
purpose. Ask: 'Does our purpose align with what, on
a broad scale, our existing and future talent wants?'
After all, times have changed and people want more,
as Andrea Mattis, host of *No More Long Talk* podcast
and currently the Global Internal Communications
Manager at Collinson, notes:

'Companies need to understand that we no
longer operate in a world where people just
work like they did back in the 1950s or 1960s.

That what you did in the morning was wake up, go to work, stay there all day and come back home and go to sleep. Nowadays, people want more. They want to explore new skills and grow in different ways outside of work that enhance what they already do for their organization. If organizations can support that, rather than seeing it as a hindrance, people will stay with them.'[3]

Company purpose must be authentic, or you risk disillusioning new employees. Shanna Wendt, who has held various VP-level communication roles at companies such as Coca-Cola European Partners and Dow Chemical, shared a story along these lines:

'An employee came into a company based on its values and what it stands for. That was the motivator for the employee to join; but then the behaviours and decisions that were being made didn't stack up to what was being externally portrayed. Then you have a situation where someone who came in thinking, "I know what I stand for and my individual purpose. I think I know what this company stands for, so there should be alignment," finds out the purpose wasn't authentic, and it doesn't work.'[4]

Another important consideration is that purpose is a journey which is never complete. We can always do more. Jesper Ambrosius, Head of LEGO Workplace Experience, reflects on this:

> 'We are a hugely purpose-driven organization. *Learning through Play* is truly at the heart of who we are, but we also acknowledge that we can and should do more to put play at the core of how we work. We can be pretty serious and corporate. We are grown-ups creating for kids; and my team and I are working right now to introduce a much more playful element to how we get things done. We want play to not be an activity but a mindset – a way of working where the characteristics of play are visible in the way we collaborate, communicate, facilitate and operate.'[5]

The four key individual purpose considerations

There are four key considerations for businesses to keep in mind when looking at individual purpose and making the business case for supporting individual purpose development within the organization:

1. Individual purpose enhances the experience of work.

2. Individual purpose is linked to internal forms of motivation.

3. Individual purpose differs by generation.

4. Individuals thrive in different cultures, and different cultures want different things from a purpose statement.

Let's look at each in more detail.

Consideration #1: Individual purpose enhances the experience of work

A large part of individual purpose is finding meaningful activities in which to engage. As part of their purpose journey employers can, and should, help individuals figure this out; but any individual can autonomously surface this for themselves. Purpose combines the pressures and needs existing in the outside world with pre-existing internal motivators to find the sweet spot of what actions will feel purposeful.

It is a difficult task to disentangle purpose from meaning, but the distinction is important. Purpose must be firmly situated within meaning. According to famed psychologist Abraham Maslow,[6] work without meaning does little to fulfil our psychological needs. While purpose is a belief in a reason for being (such as why a company exists), meaning is the value we ascribe to that purpose. If we ascribe a low value, purpose won't mean much.

Consideration #2: Individual purpose is linked to internal forms of motivation

Finding our sense of individual purpose is driven by the things that we're passionate about influencing for good, such as connecting local communities, combatting climate change, providing support for domestic abuse, etc. This is driven by a type of motivation known as intrinsic motivation.

> **Intrinsic motivation** is about harnessing internal motivators, such as doing the right thing for the sake of rightness or maybe going after a personal goal with no external reward tied to it. Often associated with altruism, intrinsic motivation can also be immoral (in the case of envy, revenge, etc). While we use 'influencing for good' in the paragraph above, there are two sides to every coin.

Consideration #3: Individual purpose differs by generation

The things people care about are shifting and a large part of this changed interest can be attributed to a changed work demographic. The days of working with just one company until retirement are over. People are happy to move jobs if they aren't finding fulfilment where they are currently. The scarlettabbott 2020 World Changers Report[7] explores this change in individual purpose and why it matters so much:

'Younger generations have never had so many choices. They can study, travel, become an influencer, kickstart a business with outside funding or join an environmental movement in south-east Nepal. A global economy means the world truly is your oyster. But that creates a lot of pressure… and there are no guard rails. Is it any wonder that these employees are looking for guidance on where to focus their efforts and how to find a sense of belonging?'

Gen Zs (often categorized as those born after 1997) are also increasingly looking for work that supports social and environmental causes. They want to make a difference, and if this is not a direct part of their roles, then their company better be committed to those causes via the company purpose.

Consideration #4: Individuals thrive in different cultures, and different cultures want different things from a purpose statement

Scarlettabbott's thoughts about company culture have been developed based on Charles Handy's famous culture framework.[8] This describes four types of culture, arranged around the elements of earth, air, fire and water. As culture could be an entire chapter (or book) on its own, we will just touch on the high-level considerations briefly. The key point is that you need to consider purpose in context with culture.

- **Fire cultures:** Mostly entrepreneurial. Driven by the purpose of the owner, and individuals must buy in to that to be personally fulfilled.

- **Water cultures:** Usually consultancies. Focused around the customer, so some individual purpose is derived from that.

- **Earth cultures:** The beefy corporations. Focused around job roles. Here, individual purpose may be driven by rank, hierarchy or how 'fancy' the job title sounds.

- **Air cultures:** Think general practitioners or academia. People derive purpose from the 'do-good' value that comes from their expertise.

(If you're unsure what type of culture your company has, talk to scarlettabbott about their culture diagnostic and audit to help you figure it out.)

How purpose supports the employee value proposition

Businesses ask employees to be engaged. They ask employees to give of their goodwill, brainpower, discretionary effort and energy in a way that moves the business towards its goals. In return for this engagement, individuals are increasingly asking businesses to provide more meaningful, purpose-driven work. This exchange is a win-win and a growing part of the EVP.

This exchange is also necessary as the war for talent rages. No employer wants to be on the losing side – and winners know purpose is an important part of their arsenal. After all, those best able to articulate the reasons to fight for one side over the other typically get the best talent. Think back to the days where the great houses took pride in their house flag or sigil. The house that spoke most passionately and memorably of what it stood for was the one that was able to inspire and arouse, the one best able to focus hearts and minds on the common foe and able to rally the most warriors behind it. While the war for talent is not a literal war anymore, you still need to satisfy that greatest of internal questions that all people ask: 'Why?'

This is the most common question out of the mouths of babes, and in the best of us, that curiosity never goes away completely. It helps us question the status quo, make better decisions, re-invent, re-imagine and improve just about anything. Joining an organization that values curiosity, that asks itself why first and foremost, is increasingly attractive to talent. Not only does it help colleagues make their own decisions at work and strive for better outcomes, it makes it easier to advocate for that business at home, with their peers or even in the pub. It helps them to answer the simplest of questions, one which we ask ourselves and are asked time and again by others: 'Why do you do what you do?' Ambrosius says:

> 'Ultimately, what we think is important about shared purpose is that it creates the feeling

of belonging. No matter what LEGO office you're at, you should have that feeling. We call it a "home-like" feel. Note, home-like, not actually a home. We do want the workplace to be a place of work and not mimic your home. Home is different. It's important for us that people actually do go home and spend time with their families and get that separation.'

Surfacing your company's purpose

Purpose is not created. Purpose is surfaced. It exists within the heritage, fabric and culture of your existing business. The job of the team tasked with a purpose project is to successfully extricate it from within. Wendt notes that, in her experience working in well-known, long-established companies, purpose is often re-examined when a company undergoes extensive change. She says:

'The moments that cause companies to look at their existing purpose is when they've gone through significant change. Whether they are re-examining their business model, their long-term strategy or going through mergers and acquisitions or other significant events – those are the moments of inflection and reflection of purpose.'

Purpose is not so much creating something new. Rather, it should be viewed as an exercise in giving back. This was the viewpoint of Gillian McGill, Global Director of Internal Communication at the British multinational insurance company Aviva. She led the team tasked with surfacing and articulating Aviva's new company purpose in 2019. If you think this is a difficult task for a newer company, imagine what it would be like if your company was over 300 years old. Aviva got its start as the Hand in Hand Fire and Life Insurance Society in London in 1696 and evolved, grew and merged over the years to form the Aviva known today. Such a journey does not come without large organizational shifts. In fact, it was a string of recent extreme changes – including changes in chief executives – that led Aviva to do some soul searching.

When the CEO left, Aviva started questioning what it was that brought the organization together. As McGill says:

> 'You started to see people talk about the things
> that galvanised the organization in the period
> without a rock star CEO and in the temporary
> absence of a clear strategy. And it became
> really apparent that people could see it and feel
> it in Aviva – but they couldn't articulate it. The
> existing set of words we had around 324 years
> of history didn't resonate with employees.'[9]

While people understood why Aviva existed, the element of purpose being a tool to help people make decisions or act as an advocate for the company was missing. Jon Hawkins, the global internal communications lead driving the purpose project at Aviva, added another dimension to the decision to reboot Aviva's purpose. Much of what Aviva had before was tethered to an outgoing member of the leadership team, 'and so we had to change, because purpose isn't about an individual.'[10]

Aviva wanted to find a way to describe what it was their employees came to work for every day – a purpose unique to Aviva that got to the heart of how people felt and described that feeling in a way that was both relatable and generated pride. As McGill explains:

'We were seeking something that would
honour 324 years of history and still work
for any future leader or any future strategy.
We wanted to build something enduring that
would buoy us through the choppy waters that
any organization faces… and stand the test
of time. Essentially, we were trying to bring
together 32,000 people.'

No small feat but Aviva was able to do just that; and the good news is – you can, too.

Seven steps to surfacing purpose

Surfacing purpose involves a mix of the right people, right stakeholders, right research, right writers and right atmosphere. It involves crucial decisions around who to include in the process. This next section outlines the seven-step process you can use to surface your purpose, with real-life examples and lessons learned from Aviva and BT:

1. Create your purpose taskforce.

2. Determine if you are going to look forwards or backwards.

3. Conduct research.

4. Take your stakeholders on the journey.

5. Use the *Surfacing Your Purpose* questionnaire.

6. Run a purpose workshop with your purpose taskforce.

7. Nail the purpose statement.

Step #1: Create your purpose taskforce

The central, common denominator of all the successful purpose journeys is the involvement of a wide variety of colleagues. For all those interviewed for this chapter, collaboration, co-creation and stakeholder engagement was one of the most difficult and most rewarding parts of the process. As a rough guide, you should include the following people in your taskforce:

- A C-level project sponsor.

- A director/VP-level representative from each part of the business (preferably a vocal one). This person should then identify the senior members of their team whom they want included in the more day-to-day taskforce activities.

- Senior representatives from internal communication and change management teams.

- The HR team will also need additional representatives. As the voice of the employees, this group is uniquely positioned to enhance the work, but also derail it, so make sure your HR teams and HR business partners have ample representation.

It is important to choose your people carefully. Do you want vocal ones, well-connected ones, or a mix of both? People from different levels, job roles and backgrounds will help ensure you get the requisite diverse thinking that will lead to a better outcome.

Step #2: Determine if you are going to look forwards or backwards

Companies surface purpose in one of two ways. The first way is by taking a retrospective approach, where they build upon the existing reason for being. For Aviva, their former stated reason for being was to '*defy uncertainty*'. This approach involves an intense internal focus on how the company and company purpose came to be. It usually involves questions such as:

- **What is that secret sauce that makes us different?** Is it culture, what we do, how we operate, our history, our founder, etc?

- **Why do we stand out?** What are we known for? What have we received positive press and attention for? What awards have we won?

- **How did we get here?** Is it our ways of working, or perhaps a series of key decisions that can be traced or other such key points in our evolution?

One key consideration with the retrospective approach is to avoid going into the territory where you simply articulate your existing reason for being. As Hawkins explains, 'If it's a purpose that's always been there, and now you just articulate a purpose that's always been there really well, how will that drive different outcomes in the future?'

Another approach is taking a prospective view. In this instance, you look forwards and reshape your reason for being to match where you want the business to go. With this approach, you might ask yourself where you see the future of your industry headed and what role you see yourself playing. If you do go this route, a critical question to ask is how far out of your comfort zone you are willing to go.

Step #3: Conduct research

No purpose exercise would be complete without bolstering your efforts with research and feedback. This is how you learn about your organization. When you do this listening activity and research, you might be pleasantly surprised to find that there are more similarities around how people describe your organizational purpose than there are differences. When you spot those similarities, those are the key points to dive into deeper.

Aviva took a robust approach regarding feedback. They approached 9,000 stakeholders, consumers, customers, investors, MPs and analysts to understand why they had bought a product from Aviva or why they had invested in Aviva. In essence, they were trying to understand what people wanted from Aviva and why they had chosen them. It was about understanding what external stakeholders wanted and what kept them coming back.

They then also looked at internal stakeholders by examining five years' worth of employee survey data. With this exercise, they were trying to get answers to the following questions:

- Why were people proud to work at Aviva?

- When they talked about Aviva, how did they articulate their connection to Aviva?

- What did people feel they needed to protect about Aviva?

- What did they tell their children about why they worked at Aviva?

- When asked about being a good corporate citizen, what were the words and language they used?

Once those general themes emerged, they were then validated with focus groups across the organization.

These smaller focus groups also allowed Aviva to examine the areas of the research that interested them more closely, as well as ensuring that what people were saying was also what people meant. Too often, there is a disconnect between what people feel and what they think, what they think and what they say, and what they say and then do. A pleasing trend emerged from these groups, says Hawkins:

> 'There were some really clear themes that started coming through. They weren't straplines, but definitely certain words kept being used. And so that theme of being there for people when it mattered, being a partner for life and that theme of being together emerged. There was also a clear theme around protecting what was important.'

Willetts explains how BT took a more light-touch approach and simply asked all colleagues if their current purpose still rang true to them. 'And we got thousands of comments back like, "Yes, it's alright, but it doesn't really get me out of bed in the morning." There was nothing wrong with it, but it didn't really ignite people.' A quick pulse check like this can be enough to put you on the path to figuring out if your current purpose is doing the job it was intended to.

Step #4: Take your stakeholders on the journey

Any change practitioner worth their salt understands a pivotal part of any successful change campaign is ensuring that people play a part in the process rather than feeling that change is something being done to them. McGill shared more of Aviva's purpose-surfacing process:

> 'We did stakeholder management like I've never ever done. We took every board member and executive member on a journey, but we took them on a personal journey. Like, we texted them the words from a workshop to show them where we had gotten to, or I read the CEO sets of words and he would tell me yes, or to go back to the drawing board.'

BT was particularly deft at this. A business as large, varied and complex as BT would demand nothing less. Willetts explains how they worked alongside leaders to get the right result:

> 'It was really important to firstly get buy-in from the chief executive and the chairman – that was crucial – so we went straight there. We didn't go through twenty committees to get to them. The second thing we did was involve all of the executive committee, because in any organization, if you're a senior leader, there is a chance you will derail things… whether or not you mean to.'

The delicate dance of involving people at the right time to benefit from their expertise without the whole show going off the rails is one you will need to perfect if you want a smooth journey to approval. BT also had a clever way of engaging the next tier of leaders, as Willetts explains:

> 'We shared the purpose with our top 800 leaders ahead of the launch to the business. This helped them to feel like they were part of the inside track. Our CEO fronted it and every single executive committee member talked about a part of it. We did it as a television show, so it was really exciting – but also really authentic. We talked about why the purpose meant something and the content was normal and gritty. For leaders to see the executive committee totally aligned helped get larger buy-in.'

BT also let the customer-facing parts of the business transition to the new purpose on their own timetable. Nothing changed on the external website until everyone was ready. This decision allowed these units to internalize what the purpose really meant in terms of the changes customers might see in how they typically interacted with BT employees.

Step #5: Use the Surfacing Your Purpose questionnaire

As we've discussed, you cannot create a purpose. It already exists. It is your job to surface it. Doing so requires a healthy dose of empathy, and since empathy starts with curiosity, the best place for you to start is where all curious people begin: asking the right questions. You can use the questionnaire below in a workshop or other working sessions designed to help surface your purpose.

EXERCISE: SURFACING YOUR PURPOSE QUESTIONNAIRE

Purpose and me

- At [name of organization] we should feel proud of...
- I believe that everything we do is ultimately in service of...
- Whatever the future holds, we will always...
- ... inspired me to join this company.
- ... makes me stay.
- The three things that are most important for me to have in my work are...

Purpose and our business

- What do we do better than anyone else in our marketplace/competitive set?
- How could having a purpose differentiate us in the market?
- What do you think having a purpose could mean to our clients/customers?
- What should we always protect and retain about our business?
- What do you think we need to change in our organization?
- Describe a time you've seen our company at its best.
- Describe in up to three phrases what you imagine your colleagues doing when they are inspired by a new purpose.

Step #6: Run a purpose workshop with your purpose taskforce

The *Surfacing Your Purpose* questionnaire is a great activity that can be done in advance of a focused workshop, or it can be used to guide the brainstorming and working session itself. The guiding principles and outcomes of this workshop should be clearly outlined to all participants. For Aviva, these guiding principles were:

- The purpose must be something that could guide action.

- The purpose must work in all languages (not just English).

- The purpose must be distinctly Aviva and not work for other organizations.

Workshop participants should be picked from all parts of your previous focus groups, along with senior stakeholders and your team of excellent wordsmiths. You'll need a brilliant writer(s) to tease purpose out of people's brains and move it onto a page. To start this process, write a narrative for each key theme emerging from your research to provide a starting point.

For Aviva, two clear themes emerged from their research: 'being together' and 'protecting what's important'. This allowed them to focus their workshop efforts on those concepts. They locked themselves in a room and got to work. McGill explains:

'We said, "OK, somewhere in here is our purpose." We set ourselves quite a challenge by saying, "Don't deviate into what the other six or seven themes were, because then you end up with the bland statements that lots of other organizations have, that are non-specific and non-Aviva." We said we had to come out of that room with it, or pretty damn close to it.'

The goal of the day was about getting underneath the words and connecting with the story and the emotion behind the purpose. Workshop activities involved dividing into groups and writing stories about what the purpose would mean to a host of everyday situations in which employees could find themselves. It was about first breaking down, and away from, the pre-existing notions they all carried into the workshop. 'We needed to be taken into a different space, because at that point you could have argued that we were too close to it. We had to break out,' says McGill. Only then could they move into surfacing the words that captured the meaning behind their purpose.

Step #7: Nail the purpose statement

At this point, you may be wondering: what purpose did Aviva land on? *With you today, for a better tomorrow.* BT's new purpose statement is similarly punchy: *We connect for good.* This is by design. Willetts describes an experience she had with surfacing purpose before she came to BT:

'We went through a huge amount of work, a
huge amount of research, and we came out
with the most beautiful statement; and it was
absolutely true. It was totally purposeful. But it
was so blooming long, no one could do anything
with it. No one could remember it; no one could
apply it. It's *really* important for it to be short.'

Six tips to run a truly purposeful business

If you've followed the seven steps above, you'll have
surfaced your purpose by now. That naturally begs
the next question: now that you have it, what are you
going to do with it? Are you ready to run your business robustly and honestly, with purpose at its heart?
'When there is a clear purpose to an organization, I
do think it's easier to hang your business strategy
and business plans off of that,' reflects Wendt. One of
the reasons BT chose to overhaul their purpose was
exactly that, according to Willetts:

'We'd had our former purpose for a very long
time, but we hadn't lived it. It would have
been very difficult to suddenly say that we're
going to live this purpose, the one that we had
for ten years, without changing it.'

Willetts is spot on. If you haven't been living your
purpose, then that means you haven't been considering how purpose impacts how you make decisions,
who you do or don't do business with, what you

prioritize or de-prioritize based on your adherence to your purpose, and what the implications are for all levels of the business. Andy Wales, Chief Digital Impact and Sustainability Officer at BT, agrees that their prior purpose wasn't fit for purpose (no pun intended):

'The old purpose was in the same general ballpark as our refreshed purpose, but it was too generic for the sector. It felt like it floated above the strategy without driving the strategy. A key consideration for our purpose was how resonant it was for the growth path that BT was on. We needed to consider how we could sharpen it and bring it to life more in the organization.'[11]

That means examining how the purpose is worked into the strategy, commercial targets, community work, stakeholder reports and even how colleagues' performance is measured and rewarded. Wales' career is predicated on that:

'My entire career has essentially been about driving business to deliver more good in a profitable, growth-oriented way. The reason I do it for businesses rather than an NGO or government is that business is one of the fastest moving and most creative institutions to drive change for good.'

There you have it. Profits and purpose are not mutually exclusive. Rather, purpose drives business growth.

the six tips to run a truly purposeful

urpose, don't launch it.

... line managers on how to steer conversations with their direct reports towards strategy and purpose.

3. Show employees how their work is purposeful.

4. Instil shared ownership among colleagues.

5. Map individual purpose to company purpose.

6. Create a mechanism that encourages people to apply company purpose to decisions at work.

Tip #1: Land your purpose, don't launch it

As both Willetts and McGill stressed, because the purpose is being surfaced, your job isn't to 'launch' it to the organization. The use of the word launch implies something entirely new has been created. It's more about *landing* it within the organization and giving back something that already belongs to everyone. You need to take this step of releasing it to your business to help ensure your employees actually know what your purpose is. It must be more than just a paragraph on your website or a slide in your new hire orientation. You can decide how big (or little) of a splash you want to make. As Maxine Goff, Head of Employee Engagement Communications at BT, explains, 'This isn't about balloons and all that sort of stuff... This is about proper leadership cascades over challenging times to guide conversations with their teams.'[12] For Aviva, it was more important to talk about the process they went through to surface their purpose than to advertise the actual words in the purpose statement. In doing so, by the time they *did* reveal the new purpose statement, the reaction was, 'But, of course, that's our purpose!' As McGill says, you don't want it to be a surprise.

When you do release your new purpose (or reiterate an existing one), business leaders must work closely with internal communication teams to make sure all communication channels and practices amplify the message. That's the approach BT took. Like Aviva, they didn't 'launch' with a lot of fanfare. 'We did it in a really simple way,' says Goff. 'It was my role to try and galvanise all of the comms teams about how to communicate this purpose and do it in a way that wasn't just a one-off fashion.'

Your message, whatever narrative you land on, better be dynamite and authentic. Internal communication teams can help once they understand your purpose and your mission, but if your purpose was surfaced correctly, it shouldn't be too hard of a sell. It should feel like the fabric of the organization come to life and captured in a simple phrase. It should reflect the experience of working for your company. Meaningful and inspiring, yet familiar.

Storytelling is especially effective in launching purpose to a business. It allows you to move from facts and figures to what something really means. The use of storytelling techniques such as videos, narratives and testimonials allow organizations to transform their purpose from words on a page to a tangible concept that people can understand and believe. One fun (and effective) idea is to use a series of videos that shows employees from all parts of the business in action living out the company purpose.

Another way to really breathe life into purpose stories is to have senior leaders talk about the purpose using their own personal experiences. 'One of the most important things is finding the leaders who are already embodying the purpose the most... and elevating and profiling them. Purpose is almost an emotion, more than anything else,' says Wales. That's why it lends itself so nicely to a storytelling format.

Plan to invest some time to discuss concerns with any employees who may be confused by the choice of a small launch. Willetts says:

> 'Because we weren't doing a massive
> campaign, some people struggled to get their
> head around it. To them, they felt that this was
> the most important thing they'd ever done,
> so why weren't we doing a big bang? Well,
> because it's not about that. It's about really
> sinking it into the business to percolate.'

Tip #2: Coach line managers on how to steer conversations with their direct reports towards strategy and purpose

In 2017, research at a large UK financial services firm found that those who had better conversations with their managers were 2.5 times more likely to understand strategy.[13] This shared understanding of an organization's goals, as articulated in a defined strategy, can help increase organizational alignment.

Organizational alignment is 'a process by which key organizational components of strategy, culture, processes, people, leadership and systems are linked to best accomplish the needs of the organization.'[14]

When someone feels aligned to the organization (and we mean that *first moment* when they discover the true connection they have to what the company is going after), and find that the company's purpose fits with what they find personally impactful, it can influence performance for the better. Your middle management team is going to be indispensable on this front. They not only need to understand the company's purpose; they need to be inspired by it to want to lead with purpose for their teams.

How do you coach your managers? Willetts acknowledges that it's part of the communication team's job:

'Our job is to gently police when we see things that go off track, because human nature means people want to make up new taglines and new goals and new purposes and, you know, just... change it.'

Providing manager guides and training sessions with clear instructions for having these conversations and showing examples of how the purpose can come to life can give them tangible and actionable ways to coach their team. It can also increase how bought-in they are to the purpose, helping them to resist the urge to change and adapt the purpose statement.

Tip #3: Show employees how their work is purposeful

This is all about explicitly and deliberately connecting what people do at an individual task and project level to the external outcome and impact of those tasks. For example, if you have a marketing manager toiling endlessly behind the scenes, share with them how an appearance on a webinar they secured led to new work or how an article they got placed in a high-profile magazine led to other opportunities.

You can also crowdsource this search for purpose by giving employees a chance to uncover this meaning for themselves. One instance of this being executed well comes from *Harvard Business Review's* report on the efforts of KPMG,[15] the giant multinational professional services firm. The article details KPMG's efforts in encouraging its employees to share their own perspective on how they made a difference by asking them the fundamental question: 'What do you do at KPMG?' A series of employee-generated posters were then created with headlines such as 'I combat terrorism'.

One of the things BT's internal communication team did to show how work is purposeful and to shine light on potentially hidden BT impact stories was to commission a documentary series. Willetts lights up when describing it:

> 'We've got two pilot episodes coming out soon and then a few seasons of it. We're calling it "We Connect For Good". It's a purpose programme, filmed not in a shiny brand way, but in a gritty, 'let's lift the lid on some of the things that this incredible company does because it connects for good' way, so you get that, warts and all. It gets right at the heart of purpose, really showing why this company is so present.'

A documentary series like this is a great idea and one that would be replicable in any organization. The more you reinforce what purpose looks like in action, the easier it is for people to start living it.

Tip #4: Instil shared ownership among colleagues

Ownership (in a psychological sense) is about feelings of possession. This can have negative connotations in some contexts, but in this context, we want people to feel, well, a bit possessive. When somebody feels possessive, a common reaction is to fight to keep what they have. You want your employees to fight to keep your company purpose alive. BT understood this. Willetts says:

'With our purpose, we wanted to make people feel something. We wanted them to hear it, read it and go, "Oh my god, that's actually quite meaningful. It's not just some fancy words on a piece of paper." It was important that it was a proper North Star to help guide people's decisions.'

Bringing the new purpose to life throughout the organization doesn't happen with a top-down approach. It happens when that emotional angle is triggered and when you give employees specific guidance on the behaviours you want to see them exhibit that embody the new purpose. This helps employees to live the purpose through the way they conduct the responsibilities of their job.

Another suggestion is to create a team of 'Purpose Pioneers'. These are your early adopters, selected for their ability to model the future state and take their peers along with them for the ride. With this group, you'll start to define the behaviours you want to drive that answer a key question: 'How will our people think and act when they are living the purpose?'

When Ernst & Young launched their *Building A Better Working World* purpose in 2014, they encouraged colleagues to share what they were actively doing to live out the new company purpose to provide tangible and tactical actions of what the purpose looked like. Use of the hashtag #BetterWorkingWorld trended on platforms such as Twitter and LinkedIn, and it remains prominent, with approximately 40,000 tweets at the time of writing.

Aviva also found an innovative way to keep purpose alive in the organization. They set up a purpose forum. The forum included a representative from every market within every function of the business across the globe. These representatives were senior folk – C-suite level, in most cases. Where C-suite representation was not available or not possible, senior leaders from across the business were nominated to take part. The purpose of the forum is to make necessary changes by identifying both the actions already in service of the purpose, and new actions arising from the new purpose.

Tip #5: Map individual purpose to company purpose

Don't make your employees do the work of figuring out how what gives them individual purpose outside of work also manifests *at* work. Rather, help them discover this. One simple way to do so is by helping them first articulate their individual passion via a series of defined questions. Sometimes, simply being asked to answer a specific question and actually putting pen to paper can help people more clearly define the different facets of individual purpose. Once defined, it is much easier to see the connections to the business. You can even work this into your employees' annual goal setting or performance management review process.

The simple exercise below can be used to help employees do this work. It is a great addition to any onboarding activities or purpose and engagement workshops.

EXERCISE: INDIVIDUAL PURPOSE DISCOVERY AND MAPPING

For you to consider	Find the connection to work
What are my core values...	To what extent does working here allow me to behave in a way that is consistent with my core values?
... for my work/career?	
... for my family?	
... in love?	
... for the wider/global community?	
... for the planet?	
Example: *When it comes to work, I believe that it is most important to have integrity.*	
What quality do I admire most in people at work/in business?	How are those qualities lived by my colleagues and company leaders?
What do I want out of a job, other than money and benefits?	How does my role align to what I want in a job?
Why did I choose to work in my current field?	How does my role support the reasons I am in my current field?
What are the top three things (besides money) that working here gives me?	

Another way to bring this to life for employees is to provide a toolkit for leaders that incorporates the corporate narrative, values and purpose. Leaders can then have sessions with their teams to work through what purpose means to each of them.

Tip #6: Create a mechanism that encourages people to apply company purpose to decisions at work

This is about putting your money where your mouth is, so to speak – and empowering your employees to do the same. Does your purpose support the business decisions you make, for example, choosing to make an investment with one company but not another because the one you didn't choose engages in activities that are at odds with your purpose? It is a tricky line to walk, to be sure. McGill explains this conflict nicely: 'I believe that an organization is driven by the head and the heart, and the purpose is the heart piece. If we start to mix the two together, I don't think you'll get the right outcome.' BT embedded their purpose into their corporate narrative to make it even more salient and more likely to be used in the day-to-day decision-making. Willetts says:

> 'We pull our purpose through into our strategy
> with the way we do business. We say we
> will be responsible, and we will identify the
> things we're going to commit to in terms of
> tax commitments or green commitments. I do

believe we are purpose-driven because it's not just our purpose; it's in our strategy now and that's been amazing.'

A great example of this was BT's work during the Covid-19 pandemic, where they supported getting the NHS Nightingale hospitals connected as quickly as possible. Willetts explains:

'We're about connecting for good. That's why we're doing it. Our CEO is really good at that. He will do little things here and there that role model how you actually bring purpose in every day, rather than saying, "Here's a campaign on purpose," or, "Here's an hour session on purpose."'

Showing these examples of how purpose comes to life in their actions makes it *much* easier for other employees to live out the purpose at work, because often we struggle to translate lofty purpose statements into tangible, everyday actions.

Back to where we started: It's not about the money

Profit is not at odds with purpose. Financial success is the outcome you don't need to focus too hard on; it comes from doing all the other stuff right. McGill says, 'To serve your customers by living the purpose in what you do for your people, for your community, and for your customers, you'll get the financial outcome for shareholders that you're looking for.'

As the adage teaches us, 'money can't buy happiness', but having a sense of purpose does feed into personal happiness. Prominent happiness scholar Paul Dolan of The London School of Economics and Political Science has studied the connection that purpose has to happiness and essentially concluded that happiness is a mixture of pleasure and purpose. Notice how money is absent from the equation.[16]

The sweet spot for purpose is reached where motivated, aligned and collaborative people all pull towards something bigger than themselves to create something none of them could have imagined or delivered individually. As it turns out, purpose really isn't about making the founders money after all. Rather, having a well-articulated company purpose is about creating a happy workforce. A workforce who can thrive – and a thriving, happy, purpose-driven workforce will bring rewards to the business far greater than a few extra zeroes on the balance sheet.

Wrapping it up: Applying what you've learned at work

Now that we know that purpose is surfaced and not created and we've provided a step-by-step guide to surface purpose in your organization, you are better positioned to take the first steps on leading your own purpose journey. If you feel your company already has a dynamite purpose statement, your next step is to create the communication campaigns, strategy directives and policy decisions that enable you to bring to life the six ways we have identified to run a truly purposeful business.

Seven steps to surfacing purpose

1. Create your purpose taskforce.
2. Determine if you are going to look forwards or backwards.
3. Conduct research.
4. Take your stakeholders on the journey.
5. Use the *Surfacing Your Purpose* questionnaire.
6. Run a purpose workshop with your purpose taskforce.
7. Nail your purpose statement.

Six tips to run a purposeful business

1. Land your purpose in your organization.
2. Coach line managers on how to steer conversations with their direct reports towards strategy and purpose.
3. Show employees how their work is purposeful.
4. Instil shared ownership among colleagues.

5. Map individual purpose to company purpose.

6. Create a mechanism that encourages people to apply company purpose to decisions at work.

Exercises and resources

- *Surfacing Your Purpose* questionnaire
- Individual purpose discovery and mapping

TWO
Change

Change management is not a dark art. Nor is it impossible. It certainly needn't be traumatic for your organization. There is truth in the notion that change management and change communication benefits from experience, expertise and a good dose of common sense – but it's our belief that the management of organizational change has evolved into a bigger and more complex challenge than it need be. Why is this? Sarah Burbedge, Head of Change at the BBC, says:

> 'It's the C-word, isn't it? When you say that you work in Change, some people recoil and find it really offensive… like, "Oh no, you're one of those 'change people', what are you going to do to me? I'm quite comfortable where I am, thanks."'[1]

In short, change has developed a tough reputation, because, frankly, too many companies get it horribly wrong. Businesses, like individuals, sometimes behave in a thoughtless and insensitive manner. Reactive, hurried, ill-conceived and tone-deaf communications get pushed out to address an immediate need, after which businesses move on to the next new project or implementation without reflecting and learning from the last. Once a collective mindset of 'we can't do change' takes hold, it's (no pun intended) difficult to change. In fact, some companies seem to wear this sentiment as a badge of honour.

The other, and perhaps *larger*, driver of this reputation is that change has become a multibillion-dollar money-making business for change management consultants. The industry advances the narrative of the change bogeyman because fear is an excellent control mechanism. Businesses are so frightened of handling change within their organizations that they spend eye-watering amounts of money to be changed from the outside in. It doesn't have to be that way. By understanding people's reactions to change (the good, the bad and the ugly), you'll be better equipped to handle change in your own organization and learn a lot of great skills along the way.

Change is easier, simpler and cheaper to implement in your business than you think it is.

In this chapter, we will explore:

- How change is about adaptation

- Understanding emotional reactions to change

- Six primary emotions people feel when dealing with change
- Seven universal barriers to organizational change
- Designing emotion-driven change programmes
- Eight tips to land emotion-driven change programmes
- Embracing change

Change is about adaptation

Here's the thing about change. People are adaptable and will generally find their way back to their default levels of happiness. As an example, one study revealed that 'lottery winners were not happier than controls and took significantly less pleasure from a series of mundane events.'[2]

Some of us are certainly better at handling change than others. A lot of it depends on our past experiences with change and the frame of reference we adopt to shape our perceptions. Handling change at work is all about adaptation. Research shows that the personality traits most aligned to handling change at work are ambition and emotional stability.[3] Some companies are also better at handling change than others. This tends to be because of the calibre, experience and values-based priorities of their leaders. For example, let's look at two different approaches to layoffs arising from the Covid-19 pandemic. Walt Disney announced the layoffs of 28,000 employees while simultaneously reinstating executive pay and salaries. It's not hard to guess how employees reacted.[4] Meanwhile, when vacation rental giant Airbnb laid off 1,900 employees, CEO Brian Chesky's note to employees was a master-class in how to handle change.[5] Why? He started from a place of empathy, acknowledged the uncertainties and the hard truths facing the business, and was incredibly detailed in how the company was handling the reductions. The note disclosed how severance, equity, healthcare and more were being provided to those impacted.

Claire Holt, a seasoned PR and communications professional with over two decades of multisector experience, is a current Global Communications Director at Capgemini. Capgemini is a global leader in consulting, technology services and digital transformation, with over 270,000 people across fifty different countries. In her experience, part of the perpetuation of the myth that people don't like change comes from the attitudes of those in charge of effecting it and the attitudes of those receiving it. She says, 'When you go in to "do change", you're naturally viewed with a degree of scepticism or mistrust, or you face a perception that you're only there because someone did something wrong.'[6]

But that doesn't have to be the case. Change should be embraced not as something that admonishes or disregards what no longer serves the business, but as a critical force of forward propulsion. Change isn't always needed because of something someone messed up. Change *should be agitated for* because there's an opportunity to get so much right.

The key for employers in charge of communicating change is confidence and being able to hold your nerve. Generally speaking, any change won't make anyone happier in the long term or utterly miserable in the short term, because frankly, they'll get over it. The lesson here is that you can do lots to agitate for, advocate for, and communicate about, change in your business to minimize the short-term impact it has on your people. To do it even better, you need to understand emotional reactions to change, which we'll explore next.

Understanding emotional reactions to change

Many change initiatives fail because the people in charge fail to consider the *emotional* impact of change. Jane Hanson, Chief People Officer at Nationwide Building Society, says:

> 'Too often, people deal with the cognitive and lay out a rational view of what needs to happen to go from A to B, which naturally implies that A is bad and B is good. And if that's done in a straightforward PowerPoint deck with a consultant lens, it misses the incredible nuances of human behaviour.'[7]

Emotion is at the heart of what drives people – plain and simple. When we don't factor emotions and how people react to what they are feeling into the change management equation, things can go horribly wrong. Take the experience of employees at a global company which was going through a classic HR transformation project: rolling out a new HR management system (HRMS). A senior HR manager at the company who wishes to remain anonymous (we'll call him Jim) shares the story of how badly it went wrong because the human element was overlooked. He says:

> 'Not only did we put in the new system, but
> as part of that, we completely changed the
> business model for HR. Originally, we had HR
> generalists in all of our different locations. Every
> single employee at the company could look
> up who their HR person was. For individual
> employees, that wasn't necessarily a big deal,
> but it was for managers. Managers are the ones
> who have to deal with HR issues, so for them
> to know who their HR person was, was really
> important to them. When we put in our new
> HRMS, we took out all the HR generalists, so
> nobody had any HR person to go to anymore.
> They now had to call a central contact centre.
> When we pulled out all those HR generalists,
> that was emotional for people; they were like,
> "Who am I supposed to talk to now?"'[8]

Even worse than not considering the emotional impact of a change is being tone-deaf to it. A senior communication director shares a story of the worst change management attempt by a leader she had ever seen as he tried to announce company redundancies. She says:

> 'The director got all of the branch and deputy branch managers together in a particular hotel. None of them were stupid; they hadn't sold enough in the last year, so they all knew why they were being summoned. Anyway, the director waltzed in, completely misjudged the mood and started cracking jokes. And then he complained about not liking the breakfast he received in the hotel. He's about to make a whole heap of people redundant and they're not sure how they're going to feed their families and he was banging on about his bloody breakfast. You could have heard a pin drop. As none of his jokes landed, he just went off script and told them that he didn't know how to say it, but they were all losing their jobs.'

These are just two of what we are sure are *many* 'change done horribly wrong' horror stories. Change done right includes factoring in emotions, so we'll show you how to do that.

Shanna Wendt, who we heard from in our Purpose chapter, reflects on the role of emotion:

> 'It's funny, emotion didn't immediately come to mind when I thought about change, but then I realised it's because I work for an organization

that is acutely aware of what emotional impact a change may have on its people. Does that mean we get it right every time? No. Is change still difficult? Yes. But any time we make a change within the business there is always recognition of the emotional impact. You can't invalidate how people are feeling.'

Let's walk through the primary emotions people face when experiencing change at work and show you how to make planning for emotion baked-in and automatic. It's about moving from a process-focused approach (which is what many large organizations take) to an emotion-driven approach focused on the employee journey. You have to nail this. People are always having emotional reactions and you can't debate emotions with logic and reason. After accepting that you can't quickly and programmatically shift feelings, your next move is to better understand these powerful emotions. Through this understanding, you can begin the process of onboarding them on the future change journey.

Martha Férez, Head of Change for Non-Financial Risk at Deutsche Bank, designed and uses a fascinating model to predict how her colleagues might respond to any given change programme her department implements.[9] With her permission, we have taken her profiling approach and developed it further. The table below will help you to recognize both how your own audiences will react to change and how to help them accept change.

How the persona reacts to change	How to help them accept change
The encyclopaedia This individual needs detail about the change before they embrace it.	Provide as much information and detail as possible in regular, digestible amounts. Be clear as to when more information will follow. Provide a roadmap for the change if you can so they can see when milestones, decisions and changes are likely to occur.
The cynic This individual may have been badly burned by a previous change experience. They do not trust the business and business leaders and they need proof that this time will be different.	Set clear expectations for them. Assure them you are using industry, best-practice techniques and tools. Communicate proof-points and progress regularly. Share a broad array of voices and experiences of the change programme, not just corporate figures and senior leaders. This provides much-needed social proof that their peers trust and believe in this change, which will help this individual to do so as well.
The fearful This individual attaches their sense of identity and security to the status quo; without the comfort of things being just as they are, they fear loss.	Design comms activities that give them back a sense of control. Focus not on what might change (structures, roles, titles), but rather on what won't change. For example, a focus on service or a commitment to excellence. Explain the external factors driving the change and the transferable skills they need to equip them to do new and different things.

Continued

Cont.

How the persona reacts to change	How to help them accept change
The indifferent This individual is perhaps the most difficult to engage in change. They don't care deeply, if at all; they prefer the status quo to the effort required in making change and they want to do the bare minimum in the organization to get by.	Make it clear that change is part of their job, not an added extra or an option. Talk about change agility and mindset as prerequisites for performance in your organization so that they can be performance managed in line with the right behaviours and attitude.

All of these characters exist in your organization. Your communication efforts should address these needs by making the change communication programme multi-faceted and multimedia, tailored, and with pick-and-mix activations for your people to choose from. Talk to your leaders and people managers about these personas so they can spot them and tailor their communication style accordingly. Leaders may need some coaching from your comms team to do this well.

Six primary emotions people feel when dealing with change

Now that you have a better idea on how people might react to change, let's take a closer look at the primary emotions associated with most change situations. They are:

1. Uncertainty

2. Fear

3. Anticipation

4. Resistance

5. Loss

6. Gain

Primary change emotion #1: Uncertainty

Uncertainty is change's uglier, scarier sibling. Uncertainty gets our backs up and it can be paralysing. Uncertainty is a threat, and our brain registers little difference between a true life and death situation and a nasty bout of uncertainty at work. When we feel mentally or physically threatened, we become laser-focused on the threat. If that's a change at work, imagine how difficult it is for those impacted by it to continue applying the appropriate amount of focus and perspective to their to-do lists and the decisions they need to make when all they can do is think about the looming threat?

Our job as communicators is to work with our leaders and change management colleagues to move our broader population from a place of uncertainty about what the change means to them, into a place of certainty which details what their role in the change is and what is expected of them.

Primary change emotion #2: Fear

Fear is predominantly generated by two forms of risk: unknown risks and dread risks. Dread risks are real and scary, like aeroplane crashes and terrorist attacks. Fortunately, we rarely have to deal with dread risks.

That brings us to unknown risks which are… wait for it… essentially the scary bits of uncertainty. These cause a state of high alert and make us feel like everything is a lot harder to do. Holt has a strong opinion on how fear enters the change equation. She says:

> 'People need to do enough work on the ground in terms of Q&As to address people's fears and we don't seem to do that enough. "Does this change mean I'm going to lose my job? Does this change mean I'm not going to be needed, or that I'm doing things wrong today?"'

Fear has been omnipresent in how people have professionally adjusted and survived through the Covid-19 pandemic, and it will be present in future societal issues we will undoubtedly face. Thornton says, 'As well as the natural fear of getting ill or loss of someone close, the fear of many associated and resultant risks and impacts have undoubtedly driven performance (or the temporary lack of it) in many organizations.' We've listed a few that she witnessed and how she advised clients, colleagues and friends to deal with them:

Fear of isolation

They said: I can't work alone. I'm an extrovert; I get my energy from others. I love the buzz of a crowd. I can't do my job in my spare room.

I said: Make time in your day job for social connections. Find your work and personal buddies who give you energy and factor them into your routine. Consider and identify what else gives you energy and build that into your day/week. You can't control the lockdown; you can only control how you respond to it. Focus on what you can control, not what you can't.

Fear of furlough

They said: I'm afraid of being out of the loop and losing touch. Am I not valued as much as those who didn't go on furlough? How do I stay relevant and as employable as those who worked through?

I said: Utilize all the channels, tools and platforms legally available to you to stay in touch with how your organization is doing while you're off. Stay abreast of your industry and what you need to know for your return. You're sitting on the bench to help your business best respond and survive during a pandemic.

Fear of return after furlough

They said: I'm afraid that my position or status in the organization has changed and I'll be treated differently. What if my colleagues resent me or think I've had months off sunbathing in my garden while they have been at work? What if it's hard to make the gear change back up to normal working pace?

I said: Time to talk honestly to your line manager and non-furloughed colleagues about how you feel and to ask them how they feel. I have heard about some 'us and them' creeping into workforces, but it doesn't last forever. Take time to reconnect with your workmates; ask for help and offer help to others. By understanding both viewpoints and sets of experiences, colleagues can reset and forge stronger bonds.

Fear of return to a workplace

They said: What? You want me to go back into the office or workplace? What will it feel like? Is it safe? Who else will be there? I've got used to working from home now. I'm not sure about that.

I said: The world of work has changed, perhaps forever, but there are many businesses whose success depends on connecting, collaborating, creating and problem solving – all things that it's been proved are harder to do remotely. Many businesses are creating a hybrid model where work from home is enabled but returning to a workplace one to two days a week is desired. Of course, businesses must provide adequate safety measures and communicate with employees clearly to provide reassurance. Pilot days are good practice. Ask your business to collect feedback from returning colleagues and to action good ideas or suggestions.

Primary change emotion #3: Anticipation

Anticipation can be both pleasurable (think about how you feel waiting to open presents on Christmas morning) or it can be anxiety-inducing. Pleasurable anticipation certainly has a role to play in change management (for example, when you're waiting to hear about a promotion or perhaps your office is being remodelled), but for our purposes let's focus on anxiety, because negative emotions are more powerful than positive ones. When we're in a state of anxious anticipation, it can negatively impact work performance.

Anticipation can also be prolonged if the change moves slowly, which is often the case in large, complex organizations. Take, for example, Jim's HR transformation story. He says:

'This project took over four years. It's funny, because there was a time when I was driving to work every day and I would go by this site the city had bought. They bought all this property, demolished all these houses and built a brand-new school in less time than we implemented a new HRMS.'

Primary change emotion #4: Resistance

We all know those people who think the rules don't apply to them, and these stubborn resisters show up in organizations, too. These are the ones who will devise convoluted workarounds instead of using a new system. They are the ones who think if they ignore change it's simply not there, or worse, they'll adopt an 'I'll wait it out' mentality. Holt from Capgemini has seen this resistance manifest itself differently in her experience. She says:

'For me, I think there is almost an apathy and an acceptance of the way things are, and unless people have bought into the vision as to why you would want to make things different or better, people will stick to the argument that that's just how it's always been, and always been done.'

The personas previously outlined in this chapter show how this resistance comes from clear places. The need for more detail. Cynicism borne from a bad experience or lack of trust. Fear of loss or status or disengagement. When you discover the root cause of the resistance, it's easier to tackle the issue with the right activations, and importantly, to approach them with empathy rather than animosity.

Primary change emotion #5: Loss

During the Covid-19 pandemic, Holt describes something she noticed about their senior executives used to travelling. She says, 'For quite a lot of them, whose identity is status-driven, they get a buzz from how many planes they use to jet across the globe for a quick meeting. I found that these individuals struggled the most.' This makes sense when we look at the behavioural science principle of loss aversion.

> **Loss aversion** explains how we are more sensitive to losing things we already have than gaining new things. This desire not to lose something is twice as strong as the thrill of gain.

Burbedge thinks that when people are facing a loss situation, the first step is to provide space and to actively appreciate that those feelings are completely normal and human. She says,

> 'Here at the BBC, we've lost team members suddenly and in harrowing and challenging situations and we've had to make space for colleagues to grieve and pay their respects while still working alongside each other. Similarly, when making a business change in which status quo shifts or disappears, where people are losing what was and looking out into something new and uncertain, we have to give them time to mourn the loss and come to terms with the new.

'The way we've been living and working during the pandemic is really weird and intense; it's sometimes hard for people to just get up in the morning and function, let alone be brave and try new things. Colleagues will call me to vent or have a little cry, and as leaders we need to reassure people it's OK to be vulnerable.

'There can be a huge and totally unproductive expectation on how people should be in the workplace; and it's total nonsense and just wastes time. People going through change, through challenge and through uncertainty should be however they need to be. And when we, as change leaders, create that safe space, the time for colleagues to engage with it, process it, to feel healthy and good with it – only then are they able to consider something new and different.'

Primary change emotion #6: Gain

Here's where we get to talk about the good forms of change, which should be celebrated.

Holt shares a great example of how a digital transformation project at Capgemini was put back on track after reminding communicators about one of the most classic change management tricks in the book: finding the 'what's in it for me?' angle. While senior leaders were on board, they had missed the boat about selling the positive impacts of change (and what that message should be) to those whose boots were on the ground. She says:

> 'We really had to sell the benefits of this. "Your career path looks very different. We're going to give you the skills you don't have, you're going to need to adapt and change, but the benefits for you in the long term are significant." If you can articulate it in a way that sells the positive and sells the future for not only the business, but for them as individuals, then you're halfway there.'

Seven universal barriers to organizational change

When you have a clear picture of what changes need to be made and you're prepared for the associated emotions these may cause, the next step to consider is the barriers that could get in the way.

If 'behaviour change 101' says people will act when it's easy or when it's motivating, then overcoming resistance to change means first understanding what's getting in the way. Understanding the cause behind the resistance will also dictate what solutions to deploy. For example, transparency is important if the reason for resistance is uncertainty, but less so if the reason for resistance is that people don't understand what you're saying. These barriers will show up in some of the personas we outlined earlier in this chapter.

Lindsay Kohler, a behavioural scientist, has worked with many companies over the years and found a pattern to the seven barriers all organizations face. Let's go through these in turn:

1. People are uncertain in times of change.

2. People don't see the need to change.

3. People are subject to choice and information overload.

4. People succumb to the status quo.

5. People won't do hard things.

6. People don't understand what you are saying.

7. People aren't motivated.

Resistance factor #1: People are uncertain in times of change

When people are uncertain, things feel risky, and people tend to do nothing. Thornton recalls a primary example of this:

> 'We worked with a prominent mobile phone giant about seven or eight years ago that was facing into the shift from selling handsets to unifying telecoms solutions. Their workforce *loved* selling handsets. They were *good* at it. They sold *lots* of them. They made a *ton* of commission. Many of their sales community

were uncertain, worried even, about the prospect of learning about the whole new and highly technical world of communication platforms for business. The business was two years into a three-year transformation strategy and the sales force were shrugging their shoulders and saying, "OK, transform me." They were keeping themselves busy doing what they'd always done, in the way they'd always done it. The task for us as communications partners to effect real, lasting change in that crucial final year of the three-year change strategy was to fully unpick and unpack what that 'scary' new communication world looked like, overcome the fear factor of learning new skills and product knowledge, and firmly place responsibility and ownership for the change with that sales force.'

Resistance factor #2: People don't see the need to change

While you cannot persuade someone to do or think something that is fundamentally opposed to who they are as a person (for example, no campaign or incentive could encourage a law-abiding citizen to commit a crime), the topics businesses communicate about do not usually fall into the realm of innate personal truths. It's often a matter of explaining the reason for the change in a way that resonates with your audience. Thornton remembers working with a large UK retail brand to help them save money lost each year to lost, stolen or damaged goods. She says:

> 'We began by raising awareness of the problem but made it personal to partners by highlighting the fact that the millions lost represented a potential 4% increase in their bonus. We then broke down the overall figure into branch-level targets and reinforced the basic operating procedures that all partners should follow in their department. People then took ownership for creating bespoke action plans for their part of the business. Finally, we equipped teams with materials to track their progress throughout the year, review, compete a little and celebrate the positive impact their changed behaviours were having on profit and their potential bonuses.'

Resistance factor #3: People are subject to choice and information overload

Choice overload is one of the more well-known behavioural science principles. While some choice is a good thing, too much can be overwhelming and can lead to decision paralysis (eg trying to find a movie on Netflix). The concept of overload also encompasses information overload. We are bombarded with too many messages from too many sources, and competition for attention is fierce. Some years ago, Thornton was asked to get to the bottom of why a recent change in strategy hadn't landed with a global financial services giant. The change strategy hinged on delivering required, different behaviours, priorities and activities from their 20,000 global colleagues.

> 'I reviewed what was out there in the employees' information line of sight. What was competing for attention, what was clear and unclear, what jumped out at me and what passed me by? I found thirty-five different levels of live projects, programmes, straplines, acronyms, priorities, goals and ambitions. No wonder people weren't clear what was expected of them. It seemed that nothing had been retired in this business for several years – just more layers and newer, shinier projects and slogans heaped on top.'

When you start a new programme or introduce a new initiative, it's as important to be clear on what to stop as it is on what to start. Some businesses seem nervous to officially put an initiative out to pasture for fear some employees think it was wrong, failed or contradictory. The old gets added with the new. Instead of giving colleagues clarity and brain space to think about, and start making decisions in service of, the new initiative, they discover a cacophony of noise that is literally overwhelming and can just result in organizational paralysis.

Resistance factor #4: People succumb to the status quo

Status quo bias explains how we have an emotional preference for the way things currently are, so any change from that baseline can be emotionally upsetting. The reason the status quo is comfortable is that a lot of the choice has already been squeezed out. There is another factor at play. When you keep doing things the way you always have, it becomes a habit. Hanson agrees this is problematic for change-makers:

> 'I think one of the biggest barriers to change are people's deeply embedded habits and behaviours. That doesn't mean they are wrong, or that they don't like change. It's not as simplistic as that. A great example is when the UK government brought in a charge for plastic bags. I'm environmentally astute and want to have a planet in the future. I have loads of reusable bags. But how many times do I find myself at the supermarket without one of my reusable bags? So, even when you have the motivation, the habit shift is really hard.'

Resistance factor #5: People won't do hard things

Sometimes things aren't easy enough. This is a major driver to encourage teams to walk a mile in their employees' shoes before sending out their communications. You're likely to uncover some potential pitfalls that you can then remedy. Kohler remembers a time when a client asked her why their 401(k) enrolment numbers were so low. She says:

> 'I did what any curious person would do – I wanted to understand the experience first and foremost to see if there were any obvious blockers to action. After about seventeen circular clicks on various websites, I still hadn't found a place to enrol. Safe to say, I had spotted the problem.'

Hanson says, 'If change is too big or too complex, you need to break it down into smaller parts. What's the one action or thing they can do differently?' Excellent advice. One brilliant, real-life execution of this idea comes from UK supermarket Morrisons. They were on a journey to modernize and bring the fight to the other supermarket giants. The incoming chief executive at the time, Dalton Phillips, asked store colleagues to focus on just three things. What's more, he made it a highly memorable acronym (since we easily remember acronyms, it was a smart play). In order to improve and deliver customer service excellence, he asked employees to do three things when they saw a customer: say *H*ello, *O*ffer them assistance and say *T*hank you. This was *HOT* customer service. Simple, effective, memorable and actionable.

Resistance factor #6: People don't understand what you are saying

What looks like resistance is often lack of clarity, so simplicity is key. Jim, from our global company, saw this resistance factor first-hand:

> 'From a change management perspective, they deliberately decided not to do a formal training [of the new system]. They thought that everything would be so intuitive that managers and employees wouldn't need any kind of formal training. They would just learn it at point of use.'

Spoiler alert: it wasn't. Marina Gonzalez, who has internal change communications experience from The Walt Disney Company and Adobe, and is the current Director of People Experience Design at Rivian, is clear on the change communicator's role here:

> 'We're here to look at the holistic experience, across every nuance and detail, to transform the complex to simple linear and engaging concepts for employees to respond to the change. That's only going to make our job as the communicator and entire project team's job easier. The goal is to avoid unnecessary triage – you're making sure, from the beginning, that the entire experience is going to be in good standing.'[10]

Resistance factor #7: People aren't motivated

Let's face it, some topics are not the most fun or exciting, so it's up to you to find what that motivating hook is. That's where utilizing emotion will help you dial up the motivation to change. Thornton recalls a multi-award-winning programme from 2013 to launch a guaranteed income pension among their 132,000-strong workforce:

'When most other employers were debunking such pension schemes, [a large UK grocery store] was launching one. A fantastic perk, but we knew that with only 10% of their current workforce in their existing scheme, it wouldn't be as simple as asking people to join a new one. Basing our engagement programme in colleague research, we developed "Save Your Dough", which tackled the truism that their people just didn't feel able to save enough money today, to invest for tomorrow. For ten months before we talked about a new pension scheme, we helped colleagues to better manage their money, making saving for the future *feel* more manageable. Our programme demystified money management and helped bust common myths like: "I can't afford it. I don't trust my employer with my savings. It's too far away to think about now. It's too complicated. I'll make my nest egg another way, with property or inheritance."'

The campaign utilized a global external expert, Alvin Hall, as the campaign frontman and created intense and emotional filmed money makeovers for real colleagues in serious financial difficulty. Accompanying this was a microsite to access from work or home with financial health checkers, cutback calculators and budget planning tools. By tackling the issues about saving first and targeting the fact that people aren't motivated to do things differently, this company tripled participation in their pension scheme in just ten weeks. A company-wide engagement survey cited that 44,500 colleagues said that the 'Save Your Dough' programme had had a positive impact on their personal finances.[11]

Designing emotion-driven change programmes

As leaders and communication pros, it's our job to tell the story, find the words and symbols and then design the activations and interventions that help move our people from uncertainty to certainty as quickly as possible, so our organizations aren't paralysed by distraction, lack of focus and a dip in performance for too long.

To do this well, we need to be mindful of the emotional impact of change and design our change communication programmes to recognize and address those feelings. Leaders need to remember to move at the pace of the slowest, not the fastest, in the organization. They must bear in mind that they may have had information about the change for much longer, giving them the ability to have processed it, found their certainty, and gained a measure of control. Coaching them to remember how they felt when they first heard the news could help remind them of the importance of giving employees further down the chain of command more time to go on the emotional journey. Gonzalez agrees:

> 'The number one thing I've learned in my career is that change can't be rushed. It needs our most valuable resource: time. Partners want to move quickly and have often questioned longer timelines. We spend months, sometimes a year or more on programme design, but forget employees need more than a five-minute introduction or one-hour training to absorb, accept and adapt.'

Unfortunately, this emotion-driven planning doesn't always happen in companies. Why? Holt has a spot-on explanation, and it's all about the need for speed:

> 'Quite often, the need for change accompanies a burning platform. We need to cut costs or do things differently because we're behind the market, we've got a new CEO or person in that's responsible for change and for delivering it quickly and they just want to "crack on and do" rather than sit down and explain the why.'

Eight tips to land emotion-driven change programmes

Let's continue putting theory into action with eight tips to design emotion-driven change programmes. You'll notice that our tips are not all communication based. Why? As Gonzalez points out, 'We've come to overly rely on communications for change management. Many think that if we communicate it, communicate it, and communicate it some more, then change is inevitable.' Our eight tips are:

1. Map the employee experience journey.

2. Actively manage periods of uncertainty.

3. Be clear if the change is positive or negative.

4. Give people back control.

5. Paint a compelling picture.

6. Enable people to be part of the change.

7. Don't take a 'one and done' approach.

8. Set the tone from the top.

Tip #1: Map the employee experience journey

When a high-end fashion house made the switch to remote working during the Covid-19 pandemic they knew it would be a big change in many aspects, but especially onboarding. Visiting the factory where their iconic cloth is made and touring the main headquarters delivered a huge emotional hit for new joiners. It was that moment that they felt awe, as well as, 'Wow, I'm part of this iconic brand.'

This retailer wanted all new employees to get that same emotional high in the new remote environment, so they devised an employee experience journey mapping workshop. In the workshop, they dissected each stage of their current process and wrote down the associated emotions. Then they collectively brainstormed ways to deliver those same feelings – just with a new set of tools under their belts. You can do this within your own organization for any change that's coming down the line. Simply plot out all the journey touchpoints, identify the associated emotions and then figure out a way to recreate them in the different environment.

Tip #2: Actively manage periods of uncertainty

Figure out what the bare minimum period of uncertainty is to mitigate the natural mental energy drainage and loss of productivity that comes when people work, operate and live with uncertainty.

Of course, sometimes we just have to live with uncertainty and cope as best we can. 2020 was the ultimate masterclass for all of us. The trick for communicators is to create structure and phasing for the change period. They must manage uncertain and weary colleagues' expectations of when the next nugget of certainty and decision-making will be.

Following the 2008 financial collapse, a large bank received significant support from the UK government, a condition of which was to separate 314 branches to create a new bank. The branches, along with a proportion of head office support staff, would become part of a new company, and as such, needed a clear understanding of the new company's history and the future of the bank. Facing such an important and prolonged period of change, Thornton advised them to regularly engage employees throughout the long separation process and actively encourage all colleagues to contribute ideas and feedback to the new bank. An accessible and visual strategic map to effectively communicate the steps in the journey was created and practical tools to help managers hold ongoing conversations with employees were developed. Thornton recalls:

'The beauty of that approach was breaking up the mass of uncertainty into more manageable chunks that colleagues could process more easily. We shared set timeframes, signposted where and when clear decisions would be taken, where changes would start to be implemented... so every future stage and gateway for future decisions was broadly visualized. All with the caveat that all those things could change, and we'd be open if and when they did.'

Tip #3: Be clear if the change is positive or negative

Nobody wants to read between the lines. If they have to work hard to figure out what you're trying to say, chances are they'll tune out. Or worse, if the change is negative and you try to sugar-coat that message to soften it, they could get suspicious. 'Looking back, I can see a lot of times where the change was a cost decision, but they'll dress it up as something else. People can see right through that,' says Hanson. What's more, there is much research connecting negative emotions to counter-productive behaviours, such as blaming others, throwing in the towel, and poor collaboration with colleagues. Gonzalez says:

> 'People are more willing to accept a negative change if you can present it to them in a manner that allows them to understand the business rationale, understand that they're going to have some discomfort, understand that it's going to take time to accept it and ultimately, understand that they are not alone.'

Férez undertakes a 'current state' and 'target state' analysis with colleagues facing into change in Deutsche Bank:

> 'I take them through an exploration of, "This is where you are now, and this is where you are going. Does the future state look better?" If they say no, I have to work with them further,

review the target, be clearer about the potential benefits. In working this through with the people facing change, they have a say and work with me to make the target state better. The next challenge is to show progress. People really struggle to understand and quantify progress because many feel that only financial value is visible, but progress can show up as deeper knowledge, or better user experience or even a less risky process. Being able to articulate progress in a way that shows value outside pounds and pence really helps take people on the journey.'

Tip #4: Give people back control

No one likes to feel like change is being done *to* them. Part of that has to do with someone's mindset, as we explored in earlier chapters, but change communicators can also give people a measure of control. Thornton recalls a brand change programme for a retail bank in which colleagues were given an exceptionally high level of decision-making by the change programme. While the brand name and ID was set by leadership, they invited a large consultation group to co-design elements like uniforms, retail floor plans and interior design and customer experiences. It was classic 'freedom within a framework'.

It proved hugely successful with their colleagues. They felt they had control over some elements of the journey, many of which were close to their heart and their day-to-day experience of work. Even though they were dealing with a high volume of prolonged change, the energy and commitment that the approach generated created tangible business benefits for the change programme.

Tip #5: Paint a compelling picture

In the excellent book *Switch: How to change things when change is hard*[12] by Chip and Dan Heath, there is a story they share that brings this concept to life vividly. In it, they describe a teacher who wanted to motivate her first-grade students to work hard and improve their maths and reading scores. Now, not only is that a nebulous goal, but it's not exactly motivating to a seven-year-old. So, what did she say instead? She told her kids that by the end of the year, they were going to be *third*-graders. That was something they could get behind. Third-graders were cool, smart, taller and – more importantly – something they saw every day, so they could get a clear picture of what it meant. Wendt agrees:

'I come at change from the perspective of making sure the end destination is clear. Does everyone understand the aspiration and what you're trying to do? I see time and time again leaders talk in features versus benefits.'

Painting this clear and compelling vision through your change narrative can be make or break for companies. Holt says:

'For me, this is where organizational change misses a trick, because when I've seen it done well, it's where leaders have spent a lot of time at the front end of the process articulating the vision and painting a picture as to what the future state looks like and what the benefits are to all different stakeholder groups.'

'The main message that you're trying to get across relies on identifying the heart of the matter – the one thing employees need to know,' says Gonzalez. 'If they read eight words and that is all, how are they going to resonate and what will be the impact?' So, whose job is it to paint the compelling picture? Who is the artist? It is tempting to point the finger at the IC team (and they have a role to play) but it's the leader's job to craft a future path. Hanson says:

'As leaders of organizations, we need to look at the context around us, the environment; we are stewards of this organization and it's our job to make sure it is sustainable for customers and employees. We need to identify the big bets we need to make and guide the organization through. It's up to us to set the vision for where we need to go – and why. It's much less about an architect, an engineer, or a project manager. They're the facilitators of what needs to get done. The important groups in crafting and shaping those choices for the future, and the pathway, are your leaders.'

Tip #6: Enable people to be part of the change

People need to feel they have a role to play in enabling the change. Thornton recalls when scarlettabbott worked with one of the largest social housing providers in North-East England to devise and facilitate a company-wide engagement programme to give every employee a voice and an active role in shaping the future strategy for the organization.

This ground-breaking project, kicked off by the CEO and Executive Board, offered all 160 employees face-to-face creation sessions where they reflected, explored and co-created how the organization could move from good to great.

It resulted in significant changes not just to what the housing group did and how they did it, but because the entire workforce was involved and felt an intense sense of ownership, resistance to the resulting changes was minimal.

Férez believes this level of involvement creates a critical component of effective change management: trust.

'Remembering that different people and personas react differently to change, the common golden thread of effectively engaging colleagues in change should all build to great levels of organizational trust. If people trust you to have their best intentions at heart, they'll go a long way with you.'

Tip #7: Don't take a 'one and done' approach

Most of the communication we undertake in business is stuff that we want colleagues to remember and do something about. If not, why bother communicating it at all? But we can impact what helps or hinders retention and recall of information.

Férez uses the sustained approach, the opposite of 'one and done':

- First, identify what purposeful change needs to happen. What part of the company vision will it help deliver? Make this narrative clear, compelling and ensure it is consistently told in your communications throughout the programme.

- Change communication must come from the top and be led by leadership. It's critical to secure their buy-in, and their commitment to provide resources and their own time throughout the programme.

- Communicate in recognition of what goes well and where lessons are being learned.

- Sustain or embed the change long after the big bang announcement and even after the implementation of the changed system or process. Ensure the people doing something in a new way are comfortable with it and have the psychological safety to speak up when it's no longer working and a new way of doing things is required.

- Over the course of a long programme, things may change, and the original target state may evolve mid-programme. Look out for this, embrace it and communicate openly if the change itself needs to change!

Tip #8: Set the tone from the top

Hanson says:

'Leadership role modelling has a massive influence on change. If you see people you respect, who you hold in esteem, behaving in the new way – it makes it acceptable. And leaders can come from anywhere. You have natural influencers in organizations who may not follow the typical hierarchy.'

'I think even senior people are frightened of communicating change, and if they get the chance to do it with an email rather than getting people on a call and getting that face time, they they'll take it,' says Holt. Burbedge believes that even more than 'culture eating strategy for breakfast', inspiring leaders eat boring corporate change approaches for breakfast:

'When I was leading the change to set up a new mobile and online division in BBC news, it was founded with a clear vision and purpose and the knowledge that it was absolutely what needed to happen. We needed to shift to reach a younger audience through digital and social platforms. We had great insights from our audience and our own staff. Rather than take a traditional, linear approach to making this happen, we set up a new digital, diverse workspace and a different working ethos.

'And the leader we appointed for this change was Fiona Campbell. She embodies what is needed to transform and build. She lived and breathed it every day, absolutely driven, purposeful and brilliant. She's the leader who didn't just get up at every meeting and say the right things in the right way, she would also be sat in a corner talking to someone about how their apprenticeship is going, giving them the most inspiring moment of their career and making opportunities and connections for them beyond. Fiona is completely authentic – she really cares about people – and is loved and trusted by her teams. The tone from the top is fundamental to change success.'

As IC, HR and change advisors, we shouldn't be too tough on leaders either. They aren't born with experience or expertise in communicating change and giving tough news – they need to learn it. If they haven't had too much experience of doing it on their way up the career ladder, they sometimes find themselves ill-equipped, nervous or being evasive when it's required by the time they reach the boardroom. Burbedge says:

> 'Some of the best advice I give leaders who might not be feeling confident about leading a change, is to try a humble leadership approach. Yes, you can be the figurehead, but you might not be the best person to share a particular message with other people. And try to keep learning throughout, be unafraid of not knowing all the answers all the time or getting it wrong sometimes. Lean into the expertise around you.'

Embracing change

The now-famous term 'survival of the fittest' from *On the Origin of Species* by British naturalist Charles Darwin suggested that organisms best adjusted to their environment are the most successful in surviving and reproducing. Férez analysed this quote from a change perspective, highlighting: 'That's the same with humans in their workplace ecosystems. Those willing and able to embrace change, because change will certainly come, are more successful and happier in their work.'

Férez considers that a great, open conversation starter for change programmes is asking people, 'What's scarier, the idea of changing what you do and how you do it? Or finding yourself outdated, outmoded and on the outside because you actively resisted the change?' To deliver what today's businesses need in a tough and unpredictable economic landscape, we must focus our efforts on helping employees to accept and work within change – because the world will move on, with or without them. 'In today's world, what we thought was a priority last year, and what we thought was important to our colleagues then, versus what is important to them now, is totally different,' says Holt. She also noticed a marked difference in who was and was not an effective leader through challenging times: 'With some of the senior guys I work with, it's been fascinating to watch how they've led. In some instances, they've done incredibly well. In other instances, some have fallen apart.'

It's not just one person whose attitude needs to change. We talk a lot about influencing the individual, but everyone in the organization must be part of it for it to work and really stick. 'In a work context, it's not just one person doing things in the new way. It's a team of 10, 20 or 18,000,' says Hanson. So even if one person does it right, if everyone around them doesn't, they face an uphill battle. 'It's a bit like your coffee cup,' Hanson continues.

> 'You're sat there in a room, ready to use your sustainable mug, when the coffee break comes

up. And someone jumps up and off they go and buy a load of coffee in plastic cups. Now, if the whole team got up and rinsed out their sustainable mugs beforehand, we'd all do it. But if the team goes, "Oh we don't have time to do that now; we just need to get a coffee in,' you go along with the bigger group."

In Chapter 4, Growth, we will talk about whether you are owning a situation or feel like something is being done to you in a situation. That applies wholly to acceptance of change. A typical employee is unlikely to be able to stop a change from happening, so what mindset will they adopt to cope best and optimize how they perform around the change?

Thornton loves the phrase her former Neuro Linguistic Programming (NLP) coach Kevin Dennison uses, which totally resonates for individuals or businesses: *people will do what people will do; what you do with it, is up to you.*

Wrapping it up: Applying what you've learned at work

People can like change. They can find it stimulating, refreshing and motivating. Better yet, when they see how change benefits them, it is exciting – which in itself generates energy and goodwill.

What we learnt on this journey into change was that there are some amazing Change and HR

professionals out there, all with very human, empathetic, pragmatic and people-centric approaches to
organizational change. When change goes bad in
business, it's because those businesses forget (or never
knew) that the change isn't the new process, policy or
piece of tech – it's the human beings they are asking to
do something differently. Remember that, and you're
onto a winner.

We looked at six primary emotions people feel
when dealing with change; seven universal barriers
to organizational change; and eight tips to landing
emotion-driven change programmes.

Six primary emotions people feel when dealing with change

1. Uncertainty

2. Fear

3. Anticipation

4. Resistance

5. Loss

6. Gain

Seven universal barriers to organizational change

1. People are uncertain in times of change.

2. People don't see the need to change.

3. People are subject to choice and information overload.

4. People succumb to the status quo.

5. People won't do hard things.

6. People don't understand what you're saying.

7. People aren't motivated.

Eight tips to land emotion-driven change programmes

1. Map the employee experience journey.

2. Actively manage periods of uncertainty.

3. Be clear if the change is positive or negative.

4. Give people back control.

5. Paint a compelling picture.

6. Enable people to be part of the change.

7. Don't take a 'one and done' approach.

8. Set the tone from the top.

THREE
Diversity And Inclusion

If purpose is the golden factor in organizational success, diversity and inclusion (D&I) is the golden
enabler. That's why, when outlining our book and
identifying the critical components for building a
better business, D&I made the first cut with ease. We
all have to build a more inclusive, accepting world
together. Thornton shares her thoughts on the subject
and the lightbulb moment when she realized that D&I
is everybody's job:

> 'I grew up in an idyllic Yorkshire village, but
> after a parental divorce, we downsized (sans
> father) into urban Doncaster, a sizeable South
> Yorkshire former mining town famous locally
> for a racecourse, good railway connections and
> dubious reputation for nightlife, sprawling fun

fairs and varied ethnic cuisine. We lived in a multicultural neighbourhood and I went to a reasonably diverse, high-performing, former grammar school and then university in Leicester.

'My working life started in Leeds, progressed to Bristol, then Manchester, Chester and back to Leeds. The organizations I worked for were reasonably progressive; I personally encountered none of the D&I horror stories that many can recount – no blatant sexism, no overt racism or homophobia… and no memory of any of the many other forms of bigotry, discrimination and bias which we as a business community are so much more finely attuned to today. I had friends and colleagues of colour, of various sexual preferences, all socio-economic backgrounds and of varying physical abilities; it felt natural and wasn't a big deal. My point is, it *must* have been present all around me – D&I inequalities, injustices and discrimination – I just didn't see any of it because it didn't hold me back. I was White, female, confident, driven and working class… I did just fine, so it didn't register on my agenda too highly.

'Fast forward fifteen years. We're in the late 2000s and I'm running my own successful and fast-growing business in York, a city not known for its cultural diversity. Suddenly, the compelling personal need to ensure that everyone who worked for me could be themselves, feel safe and valued and listened to… and that their diversity of experience was actually a huge part of their appeal to me as their employer, blossomed in me. I *awoke*.

'I'm the first to admit that I'm far from a D&I specialist. I hired some incredible, far more talented and experienced people than myself to build that firepower in my own consultancy; but I am a passionate advocate and ally. More impactful than that, I'm a leader with conviction. My appreciation of the power and importance of D&I made me not just bake it into the fundamental characteristics of my own corporate culture, but also make it part of our proposition – one of the things I want our consultancy to be famous for.'

Whatever your business does, however large or small, there are few things more important than it being diverse and inclusive. It must actively and purposefully harness the broadest experience of human existence and point all that power, value and sense of belonging at your business goals. It's a commercial no-brainer. It's also just the right thing to do. This chapter shares some perspectives, expert opinions and pragmatic considerations and ideas on how to do that in your own business.

In this chapter, we will explore:

- Why D&I matters

- The five truths of inclusion

- Seven D&I myths busted
- Unpacking fairness and inequality
- Exploring your privilege
- Seven tips to kickstart your D&I efforts

Why diversity and inclusion matters

Russell Norton, Head of Client Experience at scarlett-abbott, is a passionate D&I advocate and expert. He puts it elegantly:

'The big answer here is that diversity and inclusion is an enabler of growth in any organization when done properly. My own personal realization, from my experience as a gay man, is that as soon as you are hiding or editing yourself, you are spending energy on something that does not benefit the organization for which you work. You are instead concentrating on how you talk, how you look, how you sound, the movements you make, the way you are dressed. You aren't focused fully on your outputs. So, at its core, diversity and inclusion matters because when people are not worrying about who they are or what they are, they can fully concentrate on the task at hand. That means better outputs, greater innovation, broader perspectives, deeper customer connections and better business growth.'[1]

Andrea Mattis, who we first heard from in our Purpose chapter, is also a passionate D&I advocate. She says:

> 'D&I matters because it's all about belonging. All people need to feel that when they go to work, they receive some sort of invested payback from their company. You spend so much time at work and you need to be able to bring who you are to the organization freely. When that can't happen, it has a huge knock-on effect. Even now, I feel like some people don't see the link between D&I and employee engagement; and the reality is, it's all connected. If you don't feel you truly belong, then you're probably less likely to be fully engaged… because you'll likely feel, "What's the point of me getting involved?"'

Nadia Younes, currently a chief diversity officer (who has been in that role in multiple sectors), shines a light on this brilliantly and gets to the heart of it. 'We've never been this connected before. The world and humanity are at a place where we have some choices to make around how we want to be with each other.'[2]

Making the business case for D&I

We'd like to think the business case is obvious, but we have outlined it here as we know teams often need proof-points to make the case for the budget and resources necessary to move D&I beyond a tick-box activity and into the realm of meaningful change. Mattis predicts that, 'Companies that don't fix D&I inequalities at work are probably at risk of ceasing to exist in five to ten years.' Grace Lordan, Associate Professor of Behavioural Science at the London School of Economics, is the founding director of The Inclusion Initiative (TII) and author of the book *Think Big: Take Small Steps and Build the Future You Want.* She says:

> 'If we think about work, for the occasions that we want to create something, innovate or understand opportunities, there are risks and payoffs. You'd better care about diversity and inclusion, because that will deliver a better outcome. Diversity, as we typically think about it in society, is really just a pulse point for diversity of thought.'[3]

Norton has a clear view on how D&I done right boosts business performance. He separates the business case into two parts: the first is the financial and performance metrics we typically associate with a solid business case, and the second is a compelling moral case. The lists you see below are his work for scarlettabbott.

The business case

D&I boosts business performance because:

- Companies with the most gender-diverse and ethnically diverse leadership teams financially outperform their peers

- Doing things how we've always done them does not guarantee our continued success into the future

- Government and lobby groups are demanding increasing transparency about the make-up of our organizations

- It's a matter of compliance if we want to work with certain partners or suppliers

- Our customers care about it more and more – it influences which brands they choose to consume and which they choose to work for

- It enables us to better connect with our customers and deliver an excellent overall experience

- It demonstrates a company's purpose in action

Lordan's TII hopes to demonstrate this business case more concretely. She says:

> 'We are going to perform interventions which we have faith can move the needle on inclusivity and also demonstrate how inclusion is good for business. We need to show this from a macro-perspective – with respect to informing shareholders and also informing people who buy from these companies. To the end that you have a company that believes in inclusion, these data points will be relevant for them and they will be interested in the evidence.'

(We've shared advice and ideas from Lordan throughout this chapter, but further innovative and research-backed techniques can be found on the TII website: www.lse.ac.uk/PBS/archive/tii.)

The moral case

D&I boosts business performance because:

- People perform better when they are free to be themselves

- We all carry biases and blind spots that can cause unintentional harm

- Having diversity of experience enhances our thinking, our creativity and our outputs

- Discriminating against anyone because of something they can't change is unfair

- Enabling people to feel like they can be themselves at work is the right and empathetic thing to do

- We recognize that institutional discrimination exists in wider society, and we want to create a safe space for our employees

- Lots of small negative experiences (micro-aggressions) build up to feel overwhelmingly painful

Norton sums this up nicely: 'Diversity is a measure. Inclusion is a choice. Belonging is an outcome. Performance is the output.'

Where D&I shows up around us

D&I is everywhere. It isn't, and shouldn't be, an activity undertaken by a few people sitting in corporate offices in HR. It shows up every day in ourselves, our teams and our communities. Younes reflects:

'Diversity is, and has always been, a reality. Our exposure to it has simply increased. Equity is not a given or even a reality for a growing majority of people. Despite the current groundswell, inclusion is often still prioritized or granted by those in power. Historically, when majority and minority dynamics become polarized and magnified – religious divides, racial divides, cultural divides, education divides, wealth divides – they lead to social unrest and sometimes to extremes such as war, extreme poverty and health crises. I call these disruptions "social tectonic plates", because when there is a shift in the tectonic plates, the world opens up and there is an earthquake. It's disruptive. Sometimes it's just a safety drill warning us to pay attention to the divides among us, but sometimes buildings fall, and entire communities are left marginalized and vulnerable. When this happens, we need to consciously build back better, stronger and from a starting point of inclusive design.'

When we were evolving, it was easier to clearly identify 'us' and 'them'. Someone was either part of your trusted group or they weren't. Those tribal group structures don't hold anymore. We are more interconnected than ever; but not of all of us have caught up with the idea that it's no longer 'us vs them', but rather, a collective us. Younes says:

'This world is a mixture of differences. If you want to be in your "same, same bubble", I think that's going to be much harder to maintain or even define... You have your circle of influence and your circle of concern, but you should be aware of the broader world around you that's changing.'

Norton has devised a useful table to assist with this:

Me	My team	My organization	My community
What can I do differently, or do more of, to be more inclusive?	What can our team do differently, or do more of, to be more inclusive?	What can we influence in our organization to do differently, or do more of, to be more inclusive?	How can we show up in the wider community as an ally to marginalized groups?

The five truths of inclusion

You might be a leader of an organization tussling to do the right thing. You might know exactly what you want to do – just not how to do it. You may be in HR trying to build a case for more resource and focused prioritization. You could be an IC pro trying to generate the right C-suite level of support for D&I in your IC strategy.

Whoever you are and wherever you are in your journey, we wholeheartedly believe in five truths on which we've designed and delivered many robust and hugely successful D&I programmes for clients. They are:

1. Diversity matters to everyone, whether they know it or not.

2. It's not the role of internal communicators to communicate 'the solution'.

3. Actions matter more than ambition.

4. It's OK to say no in the spirit of fairness.

5. Fear of saying the wrong thing leads to inaction.

Inclusion truth #1: Diversity matters to everyone, whether they know it or not

Norton explains that one huge blind spot is thinking that diversity is just for people who are different:

'In many organizations, D&I activity is delivered under labels that highlight difference – "women in business" or "LGBTQ+ Network". Some people, even if they are allies, may feel that events or communications aren't *for* them.'

It's important to remember that people can feel excluded for many reasons, not just because of the visible and prominent characteristics which our D&I efforts just scratch the surface of. Of course, race, gender, age and sexual orientation are big-ticket D&I items, but what about educational background, geographic location, accent, work experience, marital status, income and recreational habits?

> **Exclusion** is when we feel we are in the minority in the context of the people around us.

D&I messaging should always acknowledge that some minority characteristics carry an additional burden or an unfair disadvantage; and even more so when multiple minority characteristics overlap. Our opportunity is to broaden the topics we cover beyond our visible differences, exploring the full range of characteristics of diversity and their impact in terms of either privilege or disadvantage. In doing so, we can frame a diversity topic in a way that resonates with everyone.

Inclusion truth #2: It's not the role of internal communicators to communicate 'the solution'

It is best practice in internal communication to always include a call to action. It's the 'So what?' It's the little thing that makes it clear *why* someone is receiving a message and what to do with it. For D&I, this isn't always the case.

Simply sharing stories about the lived experience of your employees builds empathy. Stories can show others that individuals are more than what they see on the outside and can bust myths and preconceptions. Stories are a glimpse into someone's reality, their perspective and their truth. Presented in this way, they don't need a call to action or next steps. After all, it's not the job of minority individuals to find a solution to discrimination. Nor is that IC's job. The only 'So what?' is that you feel a sense of empathy for the individual featured.

IC teams are also not always best placed to help solve embedded D&I issues. Why? Because they likely have blind spots of their own, which means it's more likely for them to miss a trick. As Mattis says:

'Even with the best of intentions, some of the people running D&I strategies haven't acknowledged their own blind spots… They can come from a position of passion and knowing this is the right thing to do – which are great qualities to have – but there has to also be a layer of acknowledgement. Acknowledgement that I don't know everything. Acknowledgement that I have unconscious biases of my own.

Acknowledgement of, let's say, the LGBT community because I haven't really been part of it. All this means that many D&I strategies can run from a place of niceness, rather than a place of empathy.'

Inclusion truth #3: Actions matter more than ambition

We often deal with future-facing messages. Visions, ambitions, strategies – these are the grand plans proffered by leadership describing how things will be in the future. When it comes to D&I, our audience has far less patience.

We still have a long way to go before true equality and fair representation is achieved in society and business. As corporations collectively wake up to the scale of the issue, they are keen to be seen to have their say. Some fall back on setting new or more ambitious targets or communicating strategies and intentions, but when people are already frustrated, we can help our businesses do better. Colleagues want to hear about what organizations are *actually* doing today, not planning to do tomorrow. They want to know how they are practically showing up for minority communities and putting their money where their mouths are. We interviewed Joanne Stephane, Principal, Human Capital for Deloitte Consulting LLP, for a *Forbes* article. She says:

'In no other area of the business would we consider leaders successful based on effort or activity. When leaders do not meet or exceed operational or financial objectives, we would dig deeper and find out what went wrong in their assumptions and approach. We should [assess] achieving Equity objectives with the same rigor and focus.'[4]

The old adage 'don't tell me you're funny; make me laugh' is completely appropriate when it comes to D&I efforts. While it's not for IC to communicate the solution, they (along with the HR and D&I teams) can be a mirror for leaders that coaches and encourages them to articulate actions, outputs and outcomes in an honest, regular and personal manner.

Inclusion truth #4: It's OK to say no in the spirit of fairness

Some aspects of D&I are far more commonly discussed and celebrated than others, so with the best of intent, our internal communication efforts may be excluding the stories and experiences of other groups. You can tackle this by defining specific timeslots in your annual messaging calendar to explore different topics. There are many well-known calendar dates to follow, for example, Black History Month, International Women's Day, International Men's Day and Pride Month. By acknowledging them, you ensure that these communities are represented and that their voices are heard.

Around and between those big moments, however, remember that it's OK to turn down news stories or suggestions for content if that diversity topic has already been scheduled and covered. By doing this, you create space for other diversity characteristics outside of gender, race and sexual orientation – for example, religion, culture, age and disability. By covering different aspects of diversity, you can appeal to a wider variety of groups, helping people to see for themselves that diversity and inclusion is relevant to all.

During Norton's interview with Kohler, they discussed whether, with all the space given and progress made toward Pride, it was perhaps time for organizations to make space for other, less represented groups. Norton acknowledges that it's a controversial topic, but he partially agrees with Kohler:

'I think there are some tokenistic Pride efforts, and it's time to move beyond them. By which I mean, simply changing your logo to a rainbow flag every June but then doing nothing else to affect change, is not putting your money where your mouth is. Are you really offering anything specific like trans-awareness training or gender-neutral bathrooms? Do you encourage employees to use their pronouns in their email signature and bios online? Because if you don't, it's performative. It distracts from the core messages of the Pride movement and unintentionally drowns out other voices.'

Inclusion truth #5: Fear of saying the wrong thing leads to inaction

The fear of saying or doing the wrong thing can lead some people to do nothing at all. As Mattis says:

'You're going to have to get uncomfortable. Let's face it. If you have to hear about somebody's story (let's say they have a particular disability that you don't share), you will never know their experiences. You might find it uncomfortable or tough to hear their story, but that's their reality every single day.'

Younes agrees with Mattis:

'I think fear can be used as a convenient excuse. When anything is deemed important enough, people can, and do, lean into their discomfort and speak up. The conditions need to be right for this to happen without fear of reprisal, particularly when power dynamics are at play... I'm not afraid of making new mistakes. I'm afraid of making mistakes that could have been avoided had I just learned from somebody else who has already been through that mistake.'

Fear is also a convenient way to make something all about you explains Lordan:

'I think the problem as humans is that we want to be in all the stories. As soon as somebody says they didn't speak up because they were afraid, well, it's not really about them. It's about the person who was being treated badly in that moment. But now you've made the emotional response all about you.'

It can be a difficult dance though. 'In some organizations, you can get in more trouble for speaking up than you do for staying silent,' says Lordan. For internal communicators, it's important to carve out a safe space to explore diversity and inclusion. It's important to look to the good and bad of your peers to avoid avoidable mistakes. It's our role to facilitate the conversations that allow people to explore their own privilege without necessarily feeling guilt or shame. It's our role to create the forums in which people can ask questions without fear of offending. It's our role to support role models to be visible while protecting them from abuse or judgement.

Seven D&I myths busted

There are few topics more important and sensitive in the world of work right now; and with that portentous weight and gravity comes anxiety and fear. Let's bust some myths, and in doing so, hopefully help to quell the fear and taboo and get more people talking. We've identified the following seven D&I myths:

1. Unconscious bias training works.

2. Employee affinity groups can fix D&I.

3. Hiring a head of D&I creates inclusion.

4. Straight, White men are the enemy.

5. We need to feel guilty.

6. A meritocracy exists.

7. D&I is too difficult to measure.

Myth #1: Unconscious bias training works

'The idea that you can educate people out of unconscious bias is really bizarre to me,' says Lordan. 'There's this rise of behavioural science consultancies who go into firms and pull a lever that might have an effect in that moment of the day, but don't have any lasting impact.' Unconscious bias training is one of those in-the-moment interventions.

The Implicit Association Test is one of the most widely used tools to uncover unconscious biases. In the test, one word at a time is presented and the participant has to rapidly place it into one of two categories. For example, 'family' could appear and the participant would have to class it as either 'male' or 'female'. Kohler remembers a time she completed an implicit association test to measure biases regarding women in business:

'I assumed I couldn't possibly hold any biases toward women in the working world. After all, all of my managers have been strong, female leaders. I was working for a female-owned business at the time. Many of my best friends had started their own successful companies. My mother always worked. She somehow managed to go to graduate school while keeping a full-time job and raising us kids. It never occurred to me that she might stay at home – even though she didn't need to work. So, I was ready for my implicit association test. I thought I would nail it. My results came back and as it turns out, I'm as biased as a 1950s kitchenware commercial.'

Unconscious bias training is effective for surfacing biases and creating a new level of self-awareness; but knowledge alone is not enough to change behaviour. It's incredibly difficult to debias oneself. Unconscious bias training is a good first step, but not a solution in itself. As we often say among our clients – awareness is not an outcome.

Myth #2: Employee affinity groups can fix D&I

Employee resource groups are communities at work that employees self-organize and lead based on mutual areas of interest or demographics that they share in common. Common examples are single parents, veterans, LGBTQ+ and those organized around race or gender. Employee resource groups are a massive driver of engagement, but the pressure of creating an inclusive environment shouldn't fall on their shoulders. Norton says:

> 'Employee resource groups should be a source of feedback and a place to share experiences, but it's not up to Black people to fix racism. It's not up to gay people to fix homophobia. It's not up to women to fix gender inequality.'

D&I is also not something any individual can *do*. It is a profession. Younes says:

> 'Many companies just hand D&I efforts over to someone who they perceive as being diverse… It doesn't mean that the person can't step up to the challenge and learn to do meaningful things in diversity and inclusion, but there is knowledge and a skillset needed to drive systemic change in organizations. You wouldn't turn to someone who happens to manage their personal finances well and make them the chief financial officer.'

Myth #3: Hiring a head of D&I creates inclusion

This is one of the biggest myths according to Mattis. She says:

> 'People think we can bring in a person who will "fix" D&I in the space of six months to a year and then you're done… They don't think about the journey or where they're currently

at, yet that's so important. Things will take the
time they're going to take, and you have to
manage expectations. Just bringing in a D&I
officer and saying, "Let them sort it out," well,
there's a big problem with that.'

The assertion that D&I issues should be centrally positioned in HR is also a mistake, says Younes:

'The best cultural transformations, clearly
aligned to purpose and improving business
performance, are rarely driven out of HR. In
most companies, HR is not where the most
business-critical programmes and initiatives
sit. Why not have D&I as part of innovation,
R&D, customer experience or the business
strategy team, with a strong partnership with
HR, rather than the reverse?'

Why not, indeed? Another barrier that HR teams face
is fatigue. Lordan says:

'HR is usually rolling out a lot of initiatives
which often don't have any kind of real roots
in resolving the problem, so the link between
their efforts and real change isn't always
there... If nothing changes and everything
plateaus despite all this work, that can be
fatiguing. I've once been in a situation where
I met a gentleman who exploded in a D&I
meeting because his company was constantly
virtue signalling. They had fantastic pie charts
asking people how they felt about various

things, but nothing had changed in years and years.'

Myth #4: Straight, White men are the enemy

There's an idea that straight, White men are threatened by the swell of D&I efforts. Certainly some are, but so many more are ready and willing to be allies. Norton says:

'If this group can reflect on the history of larger organizations to see the inequalities, and instead of feeling threatened by them, see how they can have a positive impact for future generations, then we can move on from this "us vs them" mentality.'

This positive shift in attitude has come about partially because women and other previously marginalized groups are finding their power. Younes says:

'Over the last 100 years, women have been rising, marginalized ethnic and racial groups have been rising, being out and open about sexual orientation is rising, not accepting income inequality or religious persecution has been rising, and the list goes on… The demographic patterns and attitudes about equality are shifting everywhere, so our approaches need to shift and work at the intersections as well.'

Myth #5: We need to feel guilty

Norton feels strongly about this myth. He says:

> 'There's a large idea that a lack of D&I is something we need to feel guilty about. It's not. It's something that we need to feel empathetic about. Any sense of guilt will just get in the way of us taking action, because it will just make us uncertain.'

His point about empathy is spot on. It is empathy that triggers the compassion that leads us to act, so less guilt and more empathy is a good step forwards.

Myth #6: A meritocracy exists

'I know there is a belief that we have a meritocracy and that decisions are made fairly, but it's a myth,' says Younes. 'We may intend to make fair decisions, but there's all sorts of biases and human tendencies not to; and plenty of research to back that up.'

To drive this point home, Younes mentions the now-famous paper which explains how blind auditions have helped create more gender parity among orchestras.[5] The idea is an interesting one for businesses. What other mechanisms can you put in place to reduce your biases? For a start, look at patterns in your workforce that need disrupting. Younes says:

> 'If we have a meritocracy, and you look at the patterns of who is in your workforce, where

are the sticky floors and glass ceilings? Because we know they exist. I think meritocracy is an assumption and it needs to be tested. Oftentimes, lots of women, people from BAME or other minority groups will say they have to work twice as hard to get ahead. There are clear lead and lag indicators that can be measured to check whether this is reality or perception.'

Myth #7: D&I is too difficult to measure

'There are very few people who actually track the success of D&I efforts over months, and I can't think of anyone who is doing it over years,' says Lordan. The inability to measure is likely due to a perception that it's too difficult to measure – which is patently false. Younes says,

'I'm still hearing in 2021 that inclusion is hard to measure. No, it's not. There are plenty of ways to measure inclusion. For example, where do people fall out of the application process? Who gets included in critical assignments? Who gets sponsored?'

Stephane suggests starting with data. She says:

'The data can provide a picture of how things work at the organization. Disaggregating that data by race, ethnicity, gender and other identities begins to outline a story, which can be further developed by asking questions about that data. Does it differ based on role type, level, business unit, geography or years of experience? Who is succeeding and who is not? The patterns help fill in the story.'

We also have a clear end game which helps measurement. Stephane is optimistic about the future and describes the end game succinctly:

'Equity is achieved when all systemically marginalized groups have the same power, access, and influence as non-marginalized groups and have everything they need to thrive. It will take some time for us to start to see the outcome of the actions businesses take today, but right now, with the combination of events, attention, education, and clarity on systemic inequity, I'm very excited about the commitments to take action for real, sustainable change.'

Unpacking fairness and inequality

At the heart of D&I are issues surrounding fairness and inequality. It's not so much inequality that bothers us, but rather a lack of fairness. What we mean is that if everyone has the same starting point and where they end up is unequal, then that's on them. What we know is that everyone *doesn't* have the same starting point. Ergo, life's not fair.

Let's talk about fairness in a few dimensions for your consideration as you think through your messages and policies. The first is fairness, regarding who your policies reward and who they (perhaps unintentionally) harm. For example, when the Covid-19 pandemic hit, a large fairness rift was exposed when we looked at who got to continue working from home and who didn't. Some people's jobs didn't allow for working from home, so that difference could have been (and in many cases *was*) perceived as handing out either a punishment or a reward. You must always ask yourself if some of your decisions unintentionally reward some part of your workforce while harming another. The pandemic exposed other rifts, as well, says Stephane:

'The disparate impact of the pandemic on Black and people from other systemically marginalized communities has really brought things into focus in a way that we could not turn away from. People came together and demanded better; they demanded that organizations step up and make commitments.'

We also must consider fairness in terms of engagement. Just as we see so much turmoil about inequality on all levels of society, we have to turn an eye inwards. Consider the increase or decrease in behaviours you might see because of fair or unfair behaviour. These include co-operation, reciprocation, engagement, emotion-driven behaviour and other work-critical interactions.

Decisions that feel unfair might derive from a lack of co-operation, a decrease in performance, a decrease in trust, lashing out at colleagues or superiors and more. Research suggests that organizational bias can influence who gets access to what resources. This issue frustrates people no end. Addressing this source of frustration is an issue that HR practitioners have a duty to raise with leaders. They can also work with IC teams to create educational resources, policy guidelines and managerial coaching packs about fairness.

Marina Gonzalez, who we first heard from in our Change chapter, nails the diversity workplace equivalent of this fairness and inequality concept. She says:

> 'An important business practice I see being addressed more is around parity. It's not just about equity, but about parity. People want to know – especially when it comes to compensation and rewards – that they're getting equal pay, benefits and access to career opportunities such as promotions. If employees experience parity among their peers, they are engaged and focused on their role and the company's success rather than being concerned about whether they are being treated unfairly.'

Was Covid-19 the great equalizer?

You may have heard the phrase 'we're all in the same storm but with very different boats' during the pandemic. Other than the fact that we were all facing the same viral foe, Covid-19 wasn't the great equaliser many thought it would be. Those with money and privilege were able to ride out social isolation in the luxury of their home offices while others were cramped in their small apartments with three or four roommates, jostling for space on the kitchen table and stressing the Wi-Fi bandwidth. The latter were still luckier and more privileged than others, though. They were able to work from home rather than putting themselves at risk every day in the face of a deadly disease. While Covid-19 may have spotlighted issues of fairness and inequality, it by no means levelled out those issues.

A closer look at the 2020 Black Lives Matter movement

We asked Norton to give us his reflections on the social upheaval of the 2020 Black Lives Matter (BLM) movement, an event to which some organization's D&I teams struggled to respond. He says:

'Casting our minds back to January 2020, we were still riding the wave of the #MeToo movement and gender inequality in the workplace was under the spotlight. Organizations were still responding to this, only four or five years into the gender pay gap being legally reported. Then the Covid-19 pandemic hits.

'We started seeing people of colour dying at faster rates than White people. The data showed there was some sort of social inequality at play, whether it was the jobs that people do, access to health care or access to high quality food. All the data showed a fundamental unfairness.

'And then came the brutal murder of George Floyd. Shocking certainly, but his death was not a one-off. It was a cataclysmic moment when people just became sick and tired of all of the unfairness.'

Younes also shared her reflections on how organizations reacted to the movement:

'Lots of companies and organizations came out with statements of support. Let's see how the balance of power, privilege and the true experience of greater equity plays out. Will more of the under-represented minorities remain disproportionately and negatively impacted in tough economic times?

'Will those in power seek out new solutions to existing problems (this requires diversity and inclusion), or will they resort to the same methods to solve problems as they always have: preserving the status quo rather than being willing to positively disrupt it?

'Self-preservation is a powerful force and those
with power are used to it and not showing
significant signs of wanting to share. If they
were open to a "power with" vs a "power
over" model, we'd have a lot more visible
progress by now.'

Some organizations just weren't ready to have the
conversation about race yet, nor were their external
and internal communication functions. Time and
again, communication teams indicated surprise at
being expected to say something – and found that they
didn't have a voice. They didn't have a stand. They felt
they hadn't had these types of conversations before.
The bottom line here is that this is not an excuse. D&I
has been a growing practice in business for some time
now. Part of their job is to recognize what people are
reacting to in the world around them and take a stand.

Younger generations coming into the workforce demand more

'As more young people enter the workforce, we're
seeing a shift in what they expect in this space,' says
Mattis:

'There is more of a push, and we see that
already with people who are out there fighting
for trans rights, fighting for women's rights,
fighting for racial equality. There are the people

> who have decided that they are going to create
> the change and they're not going to leave that
> at home when they come to work.'

It's a common assertion that younger people feel far more comfortable and entitled to question the intentions and actions of their employers and the brands they consume, but Younes disagrees:

> 'Increasingly, people of all ages are questioning
> perceptions of an imagined meritocracy and
> that D&I representation lowers standards in
> the workplace. Under-represented groups have
> to consistently and significantly outperform
> majority members to be seen as equal.'

There's also the question of how long that perception lasts once those newer to work get used to the way things are. Lordan is of the opinion that the shift to inclusivity plateaus over time:

> 'A lot of time people will say that the younger
> generations have different attitudes and expect
> different things, so if we just give it time, it
> will organically change. I worry about that
> for a couple of reasons. While younger people
> are more progressive, they get less so as they
> age. People's attitudes towards inclusion
> and progression are plateaued. It plateaus at
> people in their forties and fifties, so I don't
> have as much faith in the younger generation
> really creating the inclusive culture without
> another lightning rod happening at the same

time. Otherwise, they'll just adapt into the company's current culture.'

Exploring your privilege

'There's not a lot of people, including leaders, who are self-aware in terms of what they do and what they say,' says Mattis:

> 'It's not about being perfect, because there's no such thing. I think sometimes we try to strive for perfection that, frankly, causes a lot more stress than necessary. But I think if we can come from a position of understanding that we have privilege and we have biases, then that's a starting point.'

Consider your privilege

The concept of privilege was highlighted during the Covid-19 pandemic. Even though the virus did not discriminate, it was far easier for the wealthy to shelter from risk and still get their work done.

We are all three-dimensional humans with complex identities. When different minority characteristics intersect, we know that people face greater barriers and disadvantages. All too often, privilege is discussed in terms that are too simplistic and get in the way of really exploring what action you can take to be a better ally. Norton says that his experience of growing up gay was tough:

> 'I faced a lot of bullying at school and I did everything I could to hide my true identity. But now that I'm older I'm able to see that, in the grand scheme of things, I am privileged. I'm a cisgender, White, educated man. In today's society, I've benefited from these characteristics far more than I've been disadvantaged by my sexual orientation. Knowing that I'm operating with a "privilege profit" like this means I take an active choice to spend my privilege trying to lift others up.'

There are many dimensions to consider when reflecting on the extent of your own privilege. The exercise below has been designed to assist you with a few of these.

EXERCISE: REFLECTING ON THE EXTENT OF YOUR OWN PRIVILEGE

Internal dimensions

- Consider your gender identity: Do you conform to society's standard definitions of male or female? What do you notice about people who share your own gender identity?

- Consider your sexual orientation: How openly can you talk about the people you love and the make-up of your family?

- Consider your body: Do you have a physical disability or long-term health condition? Does your brain work in a different way to those around you? To what extent does your physical fitness affect you?

- Consider your race: How many role models do you have that share your skin colour? What assumptions do people make about you based on your race?

- Consider your ethnicity: What trends do you notice among people who share your ethnic background?

External dimensions

- Consider your class: How did the income of your family affect you as you grew up? What did you have automatic access to that others didn't?

- Consider your education: Did you thrive in the academic system? Were you able to attend further education? Where do you notice differences between people who have a university degree and those that don't?

- Consider where you live: Can you easily access green space? Are there arts and cultural venues nearby? What is the air quality like in your environment?

- Consider your faith: How open can you be about your faith? Has your faith (or lack thereof) made you feel different to those around you?

- Consider your appearance: Do people treat you differently compared to people who look or dress differently to you?

Having reflected on these questions, you should have a clearer idea about the extent to which you've benefitted from societal privilege. This is step one. Next, consider how other people may be advantaged or disadvantaged by these dimensions. What's vital to remember is that you can *never* assume someone's experience based on the characteristics you can see or hear. Instead, use these dimensions as the basis for a conversation. Be curious and open-minded when people share stories of their journeys to get where they are today and how these dimensions may have impacted them along the way.

The following exercise by diversity consultant Scott Horton was used to great effect in a scarlettabbott leadership event for a well-known, online UK estate agent. The intention of the exercise is self-reflection and examination of your own network. It's an interesting and enlightening exercise based on the premise that the more diverse your network is, the more perspectives, viewpoints and experiences you can tap into and benefit from.

EXERCISE: YOUR TRUSTED 10

Draw a table like the one shown below. Use it to list the ten people you consider to be your most trusted advisors, confidantes, mentors, influencers and friends, adding information under the column headings to see how diverse your network is.

Name (or initials)	Gender	Race	Age	Sexual orientation	Education level	Disability (yes|no)	Marital status	Other

Seven tips to kickstart your D&I efforts

Wherever you are on your D&I journey, here are seven golden tips to help you and your business be even better:

1. Hire the right people.

2. Get senior leaders on board.

3. Put a measurement strategy in place.

4. Use stories.

5. Remove barriers.

6. Do the right thing.

7. Gather the right information.

Tip #1: Hire the right people

You will not drive organizational change unless it is a priority to more than just the D&I function. 'Too many organizations just give D&I to somebody as a side job, or they give it to someone with a big fancy title with no resources, budget, or access to executives,' says Younes. Thornton agrees:

> 'D&I is essentially a change and transformation gig – a job that requires influencing, coaching and lobbying at the most senior levels. Changing hearts, minds and systems takes experience and gravitas – and sponsorship.

Without influence and tangible support at a C-suite level, it's hard to change anything in an organization. Of course, the relationships, networks, allies and influencers D&I needs to succeed filter right through every level and part of an organization.'

This is the one area where Lordan allows that we can use unconscious bias training – but with a time-sensitive catch:

'If you use unconscious bias training in short bursts before a decision is made, you can make a better decision. You don't need an expert to do this. Simply remind people before the interview that unconscious signals allow us to make good (but also bad) decisions sometimes, and that obstacles might be different across groups. That must be done right before the interview; and again in the moment before they make the choice. The real value in behavioural science is how we can get people to think twice in high stakes situations.'

Tip #2: Get senior leaders on board

You 100% need your senior leaders on board. Norton agrees:

'I think not getting leaders on board is a large blind spot. For example, a report from HR DataHub found that the largest reduction in the ethnicity pay gap was when a senior leader was actively championing racial equality in the organization.[6] When senior leaders get involved and influence change, the actual pay gap… the fundamental differences between Black people and White people… will be reduced.'

Mattis also agrees:

'It's always a warning sign when senior leaders aren't visible. D&I teams sometimes put things out there, but when we don't see leaders talking about it and we don't see leaders referring to it or living it, that can be an issue. As much as I've seen more conversations with middle and lower management, which is great, the reality is that people look to their leaders. If you see your leader doing something or not doing something, with the way we mimic, it can be impactful – or it can be really negative.'

One great way to get senior leaders on board is to relate efforts back to the bottom line. Younes did just that:

'When I was working for a pharmaceutical company, I took D&I to the research and development folks because we always say these platitudes around diversity driving innovation. I challenged that. I asked if we *were* consciously and intentionally pulling diverse people together to drive innovation.'

You also need to set them up for success, says Lordan:

> 'Give leaders the tools to be an experimental leader. If I were in an organization heading up D&I efforts and thinking about what I can do to move the needle, it would be getting people to experiment with different management strategies.'

Tip #3: Put a measurement strategy in place

We talked about how it's a myth that D&I is difficult to measure and Younes has provided some ideas around measurement (including looking at where applicants fall out of the process), but there's more you can do. Lordan suggests auditing career progression decisions:

> 'Audit who got promoted. Audit who goes for promotion and gets knocked back. Audit who asks for a pay rise and gets knocked back. Audit who gets a stretch assignment and who doesn't. These simple audits evoke saliency, and we know that if we're paying attention to something, we're more likely to address it.'

Tip #4: Use stories

The communication world often espouses the power of storytelling, and for good reason. Stories work.

When it comes to D&I, they're extremely effective. Norton agrees:

> 'Stories. Lived experiences. Because a personal truth is always the truth. And when presented as such, there is no challenge to it... If someone says, "This is my experience and it made me feel like this," it's fact.'

Make sure you don't feature the same two or three people repeatedly. It's a balance between sharing the stories that really matter and those for whom the company is committed to improving the lived experiences, without them being viewed as a tick-box exercise. 'If you're not careful and if your D&I efforts aren't authentic, people can end up becoming the token faces that get wheeled out on every single brochure for the sake of diversity,' cautions Norton.

Tip #5: Remove barriers

Right now, inclusion support at work is largely comprised of employee resource groups, D&I teams and senior leaders. Each has an important role to play, but sometimes D&I is about taking stuff away rather than adding more noise to an already loud conversation. For example, if there is a barrier to entry for young Black talent, you must remove these barriers. 'You can't just ship people around the edges when it comes to recruiting,' says Norton. 'The journey has to be as open and as accessible as possible; that makes it fairer for everyone.'

There are also the barriers of time and energy. D&I is often done as part of someone's job rather than their full-time job. It's then something they have to consider on top of everything else. Norton says:

> 'So often D&I is considered something extra. You've got to give 100% to your job, and then another 10% of your brain capacity to diversity and inclusion. Which is nonsense.'

You have to also remove barriers that prevent diverse conversations. Lordan says:

> 'There's no point paying for diverse talent and not including them in the conversation, not getting their views, and not getting their diverse perspectives. Some organizations have ended up with diversity without inclusion, which is quite sad.'

Tip #6: Do the right thing

A controversial question to ponder is if it matters whether people truly believe in inclusivity and celebrate diversity – or if they just take the right actions because it's the right thing to do. For an incredibly light example of what we mean, take recycling. You may put that Amazon cardboard box in the recycling bin because you know you're supposed to, rather than out of any strong desire to save the planet. You may even think that it's just one box, so what impact could it really have – but you take the right action anyway. If the action is the right one, does the intention behind it matter? Mattis finds this an interesting question:

> 'Doing the right thing is a good measure point, because you won't understand everything. I have moments where I think, "Oh my goodness, I don't have time for this," but I have to check myself and remember that just because I don't have time for something, doesn't mean someone else doesn't have time for it. It's important to them. You have to see the bigger picture, and ultimately, do the right thing. This also goes back to self-awareness, which we've talked about. When you're self-aware, you know if what you are doing is coming from a place of good intent. You also know if it's coming from a place of not wanting to do something but knowing it's the right thing to do. And that's powerful.'

Tip #7: Gather the right information

'I've said this in every organization I've worked in. There are two resources I need to do my job effectively,' says Younes. 'I need a good data analyst to create a good dataset, because good datasets help me change mindsets.' Mattis cautions that you need to understand who you've got in your organization and what they want:

'If you don't, then you're literally taking a stab in the dark. Work out how to get that data if you don't have it. It could be updating your HR system or it could be asking people to provide that data voluntarily so you can start building programmes with it. You can even use it to change your recruitment process, where you're asking more questions upfront rather than when people get into the organization.'

Wrapping it up: Applying what you've learned at work

We've shared expert and evidence-based opinions and perspectives and given you some useful exercises and tools to try, but if this chapter helps and equips you to do anything, our intent is that you feel able to have even better conversations, make stronger and more confident challenges and take the next step on your own D&I journey – both personally and organizationally.

The five truths of inclusion

1. Diversity matters to everyone, whether they know it or not.

2. It's not the role of internal communicators to communicate 'the solution'.

3. Actions matter more than ambition (or actions speak louder than words).

4. It's OK to say no in the spirit of fairness.

5. Fear of saying the wrong thing leads to inaction.

Seven D&I myths busted

1. Unconscious bias training works.

2. Employee affinity groups can fix D&I.

3. Hiring a head of D&I creates inclusion.

4. Straight, White men are the enemy.

5. We need to feel guilty.

6. A meritocracy exists.

7. D&I is too difficult to measure.

Seven tips to kickstart your D&I efforts

1. Hire the right people.

2. Get senior leaders on board.

3. Put a measurement strategy in place.

4. Use stories.

5. Remove barriers.

6. Do the right thing.

7. Gather the right information.

Exercises and resources

- Reflecting on the extent of your own privilege

- Your trusted 10

PART TWO
BETTER LEADERS

L eading is bloody hard. Leading in business is even harder. It requires courage, persistence and personal sacrifice when what you'd sometimes rather do is curl up in a ball and hope it all goes away. It will make you unpopular with some as you must challenge the status quo.

Leaders are watched intently by their followers: their language, physical cues and signs that either reinforce their messaging and rhetoric or subtly give their observers permission to do otherwise. Leaders are always on stage, which can be an exhausting place to be.

Quite simply, a lot of people don't have the energy, courage or appetite for it, and that's OK. Leading is first and foremost a choice; but it's also a wonderful privilege.

So much is written about leadership, and for anyone aspiring to improve as a leader it's tough to know where to start, but the job of a leader in any organization should never be confusing. The job of a leader is to continually drive and adapt their business to meet the demands of their future customer.

Ironically though, the leader's primary focus should not be the customer. It should be their team. The leader impacts and influences their direct team, who in turn impact and influence their direct team, who then offer amazing products and services to the customer. Big difference.

Leaders must create environments which enable others to thrive. They are the fire-starters and custodians of organizational culture. Through the consistency of their attitude and their actions, they inspire those around them to want to think and act better. By doing so, they draw others to their cause. People want to work for them, they want to be around them, they want to learn from them. Leadership happens by building a strong following.

In my experience though, too many businesses still expect a leader to do the job of a manager. They expect them to oversee already established operating models and to deliver specific results against them. That's what they're performance managed against, so that's what they focus on.

Then when competitors gain a foothold, or the market shifts, they find themselves on the back foot and become extremely reactive. Change and agility are not within the company's cultural DNA, because those at the top have never tasked their leaders with (or rewarded them for) driving those attributes.

I created the GOD principle to help leaders address this challenge. It is my call to arms for leaders everywhere: those who want to become more impactful, more inspiring and build more successful organizations. Distilled over fifteen years of leadership coaching, it is made up of three elements which every great leader I have ever worked with, known or studied has consistently focused on:

- **Growth:** The vision to see things better.

- **Optimism:** The attitude to see opportunity in adversity.

- **Disruption:** The action to drive improvements through change.

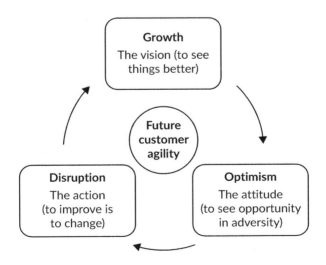

The three operate as a virtuous circle, with each reinforcing and strengthening the other. Take one away or focus on one in isolation and the power is lost.

My approach to these in each chapter is relatively simple and practical. Experience tells me that complicated and theoretical ideas and processes are the enemies of effective leadership. To that end, I have written the chapters in a workbook style so you can lift the tips and exercises off the page and experiment with them as you wish.

This will involve some courage and reflection on your part, a lot of trial and error, conscious focus and, most importantly, practice. Stay with it though, and I promise you: the results will come.

Think back to school and the teacher you remember, even now, who stood out and made a positive difference in your life. As a business leader, you have an opportunity every day to be that person for someone else. That's pretty amazing. Let's do it.

— *Charlie*

FOUR
Growth

The classic debate in relation to business leadership has always been around the difference between leadership and management. Leaders must continually drive and adapt their business to meet the demands of their future customer. Managers, on the other hand, are responsible for maintaining and sustaining those adaptations. The difference between the two is growth. Leaders must grow a business and keep it moving forwards, while managers must maintain the business and keep the engine humming. Growth is change. When something grows, it cannot regress back to its former state. Great leaders are considered great leaders because they change things for the better – they view change through a growth lens.

As a leader – and human being – growth is about far more than career development, qualifications or achievements. Growth is an appetite for life – to explore, discover, push, be better, evolve, learn and love. It's by doing these things that we feel alive, build our confidence and self-esteem; and in doing these things every day, we inspire others to want to do the same. We draw others to us and lay the building blocks for a culture of learning and exploration.

Growth is as important to us as oxygen. If something isn't growing, it stagnates and begins to decline. It is the primary rule of all living things. Businesses, and the people at their helm, are no exception.

To some extent, a measure of our growth is our legacy. What changed and what was better because of us? Some would argue that legacy is for egos, but we all leave one, whether we like it or not. Great leaders know that a successful legacy, first and foremost, is determined by the difference they've made in other people's lives – starting with those closest to them. A great leader works bloody hard to make sure they leave things in better shape than they found them.

Until the end of 2019, Hayley Macdougall was the Global Head of Talent for the International Manager (IM) programme at HSBC – arguably the oldest and most successful senior talent programme anywhere in the world. Over 150 years, with just one exception, the programme has yielded every single group chair and group CEO for the organization and provided the majority of country CEOs across the sixty-four regions where HSBC operates. Macdougall knows a thing or two about what a great leader looks like:

'Growth is probably the one that stands out and is most obvious in my mind, for how I, and many of the CEOs, would differentiate between the managers. It was a noticeable differentiator for the particularly strong managers who were picked for the great jobs and who were very much the poster children for the programme. They were the ones that demonstrated both personal growth – a huge eagerness to learn and develop and be put into really challenging situations – but were equally as interested and invested in the growth and future of the programme and the tone it set for the whole group. Despite being incredibly busy people, they would always carve out time to explore new initiatives, develop junior managers or contribute new opportunities.'[1]

Growth is about continually realizing potential. This potential can be in us as individuals, a team or a business sector – it doesn't matter. Great leaders take things and change them for the better, harnessing and realizing potential wherever they may find it. They understand that there is no limit to potential. There is only limit to our imagination and energy to realize potential.

In this chapter, we will explore:

- The three components of growth

- Growing your leadership skills

- Using the GAPS grid to fine-tune your focus

- Driving empowering feedback

- Growing your team's ability

- Growing your business relationships

The three components of growth

From a leadership perspective, growth can be broken down into three, intentional steps:

1. Visualize something better than it is now.

2. Mobilize the people and resources necessary to make it happen.

3. Pull the trigger.

Whether leading yourself, a small team or a multi-national organization, this principle doesn't change. It is that continual evolution that the 'even better' leader applies to everything. Sir Stephen O'Brien, Chair of Barts Health NHS Trust and founding CEO of Business in the Community and London First, says:

> 'It's all about self-awareness and purpose. Lots of people can define and communicate a vision, but we've all watched countless politicians and so-called "leaders" sharing visions but not meaning a word of them. The leadership difference that makes the difference is having something that you really want to do, and then working your socks off to actually

deliver it. And that nearly always means working out how to mobilize other people.'[2]

Let's look at each stage in more detail.

Step #1: Visualize something better than it is now

Effective leaders take things and grow them; they change them for the better. We all see things – services, relationships, people, products – around us and imagine them as better. A big difference between great leaders and everyone else is that great leaders commit to doing something about it. That is what realizing potential means. It's intentionally pushing the boundaries of something to see what else is possible, how else it can be done or how much further it can be taken.

Until 1954, running a four-minute mile was considered physically impossible. For decades many had tried and failed, but on 6 May that year at an event in Oxford, Roger Bannister achieved the impossible. He ran a mile in 3 minutes, 59.4 seconds. A remarkable achievement, but just as remarkable was that within two years of Bannister's achievement, nine other athletes had also broken the four-minute mile – seven of them faster than Bannister. After all those years of trying, how was that possible? Bannister had set a new standard, one which brought about improvements in the training and preparation of his successors and enabled them to push what was possible even further.

He changed not just *what* others believed was possible, he also changed *how* it was possible.

In 1995 Reed Hastings and Marc Randolph were developing their company, Kibble, which aimed to make DVD rental easier compared with the established giants such as Blockbuster. In 1997 they changed their name to Netflix, offering an online library of just 900 titles. Ten years later, they launched their first streaming product; and the rest is history. Despite setbacks, huge financial risk and, at times, ridicule, Hastings and Randolph saw the potential for home entertainment in a way that others simply couldn't imagine. In doing so, they transformed not only how we now all consume entertainment, but how the entire industry operates.

As leaders, the tougher the challenge or the more the odds are stacked against them, the more they strengthen their resolve and the harder they push to realize potential. That is what inspires others to join their cause.

As a leader, what is it you're trying to grow? What do you care passionately about that you want to see being better – for yourself, for your team and for your organization? The GAPS exercise later in this chapter will help with this, but for now, just be aware how easy or difficult you find it to answer these questions. If things come to mind easily, then what have you done about them? If you're struggling to think of things, then where else is your time and energy currently focused?

Step #2: Mobilize the people and resources necessary to make it happen

Once you have prioritized what you wish to improve, you then need to communicate this to the people who will deliver this improvement. This is where leaders need the communication skills to instil that energy and commitment in those around them.

> **Vision** is a grandiose term that is often attributed to leadership, but a vision is simply seeing something better than it is now.

What it's called – a vision, a goal, an objective – doesn't really matter (and will be dependent on the scale and ambition of whatever you are trying to achieve). What is crucial, is that you are able to explain this in a way that ensures people understand the part they, as individuals, play in the success of your vision. As Sarah Spooner, Head of Customer Experience at Vodafone reflects:

> 'If we establish a long-term vision for where we're aiming, defining what success looks like for everyone, we must then chunk that down for each individual. The key focus for any leader has to be, "Who are your team? What drives them? What motivates them? What are they good at? Where are their gaps? Do their own team fill their gaps?" Once you get this, you'll know how to mobilize them.'[3]

There are those who lead because they have the word 'leader' in their job title, but they are not truly driven to see things better. These people can achieve a certain amount but will fail to ignite inspiration in those around them, because they're not personally invested in what they're trying to grow. It's transactional. There has to be an emotional investment from the leader, something they are moved to achieve, if others are to be inspired to follow.

This can be tricky; let's face it. We're often leading projects that don't exactly excite; it's not always like putting a man on the moon. It's hard to get fired up over implementing the latest compliance regulations, a new sales protocol or rolling out a new HR management system. This is where our leadership ability to connect to something bigger is critical: taking our followers with us towards a greater good, a compelling set of benefits or a compelling vision for the future. In Chapter 1 we talk about ensuring that change is purposeful. The same applies to how we lead. Finding your personal purpose (or vision) in all you do and inspiring others to follow you on the journey is key. 'You must keep connecting back to your vision as a touch point,' reflects Spooner:

> 'Keep asking and answering the questions of,
> "Where are we going? Where we are now?
> What is it we've delivered so far? Where are we
> going next? What's the next baby step? What's
> the next big leap? How do we get everyone in
> the organization excited about this? Who do we
> need most to help deliver this? Who or what's

going to get in our way?" These are the things that great leaders do well, helping their teams understand all this with great clarity.'

The mark of a great leader is often not how impressive they are as an individual; it is how impressive their team is. A team that is enthusiastic, energetic, supportive and autonomous suggests a leader who is emotionally committed to what they, as a team, are trying to achieve. The leader has invested in building a culture which allows their team to thrive. That's why the best business leaders are obsessed with growth – the growth of themselves as leaders and the growth and development of their people. This, in turn, results in the growth of their business. Aileen O'Toole, Chief People Officer, Prosus Group and Naspers, couldn't agree more that being as close to your team as possible is the way to go:

'Be really careful about who you choose to work with, and then invest heavily in them. My advice is to avoid spending all your effort establishing your mission and too little time choosing and nurturing your team. Who you go down the path with is probably far more important than the path itself.' [4]

Step #3: Pull the trigger

A leader can have a great vision and be surrounded by great people, but unless they commit to getting started, everything else is irrelevant. This may sound obvious, but as Macdougall explains:

'It's very easy, particularly within a large organization, for leaders to make a lot of noise and be highly visible but actually deliver very little. Lots of leaders have good ideas and lots can talk a good game; but it's the ones who actually get on with it that stand out. There will always be restrictions around resources, budget and so on. That's just business. The leaders who don't accept that as an excuse, and still find ways to start, to move forwards, to try and implement even small things – they are the ones that attract more confidence, more support and more resource.'

Spooner completely agrees:

'Leaders get overwhelmed by scale – the scale and complexity of things you need to improve. I just push people to start. Just start and see how far you get. If you've improved it by 5%, brilliant. If it's 10% or 50%, even more brilliant, but just keep going. The skill of just getting started is hugely underrated. A lot of people can present what needs to happen but not enough commit to actually making it happen.'

In our experience, leaders all too easily get caught up in procrastination and analyses – the so called 'paralysis through analysis' syndrome. Leaders want almost no risk in a decision, hoping the future can somehow be predicted. Clearly this is nonsensical, but it is often the underlying cause for not pulling the trigger.

Fear is often a prevalent factor preventing the leader from action, for example, a fear of harming the company or a fear of appearing incompetent. In this instance, leaders should take a tip from Jeff Bezos, the founder of Amazon:

> 'Some decisions are consequential and irreversible or nearly irreversible – one-way doors – and these decisions must be made methodically, carefully, slowly, with great deliberation and consultation… But most decisions aren't like that – they are changeable, reversible – they're two-way doors.'[5]

When it comes to making a decision and committing to action, you would do well to remember two simple rules.

First, that you have complete control over your actions, but no control over others' reactions. Leaders must look to mitigate risks, but none of us have a crystal ball. By acting, we provoke a reaction. If we're sensitive to those reactions (and egos are kept in check) and able to remain adaptable, we can adjust our next action accordingly. Remind yourself that the unknown does not yet exist and so it is within your power to create it. This can be both exciting and daunting, but unless you try, unless you commit to doing something, you cannot complain that you didn't get what you wanted.

Second (and one that often causes frustration within leadership teams) is not allowing perfection to become the enemy of 'good enough'. All too often, projects or ideas get held up because leaders want to continually socialize and develop something before it can be launched. It is much better to develop something to the point of 'good enough', and get it out there. Then (as in the first point above), it can be adapted according to a known (ie the reaction to it) rather than an unknown (ie your perception of what the reaction will be).

Again, Bezos offers some wise council here:

> 'Most decisions should probably be made with somewhere around 70% of the information you wish you had… If you're good at course correcting, being wrong may be less costly than you think, whereas being slow is going to be expensive for sure.'[6]

In leadership, as in life, moving and adapting are always better than standing still and wondering. Build your vision, get others excited about your vision, then trust your gut and go for it. The rest you'll figure out as you go.

Growing your leadership skills

Richard Kimber, former CEO of First Direct Bank and Regional MD for Google, now founder of AI company Daisee, says:

'If you're not focused on learning and growing, your personal risk is that your career runs out of road. The potential absence of growth is your own burning platform; the existence of growth is how you guide your own future. It's your choice: do you want to be the person tapped on the shoulder hearing, "Hey, we don't need you anymore," or do you want to be the person that keeps hearing, "Hey, we want you to explore this new thing; we don't know what to do. Can you help us uncover it?"'[7]

Leaders are learners. Leaders want to develop and grow. That starts with looking forwards to where we want to go, but also looking inward and acknowledging that everyone (including ourselves) has blind spots. Think about driving a car. From a certain position, no matter which mirror you check, you just cannot see another car about to pass. The same concept applies to us as individuals.

We can reflect, looking long and hard in the mirror… but still not see things which others can. Things that (at best) can limit our potential but (at worst) could be damaging to our career. Acknowledging we have a blind spot – a gap in our skillset, a behaviour we need to adjust, a tendency toward a certain mindset – and then seeking ways to shrink that blind spot requires both honesty and humility. These are qualities essential to building trust, and they are crucial to even better leadership. 'Having a learning mindset and humility go hand in hand,' says O'Toole:

'Being curious, genuinely curious, and actually stopping to ask questions about why and what does this change; why is it that way? It only better equips you as a leader and signals to others the kind of culture you value. It's not necessarily acquiring a bunch of certificates from a business school or always being in some sort of formal education. I think it's day-to-day curiosity that can really unlock some treasures. It's the humble asking of questions... and not needing to have the answers.'

The more we're prepared to look at ourselves and seek the opinion of those we trust and respect, the greater our level of self-awareness becomes. This is key to even better leadership because it gives us choice over how we show up as a leader in different situations. For instance, if, as a leader, I have little patience for planning and analysing and prefer to quickly agree actions and get moving, that will clearly be beneficial in certain situations. The flip side, however, is I may sometimes make rash decisions and alienate those in the team whose job it is to analyse and plan. There's no right or wrong here: it's simply about better understanding our biases and drivers and how and when they enhance or inhibit us. Jeremy Petty, MD of employee engagement consultancy scarlettabbott, recalls his own lightbulb moment around blind spots and self-awareness:

'A big leap in my own growth as a leader was identifying and acknowledging my blind spot, taking responsibility. I had a tendency to point to the things around me, things weren't as good as they could be, and feel victimised by that. It took a while (and some work on me) to shift that mindset and realise that's just bullshit – it's really up to me and I can control that. That was transformational. Now I'm taking responsibility for whatever "it" is. It doesn't make it easy to change things, but at least I know that's down to me, it's my responsibility. That was a real change.'[8]

Growth is a game of focus

Sampson describes how working with elite sporting organizations brought the importance of focus into, well, focus:

'I'm incredibly fortunate to work with the leadership of some elite sporting organizations. One of my big, early learns from that environment, which I think is crucial to business leadership, is focus. Regardless of the sport, if you ask an athlete what they're working on to get better at whatever they do, they'll recount it straight away. They know, because every day they practise on improving whatever that thing is.'

Chris Brindley, former MD of Metro Bank and now chair of the Rugby League World Cup, also takes inspiration from athletes. 'I strive to be consistently excellent in my behaviour and performance, because that's what I think elite athletes do brilliantly. They turn up all the time.'[9]

Stop three people in your organization and ask them the same question: 'What specifically are you better at now than you were six months ago?' We'd be surprised if even one of them can give a succinct answer. It doesn't take a genius to work out that if we're not laser-focused on what we want to get better at, then it's highly unlikely we'll see any improvement.

We know what you're thinking. This is all well and good, but professional athletes only have to practise and work on improving their game. That's their sole job. It's true. Leading in business is far harder and more complex because of the huge number of balls to juggle and plates to spin among often clashing priorities. The idea of then building in 'practice time' on top of everything else is a non-starter.

Here's the good news: to grow and be an even better leader, you don't have to do anything additional; you just need to view everyday things through a different lens. Try small experiments to approach tasks differently and then evaluate the results. Everything you do is an opportunity to practise. The only difference is your focus. The next meeting you attend, the next presentation you give, the next one-to-one you have with a teammate – even the next email you send

– these are all fantastic opportunities to practise doing something better. Let's be honest, how many typical workday situations do we sleepwalk through, without conscious thought of the impact we intend to have or the energy we want to inject? We just show up and get it done because we have to before moving quickly on to the next thing.

Growth starts with fine-tuning our focus around what it is we want to improve and then being clear about what improvement looks like. Let's give it a go. It's time to switch on the kettle, find a quiet space to sit and spend some time being a bit more strategic about yourself.

Using the GAPS grid to fine-tune your focus

The GAPS grid is designed to help you reflect on what we consider to be the four pillars of career success for any leader. It's intended to help raise your awareness and focus in relation to your gaps. These are the things that, if not improved or implemented, might derail your achievements and aspirations. The grid will also help you figure out your vision. If you have a coach or trusted advisor, the grid provides a great structure for a powerful conversation. Alternatively, it can be completed alone. Either way, it requires total honesty and openness on your part.

EXERCISE: THE GAPS GRID

Work through the grid answering the questions for each section, but feel free to adapt or embellish the questions as you wish.

Important: Write your thoughts down. The virtual act of taking thoughts out of your head and committing them to paper allows you to view them far more objectively.

The GAPS grid has four areas. We'll look at each in turn:

1. Goals to grow
2. Abilities
3. Perceptions
4. Success

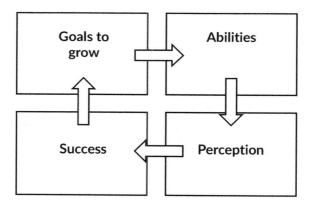

Goals to grow

As we've already discussed, growth is about seeing the potential for something to be better and then realizing that potential. It's about forward momentum and is future-focused, whether five minutes or five years from now. It's difficult to move forwards with deliberation and focus without some idea of what we're moving towards; we need something we can tie a strong elastic band around, which then pulls us towards it.

Questions:

- Do you believe you have more potential than you are currently able to show?
- What are you focused on doing to help you realize more of that potential?
- When you think about your career, what is it you want?
- What would you like to be doing that you're not currently?
- What ambitions do you have for your future customers over the next twelve months?
- How will you be better as a leader twelve months from now?

Abilities

Goals provide an important target, but it's who and what you need to become to achieve that goal which really matters. This is what we mean by abilities. These are the changes and development required in you to realize your ambitions: the new skills, mindset and experience. Often, these are the things that require the most courage and honesty to confront because they require a certain vulnerability from us to explore our blind spots.

Questions:

- To achieve the goals you've outlined above, what skills do you recognize you need to get better at?
- What skills/qualities do you see in others that you wish you had more of?
- What is the biggest change you need to make within yourself to achieve more of your potential?
- What's easiest about that and can be done quickly?
- What's hardest and will take longer?

Perception

Like it or not, your perception is your reality. What gets said about you when you're not in the room by your senior stakeholders will largely determine your career trajectory. What your team say about you behind your back will determine how successfully you can drive strategy and improvement through them. In Sampson's work as an executive coach, he's been exposed to the inner workings of many organizations and has lost count of how many times he's heard a business leader talk about their team – those who struggle, those who are steady and those who are superstars. Often, they will have limited awareness of how they are being described. If you don't know how you're perceived, you are exposed. That's not only a risk but also robs you of a huge opportunity to develop. (See the feedback section later in this chapter to explore the best way to elicit feedback and understand people's perception of you.)

Questions:

- How do you think you're seen by others when you're having a good day? How about when it's a bad day?

- How would you like to be seen? Write down some words that you'd be thrilled to hear if you heard people using them to describe you.
- How do you aspire to be seen specifically as a leader?
- Do you think you're seen differently by different groups?

Success

If you're focused on growth, then it's important that you spend some time considering what that looks like in terms of success so that you know that you're doing the right things and heading in the direction that you need to be.

Questions:

- What measures of success do you have for your growth over the next twelve months (consider this in terms of yourself, your team and then your organization)?
- How would your boss describe what success in your role looks like?
- What do your sponsors/senior stakeholders consider success to be for your performance in your role?
- Who do you need onside to smooth your path to success and who can support you? (The 'Growing your business relationships' section later in this chapter can help with this.)

Conclusions from GAPS

Having reflected on the four areas, notice what themes have become obvious as a result. Where might you be exposed as a leader? Has the exercise revealed anything you realize needs to be actioned immediately?

If nothing else, will you commit to doing one thing that will help you realize more of your potential?

Driving empowering feedback

As mentioned previously, all of us have a blind spot and the only way really to uncover what's in it and to grow is by listening to the views of others. That means feedback. If we had a magic wand and could change just one thing that can literally transform an organization, it would be the way in which leaders approach feedback. It's so crucial to any organization and culture because it acts as a barometer for things like openness, honesty, trust and ownership.

Countless books have been written and leadership programmes developed which teach you the art of delivering feedback. They are smart and well intended. We know, because in the past we've delivered many of them.

Here's the problem. In most organizations, feedback is pushed. It comes from the person wanting to give the feedback and is pushed onto the person receiving the feedback. This is often as part of a formulaic exercise such as the often dreaded '360 review', typically owned by HR, that sadly becomes more about completing a process than actually helping anyone. Just think about the logic. This is a process that will likely highlight your insecurities, is done to you, is usually owned by another part of the business, and you're expected to embrace it as part of your growth? To make matters worse, these exercises are usually done anonymously, reinforcing the very thing that creating a feedback culture is supposedly trying to change. This creates suspicion, negativity and cowardice... not words you see many organizations using to describe their values.

For any form of feedback to work, the most important element is that the recipient is prepared to own and action whatever gets said. That will only happen if they are pulling the feedback (ie if they are asking for it themselves) rather than it being pushed onto them. Inspiring leaders, inspiring teams and inspiring organizations invite feedback. They actively seek it out, because they recognize this not only helps them understand and address their blind spots, but by doing so it gives them an edge. They can adapt and improve faster than those around them because they are more informed and better focused on what needs to improve.

Jason Wilcox, former England footballer and now Academy Director at Manchester City FC, recalls:

> 'Working with my coach, I put some questions to the board asking for feedback on my leadership style and areas on which I could improve. At my next big staff meeting, I showed everyone not only the questions, but also the answers. I showed my vulnerability, but I was trying to show them the way – that we're going to have this environment where I

don't know everything and I'm trying to grow.
In many ways the team are far more talented
than me – my skill and strength has always
been in football, so I'm now working on what
type of leader I am and want to be. I can't ask
that of my people if I'm not prepared to live it
myself.'[10]

Pulling feedback with the 'ask, don't tell' principle

When doing team coaching work, the first rule Sampson introduces is 'ask, don't tell'. It's a simple but extremely powerful exercise where, starting with the leader, each team member asks for specific feedback from the group on a certain subject. This must be carefully set up in order to work. Any fear and anxiety when people first do this will reveal a great deal about the existing leadership culture.

The best businesses understand this principle of pulling rather than pushing and work hard to encourage it, but while it's great to ask for feedback, *how* you ask for it determines the quality and constructive nature of what you get back, and then how easy it is to do something useful with it.

There are three simple feedback rules:

1. Be proactive and ask for feedback before you give feedback (particularly from those who are important to your role and personal success). Always remember that people follow behaviour

before strategy, so as the leader it's important you go first.

2. Be laser-focused about what the feedback relates to. Don't ask, 'How can I be a better leader?' It's too generic. Be specific. Instead, ask, 'How can I be more effective during our catchups?' or, 'What can I do better to energize our team calls?'

3. Show that you have heard the feedback and are doing something with it, no matter what it is. If you do nothing with feedback you ask for, you will lose people's trust and kill any honesty.

As Wilcox shared, when leaders create their own personal themes for which they're requesting feedback, the exercise alone sends out a positive and strong message. It shows people they want to grow, and they need their people's help to do that.

EXERCISE: FEEDBACK

Try writing down five questions you'd like the most influential people in your career to answer in relation to yourself and areas you need to grow in. This requires you to be both brave and vulnerable, but also means you can control the focus of the feedback so it's as beneficial to you as possible.

Peer-to-peer feedback

As part of the performance management cycles for organizations, there are typically two measures of feedback. The first is measuring the 'what you did' elements, which relate to what an individual delivered over the year. Did they achieve the objectives which were agreed at the start? Pretty much all organizations have some form of this.

Then there's the second measure, which looks at 'how you did it'. You may have delivered a lot, but have you done so demonstrating the behaviours and values of your organization? This looks much more at culture – the way people behave – and focuses on human skills (typically called 'soft' skills – a term we abhor). In our experience, as the importance of culture becomes ever more apparent, most organizations are now incorporating the 'how' in some form.

A further step which needs to be introduced if leaders are serious about driving cultural change is regular peer-to-peer feedback. The problem with a boss giving team members feedback in relation to their 'how' is that the boss will have a limited idea of what those people are truly like to work with. Those who will absolutely know are their peers. If you interview members of a team individually and ask them who in the team goes the extra mile, lives and breathes the values and has everyone's back, the same name will come up again and again. Similarly, if you ask everyone who the difficult person is or the one who can't be trusted, again, there will almost certainly be a consensus.

If you want to know what people are really like, ask those who have to work closest with them. As part of your performance management cycle, introduce regular peer-to-peer feedback. It's one of the most effective ways to measure and reward the behaviours that you as a leader are trying to encourage and instils a huge sense of cultural ownership for every individual, either within a team or an entire organization.

Growing your team's ability

When we think about the performance and development of a team, it's important to clearly differentiate between each individual. No two people are motivated or operate in quite the same way. A good starting point is to break performance down into its three core components, as this makes it easier to identify which element an individual might need the most help with. To do this, we need a MAP.

The MAP

To perform well at absolutely anything, whether as a CEO, a parent, an astronaut, a spouse or a chef – we all need three things to operate in harmony with one another:

- Mindset (our attitude and focus)

- Ability (our technical skill to do something)

- Practice (have we done it before to gain experience?)

EXERCISE: RATING YOUR TEAM

Rate each of your team members on a scale of one to ten against the three areas in the list below:

- Mindset
  - Are they hungry to grow?
  - Do they welcome feedback?
  - Are they positive and optimistic?
  - Do they look to help and support others?

- Ability
  - How technically skilled are they in relation to their job requirements?

- Practice
  - How much opportunity and exposure have they had to practise different skills and improve?

You'll notice that mindset comes first. That's because it is often the largest challenge – especially for low performers. It's also the most important factor because it determines the other two. If people really want to learn and develop, then they'll proactively look for ways to hone their skills and seek out opportunities to be stretched.

Developing the MAP attributes

Use MAP to help you fine-tune your growth approach to your team members. We suspect it's likely that your strongest team member has the lowest score for practice. Your challenge is empowering them with enough regular delegation and finding them stretch objectives. Also pay particular attention to those whom you score highly on ability, but low on mindset. These people are smart and influential and if left unchecked may well bring a toxicity to your culture. They have the skills to attract others to their cause, which can severely hamper what you're trying to achieve as the leader.

There will be crossover of course, but as a general rule of thumb:

- Developing **mindset** requires you to act as a coach.

- Developing **ability** requires you to train and mentor.

- Developing **practice** requires delegation on your part.

In any team you'll see these three elements fluctuate due to personal circumstances, changes in workload, restructures and so on. The best teams are the ones where, first and foremost, the leader concentrates on continually improving mindset. Mindset is the bedrock of a high-performance culture. Where ability and practice are primarily needed to develop an individual, the leader's responsibility is relatively straightforward. Improving mindset, however, can be more complex and requires more of a coaching approach. This is not intended as a 'how to coach' chapter, but given the crucial importance of mindset, it's important we give you some highlights of the skill of coaching.

Coaching for growth

All too often, coaching is seen by leaders as some-thing that gets turned on for certain situations such as a performance review or career discussion. It becomes a technique, and for the person on the receiving end it feels unnatural and often contrived. Suddenly the person they've known and worked with for years is asking them strange questions about how they feel and what they want in life, and then sitting back and staring at them expectantly. Ever had that experience? Instead, coaching should subtly place the focus and ownership for the conversation onto the other person, allowing them to explore and challenge their own thinking from different perspectives.

On paper this might sound relatively straightfor-ward, but as Sampson says:

> 'At The Business Coaching Academy, we train hundreds of leaders every year in the art of coaching, and I'd say, even though many have done coaching programmes before, only about 20% come to us with the basic communication skills already in place: hearing (not listening),

asking challenging questions, exploring
beliefs... and often just the ability to shut up.'

A skilled communicator – through their curiosity, observations and listening – will quickly get a read on the other person's drivers, ambitions and hang-ups. This is fundamental to effective coaching, and often the hardest part for leaders. In its simplest form, to understand someone else's mindset, we need them to do the talking and not the other way around. Otherwise, we're simply making assumptions.

We'll talk more about coaching a negative mindset in the Optimism chapter, but for the purpose of coaching for growth, here are the key principles to bear in mind:

- You can't change someone's mindset for them.

- You can help them see both the impact and consequence of their mindset on themselves, you and those around them. This puts them in the driving seat of whether or not this is acceptable to them.

- If they want to change, build motivation for them by linking the change to something that is important to them – something they want. For instance, if someone is ambitious, make the links between how a shift in their mindset will go a long way to helping them achieve their ambitions.

- If someone has no obvious ambition or driver which you can leverage, then help them see the inherent danger they face. If they are content to stay as they are, but working within an organization that's moving and evolving at pace, where does that leave them six to twelve months from now? Is that what they want?

This approach is designed to help the leader place ownership for what does or does not happen next squarely on the individual. This is the power of coaching as a leader – ensuring ownership and accountability always sits with the coachee and not the coach. Help someone build enough internal pressure to want to change and that change becomes theirs. They will do it because they want to rather than because they are being told to. The difference in that person will be transformational.

Growing your business relationships

Sampson had this to say when reflecting on the growth area that most of us struggle with the most: our interactions with others:

> 'In my experience of coaching leaders, the biggest and most common growth areas aren't the "MBA business skills" such as finance, strategy or marketing. It's the quality and effectiveness of their relationships with others. Whether with their team, boss, peers, shareholders or customers, probably 80%

of every coaching conversation I've ever had comes down to a relationship challenge between my client and someone they need to work even better with.'

If we acknowledge the importance of growing our relationships – not just in business, but also in life – then the starting point and the most important thing we must realize is this: we cannot change anyone. We can only change how we approach or react to different challenges, situations and relationships.

How much of any relationship do you own?

The answer, of course, is 50%. This is the only part you have control over. Rather than investing in our own 50% and considering ways we can approach others differently or change something about ourselves to help, we instead fall into the trap of focusing on the other person's half of our relationship, saying things like:

- 'Well, if they'd only…'

- 'I wish they would just…'

- 'Why can't they…?'

You own 50% of each relationship in your life. You need to make that 50% count.

We can influence people, of course; that's core to great leadership. To try and fundamentally *change* someone means applying external pressure; and that pressure is almost always met with an equal amount of resistance. Be honest with yourself: have you ever tried to exert that control over others only to find that your attempts inevitably make things worse? Kimber sees relationship growth as a direct opposite of wielding power:

> 'It's definitely a story of give it to get it. My number one rule of negotiation is "give to get": always make the first concession. Because at the end of the day, human relationships are about reciprocity. People often say, "Look at my great network," and I always say, "What have you done for them?" It's not about what they're going to do for you. I believe what goes around comes around.'

Growth in any relationship starts with us taking responsibility for that relationship and focusing on what we can do rather than what we wish the other person would do. How do we do that with our colleagues, our teams, and even our leaders? We start by assessing the current state of the relationship we wish to influence.

The players in your growth

Completing a stakeholder map (or something similar) which helps us identify who is most influential in our career journey and can help us get to where we want to go is all well and good but poses the danger of seeing relationships based primarily on the levels of power. O'Toole agrees:

> 'Earlier in my career, all the advice was on the importance of networking, and as an introvert, I absolutely hate the thought of being in a room with 100 people with whom I'm supposed to strike up a conversation. What I always advise is, "Yes, investing in relationships is important, but there has to be a purpose to it, there has to be a reason for the relationship. Don't push an artificial investment in a relationship if there's no basis for it."'

We need to be clear about how both parties can benefit as we grow our relationships. Macdougall sums this up well:

> 'Networking is absolutely crucial, but it's a double-edged sword. I coached many international managers on this topic. They were often told they needed to strengthen their network, but it has such negative connotations for many because people don't look at it from the sponsors' point of view – only their own. I can think of a few people who believed they were excellent networkers. In one case, someone even showed me his networking diary. He had obviously been told he needed three points of interaction with any sponsor to remain relevant and front of mind. If he hadn't met his quota for

that year, he would request a meeting with the sponsor. He had no objective for the meeting or anything of value to take to the sponsor; he just wanted to touch base. This became so common that the programme actually started getting a reputation for it and I can recall several conversations with board members telling me to remove that person from the programme, or at least keep him away from them.

'The advice I gave to managers was simple. Yes, network – but do it by building true investors, ie sponsors who will want to buy you or recommend you to others because you add value. Find things of value to them and take proposals or ideas to them. Ask for time in their diaries to give them updates on projects that are of interest to them, etc… never to touch base or give them an update on your career.'

To get even better at growing your business relationships, let's define these in two distinct ways. For a leader to be effective, they require two forms of ally:

Investor: The people that invest in you and have significant influence and interest in your career. These relationships tend to evolve more gradually and have a longer-term perspective. By way of example, for a C-Suite level leader, likely investors may be key board members, the chairperson or CEO, significant shareholders or customers.

Enabler: These are the key people a leader needs to bring their vision for growth to life – those with a stake and influence in the success (or otherwise) of that vision. These don't include direct reports (as investment in them should be a given), but rather colleagues and peers. By way of example, for a head of business development, enablers may be the head of operations or finance.

EXERCISE: THE PLAYING FIELD

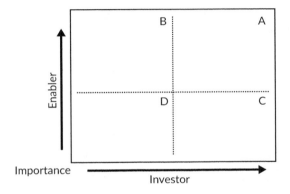

Draw out the grid above and plot the names of your top five Investors and top five Enablers onto the grid according to their level of significance to you. You may feel you have more, but the larger the number, the more you dilute the investment you can make. Some people may qualify as both.

Next, put a letter by each name using the following criteria:

- **S for Sponsor:** Someone who supports you and you enjoy a good relationship with.
- **N for Neutral:** You're not really sure how this person feels about you. In a tight spot, you don't know if they'd be your sponsor or your critic.
- **C for Critic:** This person has opposed you and can be a blocker.

Now look at who's in which box. Starting with Box A, do you have any Critics or Neutrals? If so, they are your top priority and require swift action. Then do the same for Box B, and so on. To help with this, consider these questions:

- What investment have I made in my 50% of this relationship?
- What can I do better (what can I give in order to get)?
- Can anyone else help me with this relationship?

You'll notice that after box A, the next priority box, B, is Enabler focused (rather than Investor). This is because we strongly believe that mobilizing and delivery are a leader's top priority. By doing this successfully, a leader builds their 'stock' with investors, which they can leverage to develop those relationships. A leader with little track record of actual delivery who tries to build Investor relationships quickly becomes labelled a political player and will at best be side-lined, or worst, sacked.

It may feel like a lot of effort, but as Spooner points out:

> 'Before any meeting, always work out who your stakeholders are. How are they going to challenge you and what is your answer? I would never go to a meeting, asking for time, money and effort from people, for them to turn around and say no. Because then you've boxed yourself in. Do the work in advance. Be bloody sure that if there's an influential person who's actively against what you're trying to deliver, that the other six people in the room aren't.'

There's an old saying that we've heard many successful leaders use: 'What goes around comes around'. It may not always happen, but the investment you make in others now will often be repaid at a time you least expect it. Leading without a strong network of enablers and investors is like entering a boxing ring with both hands tied behind your back. Be genuine with people, be interested and be helpful. You're going to need them.

Wrapping it up: Applying what you've learned at work

If something isn't growing, it's stagnating and will start to decline. As leaders, our responsibility is to keep pushing and realizing potential in everything around us.

Think of this backwards. The needs of our future customer are our goal. The organization must evolve to meet those needs. The team must grow to enable the organization to evolve. As leaders, we must grow to develop and empower our team. This cycle works both ways and never stops. We must set an example and first ask it of ourselves before we can expect it of anyone or anything else.

The three essential steps of growth

1. Visualize something better than it is now.

2. Mobilize the people and resources necessary to make it happen.

3. Pull the trigger.

Three simple feedback rules

1. Be proactive and ask for feedback before you give feedback.

2. Be laser-focused about what the feedback relates to.

3. Show that you have heard the feedback and are doing something with it, no matter what it is.

Exercises and resources

- The GAPS grid

- Feedback

- Rating your team

- The playing field

FIVE
Optimism

Sampson recalls the uncertainty and panic of the 2008 financial crisis:

'It was early in 2009 and the financial crisis was biting hard. Lehman Brothers had fallen in the US, Northern Rock had collapsed in the UK and HBOS had to be saved by Lloyds, who in turn had to be saved by the taxpayer. Panic, uncertainty and blame were rife, and banks had become public enemy number one.

'I was sitting in the boardroom of HSBC in Dubai waiting for the start of an emergency meeting called by the global head of retail banking. The directors sat around the table looking tired and apprehensive. A subdued silence settled over the room. Deep job cuts and drastic cost-saving initiatives were expected. Who in the room would survive? The boss stood up, thanked everyone for coming and then simply said this: "These are unprecedented times, and I don't want to waste energy today trying to predict an unknown future. There are only two things we can be 100% certain of right now. The first is that more financial institutions will not survive this. The second, however, is that some will not only survive, but will emerge far stronger as a result. Therefore, I'd like you all to do something. Please take out a pen and piece of paper and write down the three fantastic opportunities this situation presents for us as a bank."

'The energy in the room changed instantly. Heads came up, people sat forwards and everyone started writing. From that point, it quickly developed into one of the most positive and energized meetings I've ever had the privilege to be part of.'

Did this solve the crisis? Of course not, but it instantly shifted everyone's focus from uncertainty and darkness towards positive and immediate action. The overriding sense at the end was one not only of hope, but also excitement, as everyone felt they had regained some control over their own destiny.

In this chapter, we will explore:

- Why no one is inspired by 'safe and easy'

- Where optimism comes from

- Four reasons why optimists are more effective leaders

- Measuring how optimistic you are

- Managing your optimistic state

- How to tell if a leader is optimistic

- Eight habits to build optimism

- Developing a team culture of optimism

Why no one is inspired by 'safe and easy'

Uncertainty and fear are the breeding ground for great leadership, contrary to what some might think. An uncertain environment gives optimism a chance to shine. Optimistic leaders look for opportunities where others see only threats and problems. This creates hope, which generates a more proactive focus and sense of control vital to avoid any sense of panic or helplessness.

Think of the most inspiring person you've ever known or heard about. Are they someone who encountered adversity during their lifetime but didn't allow that to define them? Optimistic and inspiring leaders draw tremendous strength from adversity and use this to further improve themselves and those around them.

Why, particularly during unprecedented times, do so many struggle to step up and be one of those leaders? It's because it requires far more effort, courage and resilience to see the brightness and light visible through the mists of hard work than it does to take an easier, more pessimistic viewpoint. Being a pessimist is easier and safer. It doesn't require much more than what comes naturally for the pessimist: knocking holes, seeing faults and placing blame. The pessimist takes the safer path of predicting something won't work; they then do little or nothing about it, and, well, guess what? It doesn't work. They are proven correct, which then reinforces their pre-existing notion and viewpoint. It's a common cycle, but it's a cycle that needs to be broken for those aspiring to be great leaders.

No one has ever been inspired by 'safe and easy'. Great leaders are the opposite of our resident pessimists. They are habitual optimists. This should not be confused with positivity. Positivity on its own can be naïve, forced and misplaced. As a by-product of optimism, however, it derives from something tangible and proactive. Optimists are realists. In tough times, they will acknowledge the darkness but will still choose to focus their energy on the light.

Where optimism comes from

We talked about leaders being 'realizers of potential' in the Growth chapter. This is where optimism is so important, because optimism comes from the belief that things can be better; and we have the power to influence that. This belief typically originates from three sources:

- Our experience – have we succeeded in a situation like this before?

- Our confidence in our own skills and abilities.

- Our confidence in the skills and abilities of those around us.

If we've faced a situation before and handled it badly, we may face the next situation feeling extremely negative; but if we feel the team is much stronger the next time around as a result of the experience, we're probably more optimistic. Optimism is also partly the ability to rapidly recognize patterns around us. That said, it's important to recognize that in the uncertain and rapidly changing times we now live in, our past experience will not necessarily help us. If there are no patterns, then our confidence in our own skills and abilities needs to come into play. This is about resilience and recognizing that the past does not determine the future.

Optimism comes from looking the tough questions square in the eye and seeing the opportunity, rather than the challenges, that they present. Aileen O'Toole, who we heard from in our Growth chapter, sees this viewpoint as critical for progress. 'There are those people who are contrarians by profession, vs the optimistic people who ask questions in the spirit of moving things along to get to the right answer,' she says. That is exactly the tack Sampson took when his business, The Business Coaching Academy, took an economic downturn when the Covid-19 pandemic hit. By walking through the tough questions with his team and focusing on the positive, they were able to weather the storm. It's a real-life story in how optimism saved a business:

> 'On 16 March 2020, we were looking at our best year yet. Already ahead of our ambitious targets for that point in the year, we had numerous workshops, programmes and events booked right through to the end of the year and were looking to expand the team. Then on 23 March, Boris Johnson announced the Covid-19 lockdown, and everything vanished into thin air. Not a slow-down for us, not a reduction in revenue. All business completely gone.
>
> 'Panic quickly gave way to fear and then anger. Then we decided to practise what we preach and sort our shit out. The team meeting went something like this. We asked ourselves the tough questions, the tough questions you need to ask when any catastrophe strikes.'

Tough questions asked in the room	Straight-talk answers
Can we change or influence the lockdown?	No.
Are we going to allow this to determine our future?	No.

Continued

Cont.

Tough questions asked in the room	Straight-talk answers
Is this temporary or forever?	Temporary.
What's good about this?	We suddenly have more time.
Isn't time the most precious commodity of all, and the thing we're always moaning we don't have enough of?	Yes.
Now we have it, how can we make it count?	Let's pull our two-year digital strategy forwards and do it right now.
Can we really do that?	We don't have to. We could just sit tight, hope things change soon and slowly go out of business... Better get to it then.

'In five sleepless weeks we converted our flagship programmes into a digital format, complete with supporting videos and a learning management system containing the entire curriculum. Our first programme quickly sold out and we have since booked in many more. Being small made our rapid adaption easier. Obviously there's still a long way to go, but not only did we keep revenue dripping in during lockdown, we now have products we can deliver anywhere in the world. We're accessible to an entirely new and much larger audience. As a result of the pandemic, we are an even better business.'

Sampson's story is a wonderful example of how being determined to see the opportunities and keep a positive attitude better positioned his company for success. Those managing teams can adopt this approach, too. How will you ask the tough questions, in the tough situations, to get to positive outcomes that move your team forwards?

Four reasons why optimists are more effective leaders

People are inspired, particularly in dark times, by those who acknowledge the tough and gritty reality but still push, fight and draw others towards something better. The more adversity they encounter, the more inspiring they are to their followers. How you manage pressures can distinguish you as a leader. Research has shown that optimists are better able to cope with the stress that this adversity brings while they navigate the path to success.[1]

Not surprisingly, leaders with a more optimistic personal disposition tend to be more effective. There are four reasons why:

1. They are more likely to pursue leadership development and job opportunities.

2. They have more social influence.

3. They have better relationships with those who report to them.

4. They are more prepared to push for opportunities which may involve an element of risk.

Let's look at each of these in turn.

They are more likely to pursue leadership development and job opportunities

Throwing your hat in the ring for a leadership position takes courage, or, some might say, a willingness to take a risk. It's likely that optimists are more comfortable than pessimists in taking the type of risks required to advance a career and get into a leadership position, perhaps because optimism helps to fuel courage. As Hayley Macdougall, first heard from in our Growth chapter, says:

> 'The HSBC International Manager programme was created to provide a pool of talented senior managers who could be posted anywhere in the world at short notice. Over the years and as the world has changed, less and less managers have the appetite for the more challenging postings in some of the less developed areas of the globe, so it was the ones who put their hands up for the tougher roles that really got noticed. They could see the potential that the opportunity presented and realised they had little to lose. Even if they only achieved limited success, it was better than nothing but would be significant as a stepping stone in their careers.'

Sarah Spooner, also introduced in the Growth chapter, attributes much of her success to not being afraid to jump in and strike when the iron is hot. She says, 'I've always been a bit of an opportunist when I think I can make a difference. If there's an opportunity to do it and I can't see an immediate downside, I jump in.'

They have more social influence

While we've been clear not to conflate optimism with positivity, it is an important consideration. For example, participants in a particular study received either: a) only praise; b) mixed feedback; or c) negative feedback.[2] It should come as no surprise that they best liked the evaluators who gave only praise. When one is naturally positive, finding areas and parts of others to praise comes quite naturally. From there, it's no great leap to suggest that people who others like have more social influence – which is needed to get people to fall in line.

They have better relationships with those who report to them

People like role models. Think back to who you looked up to when you were a child. Why did you look up to them? Chances are, they were people you could see part of yourself in but who were also aspirational

– better versions of yourself, or those who had traits, qualities or achievements that you didn't yet have, but valued. Rachel Thornton reflects on this. 'I love people who are better than me at things, who know stuff I don't and who bring something different to the table. I don't think that's just me,' she says.

Optimistic people are good role models for those who report to them *because* of their optimism. Optimistic people also celebrate more, say thank you more, laugh more, blame less and have fun more – all key elements in creating and maintaining strong relationships. Jason Wilcox, who we first met in the Growth chapter, puts it simply: 'People want to work with people who they like.' O'Toole makes another point on strong relationships. She says, 'The evidence of a good and authentic leader is in how you really treat your people in your off moments.' Perhaps optimistic people work harder to have fewer 'off' moments.

They are more prepared to push for opportunities which may involve an element of risk

Optimistic leaders proactively focus their energy (and the energy of those around them) on things that they can control and influence. This conversely increases their appetite for risk, because the notion of something being 'a risk' is diminished. If you feel that you have a stake in the success of something, unease becomes replaced by confidence.

Measuring how optimistic you are

To get *even better*, it helps to have a baseline assessment of how optimistic you are today. We've drawn inspiration from psychology to take an 'even better if' view of the approaches developed by scholars over time. We're all about looking for real-life, practical applications, and a lengthy psychoanalysis across multiple dimensions and factors doesn't exactly meet the mark in our day-to-day work life. The approach we think is the most practical to use for quick measurement in the business world is the Life Orientation Test – Revised (LOT-R).

The LOT was initially created in 1985 by Michael Scheier and Charles Carver; the revised LOT-R has become one of the most widely used tests to measure optimism.[3] You can easily use this for yourself or your team.

EXERCISE: THE LOT QUESTIONNAIRE

Download the LOT-R here: https://positivepsychology. com/life-orientation-test-revised.

Follow the instructions for scoring your responses to the ten statements in the LOT-R and work out our your scores. Although Carver notes that 'There are no "cut-offs" for optimism or pessimism; we use it as a continuous dimension of variability',[4] the following interpretations of the score ranges have been suggested:[5]

0–13: Low optimism (high pessimism)

14–18: Moderate optimism

19–24: High optimism (low pessimism)

For our purposes, these score ranges might suggest:

0–13: Your glass is definitely half empty. That's OK; optimism can be learned.

14–18: You have your good days and bad days, but are moderately optimistic. You can be even better.

19–24: You are a force of optimism and believe that things can, and will, be even better.

The real question for you is: once you know how naturally optimistic you are, how will you work on strengthening the habit of optimism? Let's start with the easiest thing within your power to control – the choices you make. So: do you choose to be an optimist? Yes? Fantastic. Let's get to it then. Being an optimist is a habit you can develop and display at any time, but to do this, it's important to first understand the combination of elements which combine to create optimism.

Managing your optimistic state

Optimism is primarily a mindset – a pattern of thinking that focuses on opportunity and proactivity.

We all have days when we're tired and the world seems against us, or (as with Sampson's example at the beginning of this chapter), events may happen which can pull us towards despair. Sometimes feeling truly optimistic seems about the last thing we're capable of. It's OK (and in some ways a good thing) to show our team that we're having a tough time – we're human, and by being human we build connections. It's not OK for them to see us wobbling. In dark times, they will draw much of their strength and courage from us and how we show up; and if we present too much vulnerability, then fear and uncertainty will quickly set in.

As leaders, the skill lies in choosing how to filter and express what is happening internally (your thoughts and feelings) by consciously adapting what the world sees and hears you do (your behaviour). Leaders are then able to deliberately achieve the most empowering and positive impact on others regardless of whether they're really 'feeling it' or not. Wilcox agrees that this consistent outward projection is key:

> 'Whether it's right or wrong, I ask the team,
> "Do you ever see me devastated? Do you ever
> know when I'm having a bad day?" I've had
> some rubbish days where I have things going
> on in my personal life or I've bumped a car on
> the way in; but ultimately, when I go past the
> security guard and walk in the building, I'm
> the same every day. Because it's up to me to set
> the tone. If I want a positive environment for
> everyone, then I need to come in being positive.'

How to tell if a leader is optimistic

Here's a question: which of the leaders in your organization are optimistic? You might observe that they have a certain way of talking, or maybe there's a confidence about their body language, but it's typically quite hard to break down specifically what a trait such as optimism looks and sounds like. This makes it hard to know how to replicate it.

Every trait or behaviour we can think of (confidence, optimism, positivity, trust, openness, inspiration, etc) is a combination of what's going on for us internally, and how we project that externally. We call this our STATE. It's how we show up in front of other people; it's the energy and attitude we give off. Our state can always be broken down into four distinctive elements. By understanding these elements, you can model and replicate them to better enhance them. You can also teach them to leaders if you have been tasked to upskill your leadership team.

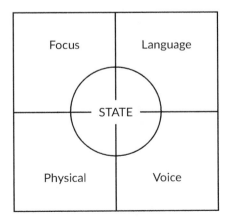

Your STATE is made up of four elements:

1. **Focus:** Your thinking and emotions.

2. **Physical:** Your body language, breathing, eye contact, movement and posture. Without saying anything, just your physicality can suggest a great deal about you in any given moment.

3. **Voice:** Actors spend years training their voices because of the power and emotion the voice can yield. Pace, projection, volume, tone… These all hugely change the impact of what's actually being said.

4. **Language:** This is connected to your voice; but language refers to the specific vocabulary you use – your phrases, rhetoric and speech patterns. Language is extremely powerful in its effect and the emotions it can stir in others.

One example of how the STATE Square can be used by leaders is in a common leadership activity: preparing for a speech.

The first question to ask yourself is how you want your audience to feel when you have finished talking. This is important, because if you want people to do something differently, then you need to fire them up emotionally. It also gives you a target emotional state to aim for. Let's assume that you want the audience to leave feeling both optimistic and confident about their future with the company.

Once you have the desired state you're aiming for, you can start with the end in mind and work backwards using the STATE Square.

Question	Example response
Focus: What do optimistic and confident speakers/leaders focus on?	The company vision, progress and successes already achieved, the amazing people who work there.
Physical: What do they look like on stage?	Probably not too formal. They're not behind a lectern. They move around the stage, they have physical energy and they make eye contact with the audience. They smile.
Voice: What do they sound like?	They project, they don't rush, they speak clearly and with intent.
Language: What words do they inject?	Opportunity, success, innovation, confidence, excited, grateful.

You now have the raw materials for a fantastic speech. By pulling these elements together into a simple structure and adding in some practice, you can achieve exactly what you are aiming for.

Of the four components above, the one where leaders can struggle most is around their focus. What if the leader can only focus on their stage fright, or what if they've had a call ten minutes before their speech about a project that's gone south? Well, here's the amazing thing about the STATE Square for when you're distracted and struggling to focus. Changing one of the four elements will change all of them. Each element is interdependent and occurs as a consequence of the others, so one cannot exist in isolation.

To make the point, sit in a chair and put yourself in a pitiful, 'feeling sorry for yourself' physical posture. Now try shouting some positive and inspiring words. It doesn't work. You'll either laugh, or feel stupid, or probably both. Your physical posture is in complete contrast to your voice and language, so your brain kicks in and says, 'Nope, this doesn't work.' Shift one part of the STATE Square and it creates a chain reaction – they all start to shift. With practice, we can 'trick' ourselves to shift into a more resourceful and optimistic state as and when we need to. Wilcox has a great approach to this:

> 'When I'm struggling to focus, as I walk to my next meeting or whatever, I make a point of lifting my head up and smiling at people. I shake hands with a few along the way and say, "Hi." When they ask me how I'm doing, I'm deliberately positive. It only takes ten seconds, and it might sound daft, but when I get to the next meeting, I feel more energized and positive.'

Eight habits to build optimism

Now that we know how important optimism is to good leadership, here are eight habits to help you

build optimism. You can either do ⟨
reflection or teach these in a leaders.
other training to upskill your team ⟨
across the business:

1. Change your lens.

2. Improve your thinking.

3. Focus forwards.

4. Set the pessimism free.

5. Be your own focus coach.

6. The optimism mirror.

7. Get some perspective.

8. Be grateful.

Building optimism habit #1: Change your lens

Small things like a late or cancelled train to really significant events such as a job redundancy or ill health
happen to all of us. We wish they didn't; but it's not
what happens to us that determines who we are and
how we lead. It's how we interpret, and therefore react,
to what's happened to us. Our interpretation depends
on which lens we are choosing to see events through.
Just as we put on sunglasses to reduce the sun's glare
to help us see better, we can change our mental lens to
view events in a way that means we can draw, rather
than concede, power. We all have two lenses:

The victim lens (it's done *to* me)

- The leader lens (it's done *by* me)

Let's look at both lenses more closely.

Is it done to you?

When we view things as being done to us, we're right there on our mental back foot and we give away our power. We become reactive and feel like a victim of circumstances. We believe that events over which we have no control are happening to us. We call this the 'victim lens'.

Mentally, the victim lens is extremely destructive and can quickly create a vicious circle of negativity. We feel helpless, anxious and stressed and resentment begins to bubble. Survival mode kicks in and we become emotionally swamped. Think about the system at work which infuriates you, the email which you haven't even yet opened (but just seeing it has stressed you out) or the colleague who got promoted over you...

All of us occasionally see things through our victim lens. This shouldn't be considered 'bad'; it's the way the human brain is wired. Over thousands of years of evolution, our brains have become finely tuned to look for threats. This was really helpful when predatory animals roamed the land or the tribe in the next valley had their eye on our cattle, but the world has moved on at an extraordinary pace. Our safety and survival are now rarely actually threatened (especially not at work), but our brains don't know the difference. That person across the board table who's challenging your brilliant idea? Well, they must be a threat, so you're triggered into fight/flight/freeze mode and lose any sense of rationale or resourcefulness. We've all been there, and know this can often lead to us doing something we later regret.

Is it done by you?

When things are done by us, we are drawing power because we have assumed fundamental control over our situation. Rather than allowing the situation or event to own us, we mindfully and proactively focus on what we can impact and influence and find strategies to move forward. This is the foundation for our 'leader lens'.

The two scenarios below will help you decide whether you view your role through a victim lens or a leader lens.

EXERCISE: VICTIM VS LEADER LENS

Scenario #1: The new CEO

You worked with your previous CEO for three years and invested heavily in the relationship. They supported and mentored you and considered you a potential successor, but they unexpectedly left and an external candidate has been chosen for the CEO role. They are younger than you and less experienced in your sector.

- Do you constantly mourn the loss of your previous boss and feel threatened by the new incumbent? You look for evidence that they were the wrong person for the role and say as much to your colleagues, OR

- Do you see the relationship as an opportunity to leverage some new thinking and new energy into the business? You appreciate that the new CEO will have their own apprehensions about coming into a new business, so offer to help and support where you can.

Scenario #2: The new sales system

A new sales system is installed in the business. It promises to save time and give you better insights into your customers, but also has a steep learning curve.

- Do you feel you can't do your job properly because you're spending more time with the system than with customers and it's going to kill your bonus? You look for other 'system victims' who share your grievances, and together you reinforce one another's negative beliefs, OR

- Do you feel that, yes, the new system is tricky to get your head around, but other people seem to be using it OK and it's clearly not going anywhere? Then it's best to invest the time getting to grips with it and making the most of what it can do for you.

If we have limited control over an event, then we can only control our reaction to the event. Imagine walking into an empty room without your shoes on and stubbing your toe on the door. What do you do? I suspect most of us will use some fairly colourful language. Now imagine that same scenario again, only this time, there's a child in the room. For most of us, we manage to hold the swearing in. That response happens in the blink of an eye, but demonstrates that with conditioning, we are still able to choose our reactions – even to the swiftest and (what we assume to be) most automatic of events.

When presented with more time to respond (which is usually the case in the business world), we can choose to view an event through our leader lens, leading to a more positive and measured reaction. Remember, it's not the event or situation which determines our future. It's our interpretation and reaction based on the lens through which we're looking. Switching from one lens to the other is a habit that requires both self-awareness and practice, but one every leader must master. O'Toole sums this up beautifully:

> 'Focus your energies only on what you can
> control and be really ruthless about that.
> Focusing on what you can't control is a recipe
> to exhaustion, sadness and despair. It's not
> about being a cheerleader or asking people
> to rally around when the situation is awful.
> Acknowledge that it's crap and then talk about
> it. What can we do within this terrible context?'

Building optimism habit #2:
Improve your thinking

To help develop the leader lens concept above, a simple but powerful way to 'check in' with either a team, an individual or ourselves is the ACT model. There are three stages:

Stage 1: Awareness

- When faced with adversity, challenge or change, what is our awareness of ourselves?

- How is our mindset impacting us and those around us? How do we feel?

- Is this acceptable to us and does it limit or empower us?

Stage 2: Control

- What can we control here and where are we focusing our energy?

- What can we do absolutely nothing about and prevent it being a distraction?

- Is our sense of control an illusion or can it be measured?

Stage 3: Think better

- How would [think of someone who inspires you] approach this situation?

- What opportunity does this present?

- What will I take ownership for to help improve this?

Building optimism habit #3: Focus forwards

Inspiring leaders acknowledge and draw lessons from the past but are laser-focused on the future. The habit to work on developing here is a future-focused mindset: to focus on something being better. The timeframe is less relevant – it could be tomorrow or it could be five years from now – but it's always about looking forwards rather than backwards.

As we discussed in both the Purpose and Growth chapters, a key component of looking forwards is having something compelling to look forwards to. Being guided by a North Star of sorts provides direction, momentum and alignment behind which people congregate. In times of crisis, when optimism can falter, the key to re-ignite optimism is by making your vision and purpose immediate and achievable so people feel they are making progress. Spooner has excellent advice on this front:

> 'How do you get people to focus on the positive? Well, you don't need to eat a whole elephant, for starters. People get stuck on, "Oh, it's going to take eighteen months and three million pounds to fix this so I might as well not bother." But what would you do if you had £2.50 and one person for a month? What could you do? So, while you need to have the long-term strategy, focus on the little, incremental improvements. What are you going to deliver this week? How are you personally going to make a difference this week?'

It's also about identifying prospective paths forward vs engaging in a game of finger-pointing when some things go wrong. As O'Toole says:

'It's really satisfying to sit around and go scapegoat hunting and look for someone or something to blame that's extraneous, but I think it's far healthier to think, "Well, what can I do; where might I be at fault; and where do I need to change my thinking?"'

Building optimism habit #4:
Set the pessimism free

Forgive the grim analogy, but pessimism is like a boil. It needs lancing in order to heal. Ignoring it, suppressing it, or worse – pretending that it doesn't exist – will only cause it to fester and spread. Spooner reflects on this:

'I'm not a natural wallower so I don't like people wallowing, but I will go, "Oh my god, this is hard." Just acknowledging it and having my team around me and creating a space where we can all say, "Oh, this week's been a particularly difficult one," or, "It's been hard for one of us," is important. We have a weekly team meeting and quite often the first ten minutes has no agenda. It's just people sharing their wins or their struggles.'

As the leader of a team, assume pessimism will inevitably exist somewhere and actively surface it, but only for a set period. Then everyone needs to move on. Imagine, as a team, you're discussing a situation or new idea (perhaps a new product or a response to a major setback). Insist that every member of the team (including yourself) assumes their victim state in turn and pictures the worst scenario possible. Dial up the pessimism massively and vent out loud to everyone else (some will find it easier than others). Stop after one minute and move to the next person.

Now here's the important bit. When everyone has spoken, start with the person who went first and ask the rest of the team what qualities that person's rant reveals about them. They are not allowed to speak, only listen. The others must share only qualities, nothing else.

The energy should already have shifted after this, but now go around the team again. This time, everyone talks for one minute about what is good about the situation. As we showed in the earlier story about Sampson's business and subsequent response, exploring the negative and then reframing it can massively transform the energy in the room. As the leader, the trick is making sure that everyone participates, so the natural pessimists 'try on' being an optimist and vice versa. This also works well as a personal exercise. We all have crap days when the dark clouds are gathering and pretending otherwise is nonsense. Indulge and vent your inner victim (away from your team) for a set time period, but then shut it off like a tap.

Building optimism habit #5:
Be your own focus coach

As we stated earlier in this chapter, optimism is largely about what we choose to focus on, and the word 'choose' is important. Imagine you've just had a catchup with your boss and they've given you some feedback on your performance. Some of the feedback was positive, while some of it focused more on your areas of development. As you leave that meeting, what are you focused on? For most, it will be the developmental feedback that you start to dissect and stew on. While that ruminating is going on, the positive feedback has gone straight over your head.

It may not feel like it, but you are choosing to do this. You could instead shift your focus to the positive feedback and congratulate yourself and then see the developmental feedback as an opportunity to learn. After all, you're ambitious, so developmental feedback will massively help you – it's a good thing. The next time something happens to you which frustrates, worries or makes you angry, try the exercise below to help you with developing this habit.

EXERCISE: BEING YOUR OWN FOCUS COACH

As soon as you're able to, find somewhere quiet and take out your phone. Film yourself looking straight into the camera and share what's happened, how you're feeling and what you're thinking. Now go and do something else for at least an hour. It doesn't matter what, but it must be unrelated to whatever has triggered those feelings in you. When you're ready, sit down and watch your video. Try and view it as though you don't know the person looking back at you. When it's finished, ask yourself these three questions:

1. How would you describe that person you just watched?
2. What advice would you give them?
3. What should they immediately do?

Building optimism habit #6: The optimism mirror

It is often hard to reframe our own thinking and see something that's difficult as anything other than that. In this case, asking someone you trust to act as a mirror for your thinking can be useful.

EXERCISE: THE OPTIMISM MIRROR

To begin with, explain to the individual that they are not allowed to go into solution mode or make suggestions as you share your problem; they must simply observe, listen and ask clarifying questions. These are the rules and it's important that they observe them. Then explain your situation with as much detail as you believe is relevant. When you're done, based on what they've heard and observed, the individual then answers two questions:

1. What do they see as positive about your situation?
2. What do they see as the opportunity it presents for you?

It may feel weird and you may both struggle initially, but hold fast and stick with it. The answers will come.

Building optimism habit #7:
Get some perspective

If you've ever had the experience of spending time on a children's oncology ward in a hospital, then you'll know that there are some things which can be painful but inspiring; they can shake us to our core and cause us to re-evaluate much about ourselves and our lives. For most of us, dealing with life and death in business is not what we do. Kohler remembers the informal motto her team at Nordstrom had when things got stressful: 'We're not saving lives; we're selling shoes.' If we didn't do our jobs, someone else would step in or step up and life would carry on. Take your job seriously – but try not to take it too seriously.

The same approach applies to us as individuals. All of us, especially when we have significant responsibilities, can sometimes get caught in the trap of believing that we are way more important, significant and relevant than we really are. We buy our own bullshit, but that belief can be paralyzing. The weight of our assumed responsibility and importance can create negativity if we're not careful. Look in a mirror now and again and remind yourself that you're not a big deal. You *are* amazing, smart, and valuable, but try not to take yourself too seriously.

Building optimism habit #8: Be grateful

A fantastic way to gain perspective on our lives, especially when we're struggling to see the forest for the trees, is by resetting our thinking and focusing on what we're grateful for, be it personal or professional. From a leadership perspective, when we hit a roadblock it's easy to only see problems and blame and we catastrophize about what might happen. As Chris Brindley, who we first met in the Growth chapter, says:

> 'I choose to be an optimist. It's absolutely a choice. The challenge is most people have not trained their brain to be grateful. You need to train the brain to be truly grateful for everything that happens in your life. It's the 90/10 principle. Typically, 90% of a job is pretty good and 10% is complete nonsense, but people often see and focus on the 10% as being the 90%.'

It helps if we're able to regularly check in on what's great and what we're thankful for. This includes things that are otherwise easy to take for granted or miss entirely. An excellent way of doing this is by keeping a journal and writing down whatever happens in our day that we're grateful for. We can then refer to this whenever we need a 'reset'. If keeping a journal isn't your thing, then there's a simpler approach, explained by Dr Laura Taylor. Dr Taylor is an urgent care NHS doctor for the South Western Ambulance service and completed her MSc researching the impact of mindfulness practices on the wellbeing of NHS healthcare staff. Dr Taylor shared this technique with many leaders who faced exceptional circumstances and stress on the frontline during the Covid-19 pandemic. She says:

> 'I like this technique because it can be done anywhere and takes very little time. To begin with, start by getting into a mindful position. Sit with a long, strong back and allow your hands to rest in your lap. Try softening your eyes and turning your gaze down toward your knees or close your eyes. Concentrate on your breathing, taking slow, long breaths in and then out.
>
> 'Now, with your right hand, take hold of the first finger on your other hand. Think about an object from your day that you're grateful for – it could be your favourite coffee cup or a comfy chair. Think about why you are grateful for that thing. Picture it in your head, what it looks like, what it's like to touch. Breathe.
>
> 'Now take hold of your middle finger, and this time concentrate on something from nature that you've experienced today and are grateful for. It might have been the sunrise when you

got up, or there's a particular tree you can see from the window. What is it about that which makes you grateful?

'This time take hold of your ring finger, and bring to mind a person that you've had contact with today who you're grateful for. It might have been an email or a text or someone you've spoken with. Really picture that person and think about what makes you grateful for them.

'Now open your eyes and look around the room. How do you feel? You can do this exercise at any time when you want to bring more positivity and optimism into your day.'[6]

Of course, gratitude doesn't have to be practised as a 'technique'. Spooner sends a weekly email to her team that covers five things they delivered that week. She says:

'It might be a tiny thing where we fixed the button on a web page that didn't work or it could be that we made a massive change or launched a massive product, but it makes a difference to people.'

Gratitude will also serve you well as a leader in times of crisis. Again, we look to Spooner, who has this reflection about addressing her team when Covid-19 hit. She says,

'Well, I'm not really a "rah-rah" speech kind of person. The speech I gave was more, "I have no bloody clue what's going to happen but we are all very fortunate that we have the technology and ability to work from home and we'll work it out together."'

Jeremy Petty, introduced in our Growth chapter, took a similar approach:

'Covid-19 is a great example where I didn't focus at all on the impact to the business because I couldn't do anything about it. How good is this team that we've got? They're really bloody good. How good is our brand and our proposition? Amazing, strong. How good's our book of work in terms of proving to new clients that we can do this for them? Yeah, fantastic. What about our relationships with our clients right now? Amazing. So, yeah, I'm 100% optimistic, because no matter what happens, it will be relative, because we'll still be a successful business.'

Developing a team culture of optimism

As leaders, we need to be optimists, but we also want to breed and develop optimism within our teams. Why? Aside from all the reasons we've already discussed, it's much easier to be optimistic when you're not the only one. If enough people are consistently optimistic, then it stops feeling like optimism and simply becomes a self-reinforcing part of your culture.

To build this optimism culture within your team, start with a few simple rules of engagement that everyone agrees to and are regularly referred to. The crucial thing is that this is not something you 'impose' on the team. The 'pull not push' concept we talked about in the Growth chapter also applies here. For example, don't tell the team you have some new ideas that you think will really help and ask that they abide by them. It has to be something they recognize the importance of and will take ownership for. They are then more likely to self-manage and hold one another accountable rather than look to you to referee.

At an appropriate time, introduce the principle of optimism to the team. Ask what it means to them and how important and relevant they feel it is. Some may raise themes such as the danger of 'blind optimism', and that's good. Get them to consider what the difference is and how it can be avoided. Highlight the importance of team optimism by asking for examples when they've seen it within the team and the impact this has had.

To encourage this as a habit within your team culture, it needs to be brought to life, so it's easily recognized either by its presence or absence. To do this, everyone must see optimism as something that is done – it is a verb and is practised.

EXERCISE: DEVELOPING TEAM OPTIMISM

Grab some paper and ask each member of the team to write down these two headings:

- It was a good week for the team because we...
- It was a bad week for the team because we...

Then ask them to think about what they would expect to see under each heading as an optimistic team. Get everyone to write down what would happen in real time in a week (how they interact, whether they are challenging one another, whether they are surfacing pessimism but reframing it, etc) – anything that will make it obvious that the team has demonstrated and encouraged optimism or not.

You should notice some consistent behaviours that emerge for both lists. Pick two or three key ones and ask the team for ways they will encourage the 'good week' and ways they will avoid the 'bad week'. How will they celebrate and reinforce optimism when it's demonstrated? How will they support one another better when they're struggling?

Note that this is about what they will do, not what you think they should do. Consider your own thoughts and suggestions, but this exercise will only encourage lasting behavioural change if each member of the team feels that they own it.

Wrapping it up: Applying what you've learned at work

Optimism is not the same as positivity. It's about focusing on the opportunity within the adversity and not allowing things outside of your control to distract or weaken you. It creates some certainty for the future because it puts you in control of the future. Some leaders are naturally more optimistic than others, but it is something every leader can improve. Notice where your focus is when you respond to setbacks and difficulties. Does this empower you or limit you? If that doesn't work, move and change your state. Sing a stupid song or do something that makes you laugh. Reflect on what you're grateful for and remember that it's just a job, not life or death. In difficult times, people are drawn to optimists.

Eight habits to build optimism

1. Change your lens.

2. Improve your thinking.

3. Focus forwards.

4. Set the pessimism free.

5. Be your own focus coach.

6. The optimism mirror.

7. Get some perspective.

8. Be grateful.

Exercises and resources

- The LOT questionnaire
- The STATE Square

- Victim vs leader lens
- Being your own focus coach
- The optimism mirror
- Developing team optimism

SIX
Disruption

Apopular quote (commonly misattributed to George Bernard Shaw) says, 'The reasonable man adapts himself to the world. The unreasonable one persists in trying to adapt the world to himself. Therefore, all progress depends on the unreasonable man.'

Chris Brindley MBE is now chair of the board for the Rugby League World Cup 2021. He has previously been voted 'Britain's Best Boss' and recognized by the Institute of Directors as the UK's Non-Executive Director of the year. In 2010, he became Managing Director for Metro Bank and set out on a mission to revolutionize the banking industry:

'I get invited to speak at leadership and
industry seminars and I sometimes go on
stage and challenge the audience to find this

229

letter. I want one copy of the following letter in existence, whether it's held by your bank, utility company, mobile phone or whatever. It says this: "I am so tired of speaking to human beings. I would like you to install an automated voice response system that keeps me waiting sixteen minutes, and then when I get through, asks me to press more buttons and eventually puts me through to the wrong person. I'm bored with humans answering the phone. Get me that machine installed now."

'There's no such letter in existence, because no customer would write it. When organizations state in their values, "We put the customer at the heart of everything," I say that's really sad, because you're lying to your customers, but even sadder, you're lying to yourselves. Any organization that has an automated voice response and puts, "We put our customer at the heart of everything we do," is simply delusional.'

Great leaders disrupt to bring about growth. That means leading and driving a culture that is focused on adapting your company to the future needs of your customer. Naturally, you want your current customer to also be your future customer, but every business needs their customer base to not just be loyal, but to grow.

Loyalty quickly becomes the justification for not disrupting a comfortable status quo. As we talked about in the Growth chapter, if something isn't growing, it stagnates and gradually begins to die. Brindley knows this:

'Disruption for us was completely intentional. If it was right for the customer, we made it happen and had a lot of fun along the way. We decided we would open up on bank holidays. People said, "You can't open on a bank holiday." I said, "Why? It's the banks choosing not to open. It's not a statutory requirement."'

'We were the only bank to open on a Sunday. People said, "Well that's not fair on your people," and I said, "Well funnily enough, we recruit people from places like travel agents and department stores – people who are used to working Sundays and bank holidays. To entice them and keep them, we just created a much better work environment. We opened more business accounts on a Sunday than any other day; all the other banks were shut.

'We put toilets in and baby changing facilities. We allowed dogs in. I was once asked by the MD of a rival bank (who thought allowing dogs was a terrible idea) what would happen if a dog crapped in a branch, to which I replied, "Well, someone will clear it up." Almost a third of UK households own a dog. That's ten million people you can instantly appeal to by changing one simple rule.'

How does a leader get even better at disruption? First, think of disruption as a verb, not a noun. What are leaders doing? What are they focused on and how are they behaving?

In this chapter, we will explore:

- The disruption challenge

- Disruption vs innovation

- Measuring your appetite for disruption

- Know your future customer

- Building a culture of disruption for growth

- Building your disruption squad

The disruption challenge

Disruption intentionally comes last within the GOD ecosystem. Disrupting without a clear reason to grow (Growth) and a belief that the thing you're proposing is possible (Optimism) is just disruption for disruption's sake; and that will erode your credibility and effectiveness as a leader extremely quickly.

You may know a leader who does this. They constantly challenge but are confusing disruption with criticism. They consider themselves to be change agents but seek change only for the sake of change. This isn't entirely their fault. Disruption has become the sexy, must-have leadership quality over the last decade. Steve Jobs wanted Apple to attract employees who could 'make a little a dent in the universe',[1] and 'move fast and break things' was Mark Zuckerberg's initial internal motto for Facebook,[2] but there's a huge difference between celebrity tech CEOs talking about disruption and the reality of what this means for most leaders working in medium- to large-sized businesses. Many of these businesses will cite disruption, challenge or entrepreneurship within their values or competency frameworks, but the truth is that if leaders actually behave in that way, they may find themselves out of a job.

As we mentioned in the introduction to this section, one of the most common reasons this happens is because too many organizations appoint someone to lead, but then expect them to do the job of a manager. Lip service may be paid to disrupting for growth, but little else. With all this focus on leadership, it's important to be clear that managers are the unsung heroes of every business. They are the engine room and keep the machine humming. As long as their market remains relatively stable, a business with great management and poor leadership will continue to be OK for some time, because their current customer will still be looked after. A business with poor management and strong leadership will break down extremely quickly, because the current customer will be neglected and so the future customer won't exist.

Unfortunately, the skill of great management has become diluted and considered the ugly sister to the more aspirational 'leadership'. As a result, both have been lessened. In too many organizations, leaders are expected to manage and are not empowered or rewarded for driving 'future focused' change; and managers don't get the credit or reward they deserve for 'just' being bloody good at delivery.

If leading through the Covid-19 pandemic has taught businesses one thing, hopefully it's that the expectation placed on leaders has changed. Most organizations have achieved things they simply would not have considered possible prior to the pandemic. At the start of the pandemic, stability was paramount and leaders had their greatest strengths and weaknesses exposed as a result, but as organizations dust themselves down and look towards the future, leaders must maintain this momentum and embrace a culture of disruption for growth if they are to survive.

Now, more than ever, leaders should be measured by what they have changed and improved, which has made their business more 'future fit 'as a result. It's this forward thinking and focus on processes, culture and ways of working in order to meet the demands of future customers, that should now define a successful business leader.

To improve is to change. Think about that. You cannot improve anything (a relationship, an attitude, a business) without changing something; and change cannot happen without a degree of disruption. If a leader is tasked with, and driven to, improving things, they must be driven to disrupt things. Likewise, if a company is committed to continual improvement, it must embrace continual change.

Disruption vs innovation

Disruption is not the same as innovation. Innovation tends to be more product related (the offering), whereas disruption is more cultural (the intent). If a company is strong on innovation but lacks the appetite and drive for disruption, much of that brilliant innovation might walk out of the door to a competitor. This is why a company can innovate, but still comfortably maintain its status quo.

Innovation tends to be a bolt-on for many businesses – a ring-fenced department responsible for generating clever solutions and ideas which the senior leadership team can accept or reject. Innovation is often assumed under the banner of 'digital transformation' or 'change' but therein lies the same problem. The people effectively responsible for ensuring the future growth of the business are working on the periphery of the business. It stops being everyone's challenge, because it's been 'outsourced' to a separate department or silo. This is a concept Aileen O'Toole from Prosus knows all too well:

> 'Some companies think, "We're going to be disruptive here," so they appoint someone to head it up and think that all will be well. But unless disruption is a core part of how you do business, simply asking someone on a different floor to think about it, is really an excuse not to change. It just delays the inevitable.'

When ideas or proposals for innovation and change are submitted to the decision-makers, those suggestions are viewed through the lens of their current status quo. If that status quo is built around a strategy of loyalty and servicing the current customers, then innovation can easily be rejected as an unnecessary threat.

All disruptive companies are innovative, but not all companies that innovate are necessarily disruptive. Let's explain that with an example. Remember Kodak? The expression 'a Kodak moment' was embedded in the public consciousness for decades whenever a camera was used. During the 1970s in the US, Kodak controlled over 70% of the photographic film market. They absolutely dominated their industry, making money from every step of the photography process. Customers bought Kodak cameras, film and flashbulbs and then paid to have their photos developed on Kodak paper. Life was good at Kodak.

At the same time this money was rolling in, tucked away in the Kodak innovation lab was an engineer called Steve Sasson.[3] He was working on something that was to prove somewhat significant to the future of his employer. Sasson invented the digital camera. He took his innovation to the Kodak decision-makers and ran a series of demonstrations to executives from different departments. He would take a picture of the people in the room and then show them their picture on a television. They didn't get it. Why would anyone want to see their photo on a screen?

Part of the Kodak internal mantra was that 'if the house is burning down, the first thing people rescue are their photographs.' They had built an entire industry out of photography being about preserving memories. They also made a fortune from selling film, which the digital camera didn't need. Sasson continued to develop his camera and in 1989 produced the first modern, single-lens digital camera, but Kodak never allowed it to see the light of day. From that point on until it expired in 2007, Kodak did make money from their digital camera patent as their disruptive competitors fully embraced the new technology, but just three years later, Kodak, one of the strongest and most admired brands on the planet, was forced to file for bankruptcy.

Kodak may have been innovative once but had long since forgotten what disrupting for growth meant. It became the tired whale being circled by hungry sharks because leaders lacked vision and had become complacent. Their strategy was built around the status quo rather than future customer needs.

Organizations that embrace, live and breathe disruption for growth place it at their centre. It is present at every board meeting, every executive committee, every town hall, every team meeting, every performance review and every recruitment decision. Leaders encourage and reward it in their teams, and in turn are held accountable for it by their board.

Where this culture of disruption for growth is combined with innovation, exciting things happen. Brindley tells the story of how they approached the issue of lost debit cards at Metro Bank. Brindley and his team worked out that customers mostly find their lost debit cards within two hours but have usually called their bank and cancelled their cards by then. It would typically take two to three days for their new ones to arrive in the post, which was extremely frustrating for the customers. After much testing, Brindley's team found a way to suspend a card while it was 'lost', but it could be reactivated if it was found again. They went a step further and installed card machines in their branches. This meant that if a customer's card was lost or damaged, they could walk into a branch and come out fifteen minutes later with a new card. That may not sound so amazing now, but in 2013 it was revolutionary, and it took other banks over four years to catch up. As Brindley says,

> 'Our job, quite simply, was to remove anything
> which prevented a customer getting access
> to their money. By combining innovative
> technology and an obsession with customer
> service, we changed the rules of the game.'

One year earlier in 2012, another highly disruptive brand began appearing on streets across the UK: Purple Bricks estate agency. Seemingly overnight, Purple Bricks changed their industry by focusing on their future customers' needs. Verona Frankish, former managing director of lettings for Purple Bricks, explains how:

'Estate agency was ripe for disruption because it hadn't embraced the innovation in technology. It had been pretty much the same for ever. The service level was effectively the same; the fee structures were effectively the same. Everybody was charging percentage-based fees but that was always up for negotiation. As a customer, depending on how good you were at negotiating with your agent meant two people on the same street could pay a completely different fee from the same agent just because they negotiated harder. There was a view from a consumer perspective that this wasn't fair. There was also a perception (rightly or wrongly) that agents didn't necessarily earn their fee – an attitude of "depending on the house and the street that I live in, my house is going to sell regardless, so effectively all you're doing is listing my property on the portals and you aren't necessarily doing anything to justify your fee."' [4]

Purple Bricks was able to be successful in that disruption and change because they believed in it enough and got enough people around them to buy into the notion that things could be better than what they were. They combined innovation with a passion held by a group of people who wanted to put their head above the parapet and champion that change and disruption.

Measuring your appetite for disruption

Innovation without an appetite to disrupt for growth is often wasted, but when an organization can combine the two, then they're off to the races. To help you build the skill and attitude to disrupt for growth, it's good to first have some idea of what level of comfort and drive you naturally have for this work.

The questionnaire below is designed to raise self-awareness around your appetite for disruption and how this might impact your leadership style. Try to answer it truthfully; then consider how that might manifest itself with those you work with.

EXERCISE: MEASURING YOUR APPETITE FOR DISRUPTION

Score yourself against the questions below, with a score of 1 being 'not at all/never' and 5 being 'very/nearly always'. Write down your scores.

- How disruptive would you say you are?
- How often do you propose changes to the way your business or team operates?
- How focused are you on your future customers?
- How often do you encourage people to try doing things in different ways?
- When a setback happens at work, do you naturally look for the opportunity?
- How comfortable are you with decisions that have an element of risk?

- How often do you try new things?
- How often do you challenge other people's opinions, even if it might make you unpopular?

Now tally up your total score:

- **Score below 15: Low appetite** – are you only tasked with managing the status quo?
- **Score 16–29: Medium appetite** – you have some appetite to disrupt for growth, depending on the situation.
- **Score 27–40: High appetite** – you're clearly a strong disruptor, but is it only ever focused on meeting the needs of your future customers?

Know your future customer

As with Kodak, if a business is being disrupted by external competitors and rapidly conceding market share, it's almost always because that business failed to disrupt first. There are always competitors and startups will always be able to react and pivot faster than more established businesses, but being long-established is no excuse for standing still.

The world-famous black cabs in London have been hailed on the capital's streets since 1948. The cabs and their drivers are more than a business; they are proudly considered a British institution. Sitting in the back of a black cab and getting life advice from the driver (whether you want it or not) is considered a rite of passage for anyone visiting London. Then along came Uber, who made it possible to hail, pay for and track a cab from your phone. Uber didn't invent the technology; they just focused on the future customer. They made the experience of travelling by taxi far easier and more convenient. Heritage and loyalty have their place but can so easily blind the leaders of a business to the changing demands of their customers. Picture the scenario. It's pouring rain, you're late and you can track a taxi to your front door by pressing one button on your phone... Heritage and loyalty didn't stand a chance.

Of course, it's easy to say these things with hindsight, but as the above example attests, leaders already have the crystal ball that will tell them a huge amount about what needs to be changed for the future growth of their business. That crystal ball is their customers. Picking up on the London black cab example above, for years customers were frustrated that they couldn't pay their cab fare on a card. Drivers only accepted cash, but it wasn't until late in 2016 (more than ten years after 'chip and pin' became the norm in shops) that it became mandatory for black cabs to install card machines.[5] By that stage, Uber had already been operating in London for four years.

Naturally there's a limit to what can be gleaned from customers, which is where innovation is so important. Sometimes customers don't know what they want until it's offered to them. Someone who knows more than most about customers and their needs is the founder of Amazon, Jeff Bezos. As he writes in his 2016 Letter to Amazon shareholders:

'There are many advantages to a customer-centric approach, but here's the big one: customers are *always* beautifully, wonderfully dissatisfied, even when they report being happy and business is great. Even when they don't yet know it, customers want something better, and your desire to delight customers will drive you to invent on their behalf.'[6]

Create a customer advisory panel

How do you get the customer voice? In the eco-system that is a business, everyone is serving someone. If you're not actually on the frontline supporting and selling to the external customer, then your role and that of your function is to support and enable those who are on the frontline to be as effective as possible.

To get an insight into your future customer needs and what might need disrupting, create a customer advisory panel (CAP). Go to your key customers and work backwards. Within your customer base, identify your supporters, but more importantly, your critics. Why are they critical? What is it about you or your products that frustrate them? Spend time seeking to understand what needs are not being met that lead to that frustration and what could be done even better.

Part of this panel should also be those members of your team who work closest with the customers, allowing you to hear and understand their experiences, suggestions and challenges first-hand. Richard Kimber, a former MD of Google, sums this up nicely:

> 'The frontline teams are the ones with their fingers on the pulse. If you're sitting in a boardroom, you don't always pick up all of the nuances and details around what customers are saying. I think that's the challenge – to make sure that the frontline teams have the power, the fluidity and the knowledge to actually feed back the signals that are showing you that the market is actually turning. We're missing business over here because something's happened, or there's a new entrant, or the new competitor or what not. I think that, to me, is one of the things most vital within an organizational culture.'

Note that a CAP is not the same as a survey. Too often customer metrics are measured according to levels of satisfaction, but these often just tell you what to keep doing – not what to do differently or better. We now live in a world obsessed with customer feedback but it's not always helpful. For example, Sampson got a coffee from a Costa machine in a garage the other day. When his drink was ready, a message appeared onscreen asking him to rate his experience from one to five stars. He chose a three and went about his day. That tells the people at Costa that their customer experience could be better. The reason he rated it a three and not higher was because there weren't any chocolate powder sachets left, but he couldn't tell them that. Bezos is not against beta-testing or surveys, but as he says in his 2016 Letter to Amazon shareholders, 'A remarkable customer experience starts with heart, intuition, curiosity, play, guts, taste. You won't find any of it in a survey.'[7]

Look beyond your horizon

We've talked about one crystal ball that leaders can use to predict future customer trends (ie the customers themselves), but there is another one. Look around and build your awareness of what others in your industry are doing, particularly in other parts of the world. Customer needs are not consistent across the globe and will differ depending on a huge number of variables, from socio-economic elements to climate. While some will still be catching up to where you are now, some will already be more advanced and so ideas can be emulated to keep you a step ahead. It was by focusing on the latter that Tom Lowe and his brother were able to disrupt the craft beer industry as the co-founders of Fourpure Brewing Co., a hugely successful brewing company based in the UK. As Lowe explains:

> 'When we started there weren't many cans around in craft beer. Cans were seen as being something cheaper and lager-based. Everyone in our industry was in bottles. We used bottles initially, but then we started going to a craft brewers conference in the US where the craft

beer market is much bigger. We'd look at the
trends because they were slightly ahead of
us; and we saw that a lot of breweries were
putting their beer into cans for better quality.
Beer gets staled by air and the seal on a can
is much better. Beer is also staled by sunlight,
which doesn't affect a can. You can also get
much more space for branding on a can. We
took a risk and went all in with the can and it
became a differentiator.'[8]

It became such a differentiator that most of Fourpure's
competitors have now switched to cans. Even Carlsberg, one of the global beer giants known primarily
for lager, has had to sit up and take notice. Craft beer
is known for its experimental flavours and brand trib-
alism and Carlsberg recognized they were fast losing
customers to this emerging market.[9] Carlsberg were
still marketing their lager for the mainstream, but
the mainstream had moved on. As a result, they've
changed both the ingredients and recipe for their beer
and created a new label design. It's too early to tell
whether that will be enough, but the lesson here is
that it's better late than never to adapt to your future
customer.

David vs Goliath

Both large and small businesses will claim to be customer focused, but they'll approach this in very different ways. Startups want the clout and success of

established businesses, but without losing the agility and energy that made them successful as a startup. Established businesses want the agility and energy of a startup, but without taking risks that may harm their brand. As an entrepreneur in the brewing industry, Lowe has an amusing take on this:

> 'When big business tries to act like a startup, it's like dad dancing isn't it? There's loads of stuff you do as an entrepreneur that doesn't make sense to a corporate customer because it's too risky. For instance, the way we often made decisions was based on feel. We cut through all the corporate decision-making process because we could. We made most of our big decisions there and then in the room. That was something we could do that big business couldn't. If it was something we could retract if it didn't work, then we'd do it. The key was to focus on, "What can we do that they can't?" I came to the conclusion that on product innovation, the marketing side, and culturally, it's really hard for them to be innovative because they're encumbered by certain rules due to shareholders and everything else.'

What can you do that your competitors can't? Play to your strengths and use your size, supply chains, infrastructure and expertise to your advantage. Once this is established and leveraged, the difference between success and something never being more than just a good idea is usually autonomy. Are you truly empowered to take that thing and try it?

This is a huge challenge for big business, partly because leaders are often tasked with being effective managers, not disrupting for future growth. They are expected to deliver on process for the sake of the process, not because it's the right thing for the customer. When asked what advice she would give to leaders working within larger, more established organizations, here's what Frankish from Purple Bricks had to say:

> 'Make sure you've got the right person in the right role. That's the first step. The second thing is to give them autonomy and empowerment to make decisions. Set rules – be clear where the decision-making line sits, and what you can and can't make decisions on. Agree what the longer-term strategy and set of objectives are and make sure that everybody is clear on that. People can then make decisions and be empowered within their role to progress the business. If every single decision has to go through the person at the top, you won't be agile. You won't pivot. The team won't feel valued and admired and trusted. They'll feel like they're just a messenger to get to the top, and that is not meaningful or satisfying for anybody in any role. That applies right up to board level. Every single level must question the next level down and ask, "Have I got the right people in my team and am I creating the conditions for them to be successful

and feel like they are making a difference and adding value on a daily basis?" If they're not, there's something not quite right.'

This advice from Frankish comes with a healthy warning:

'I really struggle when leaders say they want autonomy and they want to be empowered, but they don't want accountability. They think that it's always someone else's responsibility to make things happen. They'll say, "You need to bring me in, to get me involved in these things; you need to give me the autonomy to make it happen," but then they never actually do. Then when things aren't going to plan, it's someone else's fault. I have a real problem with that. If you want power, then you have to accept the responsibility that goes with it.'

You could argue that such advice, coming from a newer and smaller business, is all well and good and that autonomy for them will be much easier. If you believe that to be true, then your business is in trouble. As the next example demonstrates, where leaders are given real autonomy, even the oldest, largest and most bureaucratic behemoth can adapt. Over to Hayley Macdougall, former global head of international manager talent for HSBC:

'During my time at HSBC, senior executives often compared changing anything to being like "turning an oil tanker". Given the size

and complexity of the organization, this
made sense, but it became a self-fulfilling
prophecy to the point where it became a global
joke. Both staff and customers would say
that HSBC stood for "How Simple Becomes
Complicated". Staff didn't share their ideas
because it was just too painful to get anything
implemented.'

Then in 2015, HSBC was given an opportunity to
shake things up. After the fallout of the financial crisis
in 2008, as part of government reforms, all banks were
forced to ring-fence their UK operations. If the global
bank got into trouble, it wouldn't then pull down their
UK business. As a result, HSBC established HSBC
UK, a stand-alone entity with separate leadership and
operations from the global group. Macdougall says:

'Effectively, it felt like a new bank. New
premises in Birmingham and new leadership
determined to learn lessons from the past
and take advantage of this opportunity. They
deliberately set out to create a new, UK-specific
culture and recognised that as the leaders, this
had to start with them.'

Learn lessons they did. In 2019, two staff members
raised awareness of the difficulty people with no
address or photo identification faced in opening a
bank account. A pilot was quickly launched in Liver-
pool, and by the end of that year HSBC had teamed
up with national homelessness charities Shelter and

Crisis and launched its 'no fixed address' service. This allowed people with no address or photo identification to still open a bank account – essential for claiming benefits, getting a mobile phone, being paid a wage or renting somewhere to live. This service is now available in over 100 branches and 300+ members of staff have been trained to offer specialist support. All in under two years.

On the surface, a bank investing in people with little money doesn't make a huge amount of sense, but that would be missing the point. HSBC took a hammering after the 2008 financial crisis, with huge fines imposed for money laundering, and they nearly had their banking licence revoked by the US government. Even now, most people are suspicious of banks, seeing many of them as faceless corporations focused only on huge profits and wealthy customers. HSBC UK saw an opportunity to disrupt this and show a humbler, ethically driven and community-focused approach to financial services. It was bold and was an investment in the long term. Guess who all those qualities are becoming increasingly important to? That's right. The future customers of banks.

HSBC UK listened to what their people on the frontline were telling them. They simplified and accelerated the decision-making process by reducing bureaucracy and empowering their leaders and they invested in something deliberately focused on their future customers. Regardless of the circumstances, if one of the largest organizations in the world can do this, then there's a powerful lesson here for every leader in every business.

Building a culture of disruption for growth

There can't be many people on this planet who've not heard of Steve Jobs. His story is one of legend; he's known as the guy behind the tech that changed the world. The absolute rock-star product that was produced under Jobs' leadership was the iPhone. Statistics published in a 2020 article estimated that Apple have sold over 2.2 billion of them, bringing in around $1 trillion in revenue.[10]

What you may not know is that Jobs thought the iPhone was a terrible idea and for years, he refused to even consider it. He hated mobile phones. In fact, his team worked secretly on it for months as they tried to chip away at his negativity. The team around Jobs were future customer-focused, but in a different way to Jobs. They saw something he didn't, and for a long time his ego got the better of him. He believed he was right. In the end, his team finally won him over. As the story goes, it was Apple vice-president, Michael Bell, who finally convinced him to consider a phone. Bell helped Jobs to see that smartphones would almost certainly kill off the iPod and competitors such as Microsoft (Apple's archnemesis) would be rushing to take advantage of this opportunity.[11] This was a clever way to leverage Jobs' ego and spur him into action; but should it have been that difficult or taken that long?

A culture which embraces disruption for growth is one that removes obstacles to change, and so accelerates the delivery of products and services for the future customer. It is a culture where challenge and tough questions are the norm, allowing disrupting thinking to not only flourish, but be acted upon. Individuals at all levels feel genuinely empowered to think and share their thoughts because they are listened to and good ideas get actioned. Steve Jobs founded what many consider to be the most disruptive business of our time; the true disrupters for growth, though, were often those who worked under him. Jobs was lucky that his team had the passion and commitment to sometimes act *despite* their leader.

The lesson here is that often the blocker to achieving a culture which disrupts for growth is a leader's stubbornness, overconfidence and/or ego. When this becomes a significant blind spot for the leader or leadership team it will strangle everything else. Sampson shares an example that he has seen often:

'On many occasions I've met with the senior leadership team of an organization to discuss a brief around developing their culture. They will say things like, "How do we get people to live our values, how do we build more openness and honesty and more of a coaching and feedback culture?" It's obvious that the team see everything they are discussing as being "for the organization", but not for themselves. They see it as a problem that sits outside of the boardroom walls – something to be debated and fixed as though it were a new product which can then be rolled out. But of course, culture is behaviour. It has to start at the top.

'I ask one simple question: "How much of everything you've just shared about the challenges within your organizational culture exist within this team?" I'll be honest, this often doesn't make me popular, but the truth is that unless those leaders are prepared to hold up the mirror to themselves first, trying to impose things further down the organization will serve purely as a box-ticking exercise.'

People will do as you do, not as you say. If a leader is looking to build a culture that disrupts for growth, then they must lead by example. Leaders who openly accept that they will need to change in some way if they wish to improve, build both humility and trust. They are not threatened by the brilliance of others. They acknowledge that, often, their job is to let others shine brightly by just getting out of their way.

It's important to re-iterate here what we said in the introduction to the GOD chapters. A leader's job first and foremost is to create an environment which allows others to operate at their best. We're assuming you hire brilliant people for a reason. Help them become even more brilliant.

Threat of extinction

This is a relatively easy and quick way to highlight and uncover priority areas of your team or business which need addressing. It gives licence for people to air their frustrations and challenges with their current setup, but in an extremely positive and non-confrontational way.

It offers a way of proactively considering ways to innovate and develop, but also consider current processes, procedures and culture which pose a threat that a competitor could (and almost certainly will) easily exploit. The exercise is extremely effective for developing a holistic, organizational strategy, but works just as well for specific functions within a business.

EXERCISE: THREAT OF EXTINCTION

To encourage as much disruptive thinking as possible, split the team into groups of four to six. You (or whoever is doing this exercise) are a new team tasked with creating a blueprint for a new organization – one that you are intentionally building to not only compete with your actual organization, but to systematically take its market away and drive it to extinction. You want to crush your current employer by offering a better service, better products, a better experience, etc.

A few notes to guide the exercise:

- You only have the resources available in your real role and you can only suggest things which can be owned and achieved by those doing the exercise.

- This is not the time or place to moan about all the things you dislike about your company and the things it does badly. It's fine to highlight a negative, but only if you can propose a more positive alternative.

- View everything through the eyes of a potential rival. What do you notice about the business that could be done better? What opportunities are being missed that you propose doing instead?

- Be specific about what you are focusing on for the exercise. Is it products, customer service, business development, culture or perhaps a mixture?

Give the groups whatever materials they need and set a strict timeline. When done, the groups come back and present their ideas.

This is the important bit: people typically find it easy to come up with improvements and ideas, but how do you narrow them down to those that are realistic?

Put this back to the group. They will have to action and own their ideas. Get everyone to vote for the things they felt really stood out from all the presentations. What ideas provoke a sense of buzz and energy? Look at the top four or five, and then narrow them down to just three. Then simply ask: what is the consequence of not doing this?

You'll know instantly whether there's the commitment and energy to make it happen or not.

Appoint your non-executive directors

Where your CAP can tell you what you need to be changing and developing, your non-executive directors (NEDs) can help you understand how best to do it. The Institute of Directors website,[12] describes the role of a NED as follows:

> 'Essentially the non-executive director's (NED) role is to provide a creative contribution to the board by providing independent oversight and constructive challenge to the executive directors… The normal role of the NED in strategy formation is therefore to provide a creative and informed contribution and to act as a constructive critic in looking at the objectives and plans devised by the chief executive and the executive team.'

Does that sound like something that could be helpful for you and your team? Does it also perhaps create an opportunity to bring key enablers into your business area to build better support and awareness? Leaders are obviously extremely busy people, but can you think of two or three who would be willing to act as unofficial NEDs for your team? Perhaps they can attend your team meeting every six months or when a significant initiative is being considered?

Often, the most valuable role a NED can play is that of devil's advocate. They challenge and disrupt the board's thinking, introducing fresh perspectives and different insight. Ultimately, this enables the board to reach more robust and better-informed decisions. Even if you don't sit on a board, perhaps consider introducing the same thing for your team.

Disrupt to construct

The reality is, being truly disruptive for growth requires courage and tenacity, and often where that's toughest is lower down an organization. As O'Toole shares:

> 'I think the more senior you get, you probably don't need as much courage to ask a difficult question as you do when you're in the middle or just starting… There's a risk of being unpopular, there's a risk of being perceived as irrelevant. I think courage is a huge part of it, but I think it's the responsibility of leadership to ask tough questions.'

The problem here is that it's often the less senior leaders in the gap between operations and strategy that are best placed to notice trends and things that need to change, but they often won't speak up or challenge for fear of the consequences. This it's why it's so crucial that leaders must first create an environment where people feel safe to speak up, challenge and be heard if they are determined to build a culture of disruptive growth. We talk more about this in Chapter 8. It is just as important that everyone understands that the intent for challenge and disruption is only ever for one purpose: to grow. The simple five-step question-naire below will act as a filter to ensure any disruption is viewed through a growth lens.

EXERCISE: DISRUPTING VIEWED THOUGH A GROWTH LENS

1. How does this help us better serve our future customers?
2. What is the consequence of not doing this?
3. Are we OK accepting this?
4. What level of disruption is required?
5. Is that outweighed by the answer to Question 2?

We talked about the importance of autonomy ear-lier, but often leaders are reluctant to delegate more authority as it poses a risk: what if the person you del-egate to then screws things up? Be honest with your-self about why you have a team member who you're not fully prepared to empower. Are they not capable? (If not then what have you done to help them?) Do you not trust them? (If not then why are they still in your team?)

Delegating authority can be scary, but there are ways to continually assess how much authority someone is ready to receive and minimize the risk of something blowing up. Get in the habit of testing and challenging the thinking of your team members to see how they respond. If someone asks your advice on something, ask them what they think you would do. If someone has an idea, ask them who is impacted by it and what supporters they have for it. If someone suggests a process change, ask them why now, and how this will contribute to your vision as a team.

Always be exploring and testing thinking to understand who is ready for more empowerment and then help prepare them for when it comes.

Make decisions like a startup

One of the biggest differences between a disruptive startup and a larger, established business is the speed with which they are able, and prepared, to make decisions. Amazon, an organization with over half a million employees globally, has proven time and again that if the right cultural elements are in place, size is no prohibitor to speed. Amazon founder Jeff Bezos determines decision-making quality by classifying decisions as either Type 1 (if it doesn't work, it's irreversible) or Type 2 (it can be reversed if needed), but to help with decision velocity (speed) he endorses an approach he calls 'disagree and commit'. He outlines it in his 2016 Letter to Amazon shareholders:

> 'If you have conviction on a particular direction even though there's no consensus, it's helpful to say, "Look, I know we disagree on this but will you gamble with me on it? Disagree and commit?" By the time you're at this point, no one can know the answer for sure, and you'll probably get a quick yes.'[13]

You need faith and confidence in your team for this to work. Look for opportunities to try this approach so you can assess the effectiveness, but also be mindful of how your team respond. By giving them more trust and agency, do they step up and find another gear?

Death by email

This is simple but powerful. Kill your 'email first' culture. A culture that disrupts for growth has to be built upon open, honest and fast communication. One of the reasons entrepreneurs are far more agile is because their size allows them to make important decisions at speed. There is no long approval process requiring multiple signoffs and continual debate. Things are hashed out and agreed to and then they move on. In larger companies, email is often the antithesis of this ability.

Email has its place, but one way to encourage more agility is to break the habit of communicating with email first. Research conducted by Mail Manager found that a third of employees spend nearly one day a week just managing their inbox, and that 70% believe email is one of the biggest drains on productivity.[14] Aside from the sheer number of emails received each day, the written word can be misinterpreted. Challenge and disagreement (even if done positively and with the right intent) will not always be received the way the author intended, but if something is misinterpreted during a 'live' conversation it can be clarified and may even further improve the conversation.

As a leader, think about the email culture within your team. Are people copied in to everything (often a sign of a 'just covering my back' culture)? Does this suggest a lack of trust and accountability? Do people send emails when they could literally just walk ten yards and talk to that person? Think about how you might get the team to introduce some simple rules around the use of email. Encourage people to think, 'If I send this email, what am I asking of the recipient?' If it's just an FYI, will they even read it? In their survey, Mail Manager also found that around one third of emails are never opened.

An example we've seen in a few progressive organizations is to ban any work emails being sent internally between 6pm and 8am – something you *must* lead by example with. You can't stop people working, but you can ask them to save their work until the next day. If something is urgent, then pick up the phone.

Building your disruption squad

This may sound like something Elliot Ness from *The Untouchables* would do: bringing a crack group of honest cops together to bring down Al Capone. This isn't exactly that (fewer hats and guns), but in some ways the same spirit of adventure is similar. It's the energy and sense of camaraderie that comes from heading into unknown territory which often gives startups their edge over larger competitors.

As a leader trying to disrupt for growth, your efforts will have a lonely and unsuccessful existence if you don't bring others who will support and believe in you on board. To get things from, 'Are you serious?' to, 'My god, you were right,' every leader needs to build a disruption squad. Carly Fiorina was the first ever female CEO of a top Fortune 500 company, taking the helm at Hewlett Packard (HP) back in 2000. Fiorina had a reputation for being bold and disruptive so she was an obvious choice as CEO for a company that had become bogged down by its heritage and size, but after six years she was fired. She went on to run as a Republican presidential candidate. During an interview with CNN, she discussed how her departure was because of her challenging the status quo in a boardroom brawl. She says, 'It's what leaders must do… When you challenge the status quo, when you lead, you make enemies. It's why so few people lead.'[15]

Fiorina was known as a formidable strategist with an incredible sense of vision and her quote echoes much of what we've said about the courage and tenacity required for leadership; but she was criticized for focusing so intently on her disruptive vision that she failed to build rapport with key individuals and so she never got complete buy-in or support for her initiatives.

Your disruption squad are the people who will support and help you action your disruptive growth strategy. Without them, you can quickly build a reputation as nothing more than a trouble-maker. In the Growth chapter we shared an exercise called 'The Playing Field' to help leaders identify their Enablers (the people they need in order to bring their vision for growth to life). If you've done the exercise, you'll have identified most of your disruption squad.

To build relationships is one thing, but to build advocates who will join you in the trenches when there may be significant upheaval and risk involved requires seriously finessing your influencing skills. The challenge is two-fold. Firstly, you need to get a read on your would-be supporters: what makes them tick? Then you need to figure out how to adapt your approach to each individual to gain their support.

Four energies of the LEP

To help with this, we're going to draw from the adaptive communication tool, Leading Energy Profile (LEP). LEP was created and developed by The Business Coaching Academy over three years and derives its origins from three scientific sources: individual differences, biological psychology and cognitive behavioural therapy. LEP is based on the premise that we are driven by a combination of four distinct cognitive energies – in essence, four thinking biases. Everyone has all four energies, but one will typically dominate, and one will be weakest. Both will reveal distinct characteristics about us and how we prefer to interact and work with others.

LEP is a licensed product, but here's a snapshot to help you better prepare for ways to approach and win over your disruption supporters. The four energies of LEP are associated with the four parts of the human body, providing a simple metaphor that makes them easy to understand and put into practise:

1. The person who thinks with their head

2. The person who thinks with their heart

3. The person who thinks with their legs

4. The person who thinks with their hands

Let's look at each in turn.

The person who thinks with their head

This person has a bias for process and analytics. They tend to be organized and consistent, act dutifully and prefer planned rather than spontaneous behaviour. They can often appear quite formal and may be quieter than others in a group setting, as they like to reflect and gain clarity before speaking. They will not tolerate cutting corners or any sense of disrespect.

- **To win their support, do this:** Ensure you approach them with a clear business case, citing data and analytics which support why you believe something should be changed. Send them your research to read and digest before your meeting.

- **Don't do this:** Never lead with emotion or instinct. Don't be loose or vague about the facts and any potential risk – be absolutely honest. Don't dismiss the need for process and procedure, no matter how urgent your timeframe. Don't push them too quickly for their commitment. Give them time to reflect.

The person who thinks with their heart

This person has a bias for people, connection and co-operation. They place significant value on relationships and are genuinely concerned about others' emotional state and wellbeing. They'll always encourage input and openness from others and will typically place people at the heart of their decision-making.

- **To win their support, do this:** Take the time to connect with them as a person first and a sponsor second. Find some common ground (family, hobbies, etc) and show genuine interest. Build your business case around the people agenda and the impact your proposed disruption will have, whether on staff, customers or both.

- **Don't do this:** Don't ignore the impact on others of what you are proposing, even if it may appear negative. Be empathetic and don't overly confront or challenge them if they disagree. They will simply smile, say thank you, and you'll leave none the wiser.

The person who thinks with their legs

This individual is all about pace, action and forward momentum. They want things done quickly and have little interest in the detail. They can be outspoken and typically prefer driving rather than being driven. They will be noticeably frustrated by holdups or perceived barriers to obtaining a result.

- **To win their support, do this:** In a business case, start with the end in mind – specifically, what does the disruption deliver and what is the measurable result? Be clear what the timeline is and what your ask of them is. Highlight how this benefits them directly.

- **Don't do this:** Don't bore them with data or process. Get to the point and keep it short and sweet. Don't show confusion or uncertainty in your own thinking – be bold and concise.

The person who thinks with their hands

This person is energized by change, flexibility and new ways of doing things. They are drawn towards creative, innovative approaches to challenges and encourage options and alternative perspectives from others.

- **To win their support, do this:** Clearly show how what you are proposing is different than what's gone before. Allow your passion and belief for your proposal to come through, and emphasize the original, and possibly contentious, thinking that has gone into it. Build a sense of adventure to your goal and excitement around what this could mean for the future.

- **Don't do this:** Don't restrict their flexibility and tie them to one option – give them choices to explore. Don't be closed or overly traditional in your own thinking. Don't use words or data where images and stories can do a better job. Don't mistake enthusiasm on their part for commitment.

Of course, nobody is ever one thing or has only one style. We are all fluid according to the situations we find ourselves in. Consider your enablers who approach things differently to you. Can you see how you may need to adapt your style and approach to win their support and build a more beneficial relationship?

Wrapping it up: Applying what you've learned at work

Leadership requires courage, tenacity, optimism, and often, personal sacrifice. We believe that leaders are tasked with building organizations that have one primary purpose – to continually adapt to meet the needs of their future customers. To do this, use the GOD principle to guide you and help you stay focused: Growth is the vision. Optimism is the attitude. Disrupting is the action.

Four energies of the LEP

1. The person who thinks with their head

2. The person who thinks with their heart

3. The person who thinks with their legs

4. The person who thinks with their hands

Exercises and resources

- Measuring your appetite for disruption

- Threat of extinction

- Disrupting viewed though a growth lens

PART THREE
BETTER SELVES

I started my career communicating to employees about their health and financial benefits. A lot of the time, that meant creating educational campaigns around why staying healthy is good for you and how saving for your future is important. These were usually accompanied by a call to action to participate in a wellness programme or increase contributions to retirement plans.

These campaigns weren't very successful. Looking back, I don't know why I was so surprised, but it was my first glimpse into the hard truth that education alone is not enough to change behaviour. Let me say that again, because it is the most important point I will make in all three chapters of this section. *Education alone is not enough to change behaviour.* If it were, no one would eat fast food, smoke, drink too much, have an accident at work or go on a needless spending spree. Yet, those behaviours persist.

I found myself looking outside of the standard marketing and internal communication advice and best practices for anything new that I thought could move the needle and get me the results I was looking for. Then, in 2010 a colleague who managed the 401(k) defined contribution plan at Nordstrom (where I was working in benefits communication at the time) gave me the book *Predictably Irrational: The hidden forces that shape our decisions* by Dan Ariely.[1] I couldn't put it down. I suppose that was the first step that would culminate in me going back to school to get my MSc in behavioural economics almost a decade later; but another thought I had while I was reading Ariely's book was: *some of these interventions are so simple. Why aren't we applying this to our work?*

When the time came to run our annual 'Meet the Match' campaign encouraging employees to save at least enough for retirement to earn the full Nordstrom matching contribution, the 401(k) manager and I politely informed the consultancy that usually handled the campaign that we would be writing the copy that year. We were tired of seeing the same campaign year after year, with only the colour perhaps updated if we were lucky. We wrote it ourselves, and lo and behold, we had almost 50% more employees choose to increase their contribution than the same campaign from the year before. What did we do differently?

First, we leveraged the principle of *loss aversion* by providing employees with a personalized calculation showing how much money they had missed out on last year by not meeting the full match. We also utilized *social proof* by telling them how many of their peers were contributing enough money to receive the full match. These two simple principles from behavioural science made an enormous difference, and I was hooked.

Now it's my mission to apply behavioural science to traditional internal communication and human resource activities to enable them to help their employees be healthier, safer and more financially sound. In this final section, we'll explore specific behavioural science interventions for:

- Health and wellbeing: What is the one key principle that prevents people from taking the actions that are in their own best interest… and what can businesses do about it?

- Safety: What are the routines and policy decisions that are unwittingly putting us at risk; and how do we measure and improve psychological safety?

- Financial wellness: What are the key barriers that make being good with money so difficult; and what are practical interventions HR teams can take?

— *Lindsay*

SEVEN

Health

A good meme is truly the internet's gift to the world. One about workplace wellness made the rounds that, unfortunately, is often too true at many places of work. It goes something like this:

Employer: Managing stress is important, and we're committed to helping our employees find ways to feel less stressed.

Employee: Great. Can you pay us more, hire more people, and provide flexible working so I can achieve work/life balance?

Employer: Oh no, not that. We were thinking we'd just reimburse some yoga classes or something…

Employers have a tremendous opportunity to positively impact their employees' lives through the programmes they provide and how they motivate people to engage in them. This influence for good is more important than ever, for both physical and mental health issues. Let's look at mental health first. Stress, mental health and loneliness are not necessarily new conditions, but their prevalence is rising. The loss of social connection and its subsequent impact on health was abruptly and keenly thrust into the limelight during the Covid-19 pandemic. When millions were forced to make the shift to remote working and social distancing, the lack of regular in-person connection and its subsequent effect on mental health was well documented. In a survey conducted in the UK regarding the specific effects of Covid-19 on wellbeing, 79% of participants reported that their quality of life had been reduced.[1] The same report went on to make the bold statement that levels of wellbeing were the lowest that they have ever been since records began.

Emotional wellbeing is just one health challenge that businesses face. Physical issues such as high cholesterol, diabetes, cancer and so much more abound. Throwing money at these issues won't solve the problem. America spends more of their gross domestic product on healthcare than any other high-income country, yet still has the highest rates of obesity.[2] No matter which countries their people are based in, this is very much a problem for businesses. 'The time has come where we are finally seeing the moral case for wellbeing coming out,' says Dr Richard Caddis, Chief Medical Officer of BT:

'What that means is we're going up and down Maslow's hierarchy of needs. We focus on evidence-based approaches rather than what 'feels nice'. People want to know if their workplace is safe. They want the right support to do their job well and do their job safely. They want to know they have someone to speak to when they don't feel safe.'[3]

That means businesses aren't only operating at the top of Maslow's hierarchy pyramid in the realm of self-actualization. We're down on the lower rungs of safety and security. Businesses know there are many benefits when they get employees engaged in healthier behaviours. There's just one problem: employees would rather not.

In this chapter, we will explore:

- The conflict between want and should

- Five motivation and mindset barriers to good health choices

- Mental health, psychological safety and the moral case for wellbeing

- Six workplace interventions to help employees make healthier choices

- Loneliness at work – a growing health and wellbeing issue

- Two workplace interventions to battle loneliness

The conflict between want and should

To get to the one, root cause behind the most common health and wellbeing challenge businesses face, we'll need to play the most boring, but insightful, game of 'Would you rather?' For those of you who have never played before, it is a party game people play to explore ridiculous trade-offs around two unpleasant things. For example, 'Would you rather only be able to use a fork for the rest of your life, or a spoon?' Questions can get quite raunchy and uncomfortable, but we'll play the behavioural science equivalent of the game instead.

EXERCISE: WOULD YOU RATHER...?

Start each question by asking yourself, 'Would I rather...?' and choosing your responses from the following columns:

Go to the gym after work	Grab a drink with friends
Cook a healthy meal after a long day	Grab something fast and easy from the drive-through after a long day
Go for a long run	Sit on the couch and binge-watch Netflix
Eat a salad	Devour a plate of nachos

Now consider your answers. It's not hard to guess that you probably chose the options in the right-hand column. These questions are just a smattering of the trade-offs employees are asked to make decisions about every day.

Your employees are ticking those boxes, too. An exercise like this or an interactive quiz is a great internal communication technique to start to bring this tendency to your people's attention. When we are more mindful of what is preventing us from hitting our health goals, we can do a better job of reaching them.

This simplistic game gets to the crux of most unhealthy behaviours HR teams aim to solve. Whether they are trying to create change via onsite interventions, events or facilities, or they are trying to equip employees with the tools and motivation they need to take health into their own hands, the largest barrier comes down to this: people prefer to do what feels good in the moment vs what they know to be in the best interest for their future selves. Simple as that.

It's paramount to understand that many standard health communication campaigns that companies run for their employees fail to achieve the desired action because they don't factor in that life is a perpetual game of balancing 'want' against 'should'. Understanding the depth and strength of the present's pull on employee decision-making is vital in understanding why your people make decisions that are clearly not in their own best interest. In other words, it explains why employees sometimes blatantly ignore your thoughtfully crafted wellbeing campaigns.

When we understand the underlying psychological mechanisms behind why people make the decisions that they do, it can help us to better understand how the different health and wellness contexts we come across at work – activities such as asking someone to get a flu shot, participate in a wellness programme, or join a running club – might be viewed by employees. Even better is that you can also deploy tactics and strategies to help counteract these tendencies, which we will explain further in this chapter.

Five motivation and mindset barriers to good health choices

This next section breaks down the additional behavioural barriers to making good health choices. When we understand the theory behind the resistance to good health behaviours, we can design better solutions. The five largest motivational and mindset barriers to making good health choices are:

1. People choose the instant hit.

2. We think 'future us' will make better choices.

3. We think of 'future us' as a different person.

4. Poor employer incentive models.

5. A scarcity mindset.

Barrier #1: People choose the instant hit

We're suckers for instant gratification, and this temptation is even stronger with visceral emotions such as anger, sadness or hunger.[4] Why? Because these sharp emotions have an overly large influence on our behaviour. Essentially, visceral emotions are so strong and powerful that they are able to crowd out common sense and virtually any other goal we may have in the moment. They narrow our attention to focus only on the present want in front of us. It's why the old adage, 'Don't go grocery shopping on an empty stomach' is actually terrific advice. This desire to do what feels good now is at the heart of most of our poor health and wellbeing choices. Unfortunately, we usually choose the naughty and unhealthy choice... *because it feels better in the moment.*

Barrier #2: We think 'future us' will make better choices

Even with the best of intentions for many things in life, we still fall short. This is partially explained by our tendency to vastly overestimate our future self-control and performance. We make, in the present, what appears to be a rational decision about future consumption. Why wouldn't I take that new special rate my gym is offering – of course I'm going to go to the gym four times a week. A study aptly named 'Paying Not to Go to the Gym' looked at gym attendance from three US health clubs over the course of three years and found that those who paid a flat monthly membership fee on average forfeited about $600. It also found these customers paid a whopping 70% more than they would have if they'd chosen the 'pay as you go' option.[5] Anybody who has ever bought a gym membership as a New Year's resolution only for it to promptly go unused can relate.

When designing workplace programmes for employees, especially those that involve perks around gym memberships, sending a targeted message highlighting the monetary loss of *not* attending once people have signed up with your member gyms can be quite a persuasive tactic. For example, you could check the gym attendance data monthly and send an email, text or other such communication letting someone know that they have thrown $150 down the drain (or whatever the cost of their specific membership is).

Barrier #3: We think of 'future us' as a different person

American comedian Jerry Seinfeld does an excellent skit that beautifully illustrates this disconnect between present and future self. He talks about this conflict in terms of willpower and ego depletion. Most of us can agree with his statement that, 'No one wakes up, eats a healthy breakfast, and then destroys a box of brownies.' He talks about 'Night Guy' vs 'Morning Guy' and makes an insightful point when he says that they're like two different people. Night Guy is action guy, he's an 'I don't give a damn' type of guy... but Morning Guy, he's gotta go to work. Night Guy doesn't care about Morning Guy. Night Guy always screws Morning Guy.[6] What Seinfeld stumbled upon in the pursuit of comedy is well evidenced by behavioural science:

we actually think of 'future us' and 'past us' as different people.

Perhaps one of the clearest demonstrations of this disconnect between how we view our present selves vs how we view our future selves – and one that can inspire future health campaigns – was in a series of studies that asked people to envisage something quite simple: having a meal. Participants were assigned to one of five conditions and asked to shut their eyes and visualize a specific meal that occurred at various points in time such as their childhood, yesterday or in the distant future (eg when they were over the age of forty – apparently that's distant when you're a college undergrad). They were then asked if they had seen this meal through their own eyes and so did not see themselves in the image, or if they saw the meal through the eyes of an observer and so could see themselves in the visualization. The majority of participants asked to visualize their meal when they were over the age of forty reported seeing themselves in the image (and not through their own eyes) as if they were a different person.

Barrier #4: Poor employer incentive models

About a decade ago, employers in the US started implementing outcomes-based wellness-incentive programmes. Desperate to reduce the amount of money spent on medical claims while simultaneously improving their employees' health, the idea behind these revolutionary programmes was to reward employees for meeting certain biometric goals such as falling into widely considered healthy medical ranges for blood pressure, cholesterol and body mass index. Rewards were also given for engaging in certain activities such as completing an online health risk assessment or participating in health coaching. (An important note here is that this type of monetary incentivization strategy is almost solely a US construct.)

Nate Randall, founder and President of Ursa Major Consulting and host of the *Illuminate HR* podcast, was on the team at Safeway who rolled out one of the first such programmes in the US. The work Safeway did made its way into the Patient Protection and Affordable Care Act, colloquially known as 'Obamacare'. Casually known as 'The Safeway Amendment', this provision allowed employers to use 30% of the total cost of employees' health insurance premiums as outcome-based incentives for employees.[7] 'On the surface, whether or not there is a behaviour change, the idea of premium differentials based on risk was new,' says Randall. [8] He likened it to how car insurance providers determined premiums. If they deem a driver risky due to a factor such as age or their previous driving history, the driver pays more. Safeway wanted as many people as possible to be able to successfully complete the programme. Randall says:

> 'It was actually pretty easy. The concept
> was you could pay your higher premiums
> based on whatever [health] triggers were in

there for the various biometric tests, but you could earn them back by making incremental improvements. It wasn't that you were morbidly obese and had to become a healthy weight by the end of the year in order to get your money back. For example, you could always get a note from your doctor to [address the issue].'

From Randall's perspective, the programme was a success in that it worked much as it was intended to from a financial standpoint and in nudging people the right way. However, if the programme was easy to complete – a key ingredient in any behaviour change – why did some struggle to complete it? In hindsight, it's clear what a key problem facing this and other internal health and wellbeing initiatives is: motivation.

Those who were already intrinsically motivated to be healthy were the ones eagerly embracing the new programmes. Those who loved their early morning jog would keep running and those that swore off sugar, carbs and alcohol were going to continue eating well. The new incentive would not change those existing good health habits. For those not already meeting the threshold, a small incentive (usually in the form of a discount on their medical plan deduction on their pay cheque) was not going to be extrinsically motivating enough for people to change behaviour.

The US looks to reduce medical premiums but that's not the case globally. 'In Europe, we focus on the reduction in sickness absence. We stop people from becoming ill. The drivers of wellbeing are very different,' remarks Caddis. He also calls out the problem with data that these types of models as seen in the US have:

> 'The problem is getting the data on it. Because ROI can take a decade. For example, if we were to do a diabetes program tomorrow, the ROI is ten, fifteen, twenty years away when we talk of strokes, heart attack and death.'

Barrier #5: A scarcity mindset

Randall brings up another interesting point regarding lack of completion – one that employers would be wise to pay heed to. He says:

> 'When you look at it from a population health standpoint, high blood pressure, high cholesterol, diabetes, overweight… All of these things disproportionately affect lower income populations and certain ethnicities. That's the hard, negative truth.'

These programmes can put a lot of pressure on people just trying to get by, even though they're the ones who would potentially benefit the most from such incentive schemes. When you're focused on just making ends meet, well – sometimes that's all you can focus on. It's called a *scarcity mindset*.

> A **scarcity mindset** is what one adopts when there is not enough of a certain resource. This scarcity mindset focuses attention on whatever it is that someone has deemed scarce.

Randall thinks that this scarcity mindset in some is partially to blame for dismal wellness programme completion rates in certain portions of the population:

> 'They can't get to real, lasting change because they can't make their car payment and they're stressed out about it, or they're trying to save for their kid's university and they're stressed out about it. These really important "in your face" things are the behavioural blockers for really doing true, lasting wellness.'

We'll explore the concept of scarcity further in Chapter 9. Given the double-whammy of a non-motivating incentive and the implications of a scarcity mindset, should workplaces abandon the idea of paying incentives for healthy workplace behaviours? Probably. Don't fret, though; there are plenty of other behavioural levers, discussed later in this chapter, that you can use to encourage healthier behaviours at work.

Mental health, psychological safety and the moral case for wellbeing

The first two episodes of Season 5 in the US version of the popular comedy *The Office* are entitled 'Weight Loss', where the Scranton branch of the Dunder Mifflin Paper Company participates in a company-wide weight-loss challenge. The branch that collectively loses the most weight gets an extra three days of vacation. How do they measure this collective weight loss? With a public, group weigh-in on a giant scale. Enthusiasm for losing weight quickly turns to excessive competition and some participants resort to rather *extreme* measures. 'I'm totally gonna slaughter at the weigh-in today,' says one character. 'All I had to eat this weekend was a chicken breast and a case of Diet Coke,' says another. Someone replaces all of the items in the vending machine with fruits and vegetables. Toward the end of the competition when weight-loss efforts start trending flat, tempers rise. 'I need these five days for my honeymoon! Who is slacking? I want names!'

This was just a scenario for laughs in a sitcom and it would be unimaginable for companies to sanction a weight-loss competition that involved a public weigh-in, but it does raise the issue of what expected behaviours in a workplace should be. Social normative behaviours around what can and cannot be discussed in the workplace often dictate how comfortable people are (or aren't) with certain topics.

Arguably the most powerful intervention that employers have is to shed light on the fact that stress, anxiety, depression and other mental health states impact us all – and that it's OK to talk about it. We'll talk more about creating a psychologically safe environment in the next chapter, but one key to this is opening up the conversation around mental health. What this does is normalize the issue – it moves it from the margins of what it's OK to talk about, to a widely accepted practice. Marina Gonzalez, who we heard from in earlier chapters, says:

> 'For some organizations, wellbeing has been a sleepy topic in that it's put out there and talked about, but it's not until the last two years – especially with Covid-19 – that emotional wellbeing and the mental health of employees has become a business imperative. As a result of the pandemic, employees are much more conscious and educated to the effects of burnout, anxiety and stress, and will hold their company and managers more accountable to role model a work/life balance.'

One standout company in this space is professional services firm Ernst & Young (EY). After experiencing mental health crises where individuals in several offices had taken their own lives or there were fatalities due to substance abuse, EY colleagues were left with a profound feeling of grief and shock. Lori Golden, Abilities Strategy Leader at EY, shares how some employees were also left with an intense feeling of guilt. 'It was this guilt of, "Should I have noticed something I didn't pick up on, or was there something I should have said?"'[9] While EY had a terrific Employee Assistance Programme, it wasn't the same as equipping employees to proactively spot signs of their colleagues struggling. It was more than that, as Golden explains:

'For the first time, it wasn't just about services to protect the individual's mental health. So many people have friends or family members with substance misuse conditions or mental illness, and the role of a friend, lover, supporter, child or caregiver can be overwhelming. It can become toxic with someone else's issues.'

While researching what else was out there in the space, she came across a video series initiated by students at the University of Minnesota where they said things such as, 'Hey, I've been impacted, and we need to talk to one another.' That was the lightbulb moment. It wasn't a campaign from the administration. It was a campaign from student to student. EY hatched a plan to not only give people a basic education on how to spot if somebody might be struggling so they could play a more active role in supporting one another's mental health, but to also give a safe space to start a conversation. They called it 'r u okay?' The name was borrowed with permission from an Australian suicide prevention charity,[10] and the campaign launched in the autumn of 2016. Careful not to put colleagues in the position of actually intervening, the campaign focused on quick ways to approach one another and made a tremendous impact on helping people feel less alone. Over time, they evolved the name. '"r u okay?" is a point in time and assumes a negative,' Golden explains. 'We wanted to broaden the frame to say we care about one another and there are many ways that plays out.' Now operating under the broader term 'Better You', EY continues to see high demand and engagement. Bruce Greenhalgh, Global Health and Wellbeing Clinical Lead at BT, shares the pioneering work they did in this space:

> 'We signed up to the charter Time to Change as
> a corporation over ten years ago, which gives
> you an idea of how long we've been talking
> about mental health. When we signed up for it,
> we were already two years into a programme
> educating managers, thousands of managers,
> in mental health. That programme is similar
> to Mental Health First Aid, which we first
> had people on the pilot for in Scotland. Then
> we developed our own programme tailor-
> made for the corporate environment, and
> BT in particular. Programmes like this train
> managers to help support their people with
> mental health.'[11]

That was a good start, but Greenhalgh notes that the need for mental health support doesn't magically go away once someone becomes a manager. 'It was a naivety that I laugh at in myself, because we felt we were training the managers to help employees with their mental health – forgetting that the managers needed support, too.' So, BT expanded its offerings. In addition to the aforementioned programme, they also launched a mental health service providing treatment using cognitive behavioural therapy, a peer-to-peer support network trained in mental health first aid, a suicide prevention programme and more.

Six workplace interventions to help employees make healthier choices

The six interventions outlined in this next section tackle two key considerations for behaviour change: they make unhealthy behaviours harder to do, and they make good behaviours easier to complete. The six interventions are:

1. Guard against future temptation.

2. Find the 'today' hook.

3. Pair the fun with the not so fun.

4. Influence the environment.

5. Try implementation intentions.

6. Use commitment contacts.

Intervention #1: Guard against future temptation

One of the most effective tools at an employer's disposal is helping to prevent unhealthy behaviours *before* they happen. It's about pre-emptively putting guardrails in place because we know 'future us' likely can't be trusted to resist temptation if it's around. These 'Ulysses contracts' as they are called (they get their name from Ulysses' encounter with the famed Sirens in Homer's *The Odyssey*) have become an extremely valuable tool in health.[12] They can be considered an advanced directive of sorts, and work by thwarting future bad behaviour rather than encouraging current healthy behaviours. For example, if the authors of this book do not buy wine at the grocery store, it won't be in the house to open later on – because future us cannot be trusted to not open the wine. This type of intervention doesn't rely on willpower; rather, it employs the trustier tools of external constraints. Having employees make their own Ulysses contracts as part of a health and wellbeing campaign can be highly effective.

Intervention #2: Find the 'today' hook

As communicators, we often talk about making sure we always include the 'What's in it for me?' angle to capture the employee viewpoint. It's one of the ways to put yourself in the employee's shoes and to start to gain insight as to why they should care or pay attention to what you have to say. HR practitioners and internal communicators have an opportunity to take that one step further and transform this saying into: 'What's in it for me... *now*?' For example, many marketing campaigns on health talk about the long-term health benefits of whatever activity they are promoting. Many of these fail.

Instead, find something incredibly simple that someone can relate to in the moment and use that to lead communication efforts. 'Get an instant energy boost' or 'Zip up your skinny jeans' can work quite well. How are you creating a compelling, high-definition picture for employees to embrace?

Intervention #3: Pair the fun with the not so fun

Considering that we often choose what's gratifying in the moment, common sense dictates that we should find ways to make anything we ask employees to do immediately motivating. Taking that into account, what if there was a way to combine that instant gratification with an activity that's actually good for people? Well, there is. That's the idea behind *temptation bundling*.

> **Temptation bundling** pairs together an activity we don't want to do with one that we find pleasurable.

Let's look at a couple of examples of temptation bundling at work. We'll start by using an example based on personal experience. As the authors, we employed temptation bundling by taking something we didn't want to do (but was good for us), such as completing the next chapter of our book, and combining it with something pleasurable, such as ordering a nice glass of red wine. This technique has proven to be quite effective in motivating good behaviours. In one study, researchers would only let participants listen to a really in-demand audiobook when they were at the gym. The group visited the gym 51% more often than the control group who didn't have that enticing audiobook to listen to.[13] Can you pair something fun with the 'not so fun' thing you're asking people to do in the workplace?

Intervention #4: Influence the environment

A large part of the actions we take comes down to what is easiest to do. Another side of that coin is about making the not so desirable activities *harder*. We can control the environment at work to make poor health choices harder to do.

Brian Wansink, a top food researcher out of Cornell University, studied myriad ways in which to make unhealthy food consumption more difficult. Before we outline some of his top ideas for workplaces to implement, it is important to note that there has been some controversy with his research.[14] However, the ideas he tested do have some merit, and some researchers are working to replicate his results. A few ideas Wansink has suggested that you can pilot in your own workspaces to see what impact they may make include:

- Make healthier food more available. For example, replace the snacks in vending machines with healthier options, or have a policy of only stocking water, tea and other healthy beverages in office kitchens vs keeping soda and sugary juice drinks on hand.

- Make healthier food the first option people see. In one study of how people chose items from a buffet, whatever food they saw first tended to be what they loaded their plate up with. If fried potatoes, cheesy eggs and bacon appeared first, people went to town on those items. If yogurt, fruit and granola appeared first, that is what people chose.[15]

- Make healthier food more attractive. Try placing fruits, vegetables and salads in fancy bowls or platters under nice lighting. In some of the Wansink studies this was shown to increase uptake.

- Make healthier food easier to eat. It's the simple things such as pre-cutting apples into slices that can make people more likely to choose an apple as a snack.

Google took these lessons to heart. They reduced portion sizes for meat and desserts. Careful choice architecture guides people to appealing spa water over sugary soda and fruit juices. Delicious meals are self-served on smaller plates. Micro-kitchens across campus deftly place fruit and healthier snacks within a clear line of sight, whereas unhealthier snacks get opaque jars or are hidden in drawers. A series of small interventions can add up to some serious health benefits over time.[16] While Google is well known for their free food perks, you don't have to be Google with a world-class cafeteria onsite to incorporate some of the changes they did to help their employees make healthier choices.

We also saw a new take on influencing the environment during the Covid-19 pandemic. Facilities teams rushed to put up signage for one-way systems, plexiglass dividers and furniture arrangement to keep social distancing. These interventions do one thing: they make accidentally being too close together harder to do.

Intervention #5: Try implementation intentions

Sometimes, things feel too big for us to even know where to start, so it can be tempting to give up before we even begin. This is often the case with workplace wellness campaigns. We provide all the tools, but don't always provide the most important one: how to take the first step. One way to make the act of getting started easier is with *implementation intentions.*

> **Implementation intentions** are a specific type of goal-setting strategy, often structured as 'if-then' statements.

First described by Peter Gollwitzer, implementation intentions are a type of goal-setting strategy for those already motivated to change their behaviour.[17] They are structured as, 'When X happens, I will do Y.' For example, if your goal is to be better at flossing, your implementation intention could be, 'When I place my toothbrush back in its stand, I will reach for the floss.' Implementation intentions work because making specific plans on when and how to act can help people overcome the often-daunting barrier of getting started. Implementation intentions take classic goal-setting a step further by adding extra clarity and context to your goals.

For example, a common workplace wellbeing initiative is encouraging employees to get their annual flu shot onsite. A typical campaign might say: 'Get a flu shot!' While the reminder is nice, it is also often out of our minds as soon as we delete the email or walk past the poster. The same campaign with an implementation intention would leave spaces for people to write in specific details: 'I will get at flu shot on [date] in [location] at [time of day].' The message to 'Get a flu shot' is aspirational and educational; the transformed message is practical. It's as if it's already a foregone conclusion. The hard part – figuring out what and how – has been handled. All the person needs to do is follow through.

Researchers tried implementation intentions in an office setting to study if there would be a change in participation rates to get an onsite flu shot. Sure enough, vaccination rates increased when these implementation intentions prompts were included in the mailing advertising the flu shots.[18] The vaccination rate among the control condition was about 33.1%. Employees who received the prompt to write down just a date had a vaccination rate 1.5 percentage points higher than the control group, a difference that is not statistically significant. Employees who received an *even more* specific prompt to write down both a date and a time had a vaccination rate 4.2 percentage points higher. That may not sound like much, but it is a difference that is both statistically significant and of meaningful magnitude. It's quite easy to add in a 'fill in the blank' section on your communications for people to create their own implementation intentions and this technique is well evidenced to be effective in a workplace setting.

Why do these written commitments work so well? Well, the more work we must put into making a commitment, the greater its ability to influence our attitudes and intentions. It's similar to when you build that pesky IKEA furniture and you've sat for hours with a backache meticulously counting the number of screws, washers and panels and prayed to God you didn't miss something in the seventeen-page-long instructions booklet. Don't you feel prouder of and more attached to the final product when you're done? That's an extreme form of what written commitments can do, but it illustrates the point that the act of writing, building or creating reinforces our thoughts.

Intervention #6: Use commitment contracts

Commitment contracts are a well-known and well-loved behavioural science tool to help people follow through on their goals. They essentially formalize your goal (eg to stop smoking) and are often structured with either a reward for following through or a penalty for *not* following through. The cherry on top is that they are often declared publicly for additional accountability. Greenhalgh shares an example of how BT used the idea of commitments to help employees reach their goals:

> 'I kept being asked to speak on wellbeing. What I would say to people is, "You've invited me back, but I did this same thing about a year ago at your Christmas event. In the weeks that followed, every time I saw someone walking down a corridor, they ducked away." They didn't want to look me in the eye because they hadn't been following any of my wellbeing advice. So, I changed tack. I got people to pair up. They chose who they wanted to pair up with, and then within that pair, they shared what they were going to do to implement one of our five ways of wellbeing into their lives. For the next month, they checked in once a week with their partners on how they were doing.'

Here are four top tips for making the ideal commitment contract:

1. Choose your reward or consequence.

2. Make it specific: 'I will hit 15,000 steps a day for one month,' is better than, 'I will walk more.'

3. Choose your timescale.

4. Choose your referee: Who is going to hold you accountable?

EXERCISE: FIRST STEPS TOWARDS A HEALTH CAMPAIGN GOAL AT WORK

Step #1: Identify a pressing health problem at work. For example, the need to get more people to sign up for telehealth services.

Step #2: Pick one of the six interventions above. In our example, we could use the 'find the "today" hook' intervention.

Step #3: Now work through how you can apply the intervention. With the 'today' hook, finding and sharing a compelling vision for something they can do now will be the key. The 'today' benefit is the satisfaction of ticking something off a to-do list that they know is good for them. The call to action needs to be easy and specific. A good one in this instance would be: 'Take two minutes to download the app for peace of mind.' If employees do this, they know that the next time they are sick, they won't have to get out of bed, drive to the doctor, sit in the waiting room and wait to be told what's wrong with them. They can just open an app.

Loneliness at work – a growing health and wellbeing issue

Covid-19 may have put loneliness in the spotlight, but loneliness had received attention prior to the pandemic. When former UK prime minister Theresa May appointed a minister of loneliness in 2018 to address the issues raised in the 2017 report released by the Jo Cox Commission on Loneliness,[19] some laughed (those Brits must be a truly miserable lot!) but the statistics shared in the report are no laughing matter. It reported that in Britain alone, 43% of those aged seventeen to twenty-five experience problems with loneliness; 50% of disabled people will be lonely on any given day; over half of parents have had a problem with loneliness; and for 3.6 million people aged sixty-five or over, television is their primary form of company.

But Britain is not alone in, well… feeling alone. Former US Surgeon General Vivek Murthy specifically called out loneliness as a rising global epidemic and named it as not just a health issue, but as a *workplace* issue. In an article Murthy penned for *Harvard Business Review*,[20] he shared the startling observation that the largest pathology he saw in his years of caring for patients wasn't the usual suspects of heart disease, cancer or diabetes. It was loneliness.

Why is loneliness also a workplace issue? Well, it can limit creativity and reduce performance, for one thing. Loneliness often involves feeling estranged or separated from people and one's environment, including the workplace, and that detachment can lower performance for a variety of factors. For example, it takes a lot of energy to self-regulate behaviour and emotions under the best of circumstances, but when one is lonely and feeling removed, the energy expenditure required to 'act normal' can take people's attention and focus away from task completion.[21]

Two workplace interventions to battle loneliness

At the start of this chapter, we opened with a brief mention of the loneliness epidemic. New ways of working such as the rise of remote workers and the increasing lack of connection in younger generations have the potential to exacerbate this issue. In the past, the office was often a key social gathering point where adult friendships were formed. The token 'water cooler' was the gathering point and key locality where connections were made. Those casual connections are harder to come by these days. Here are two interventions that you can use to assist with combatting the issue in your workplace:

1. Understand and monitor what support your employees want and expect.

2. Increase connection and feelings of community.

Let's look at each in more detail.

Intervention #1: Understand and monitor what support your employees want and expect

Companies regularly ask employees what they are struggling with, and where they could use more support. Sometimes those activities can feel like a 'tick the box' exercise, or worse, insincere. Don't be the employer that offers employees free yoga classes in response to their pleas to be less stressed and find more work/life balance. There is a nuance that must be captured in discussions with employees as companies seek to beef up their mental health initiatives.

Hewlett Packard Enterprise (HPE) is a leader in investing in the wellness of its employees across the globe. Allison Stark, Global Wellness Programme Manager at HPE, spoke about the development of their behavioural health programme, titled 'For Real Life'. She says:

> 'Behavioural health [claims] were increasing and had a significant effect on costs. But more importantly, the driver was that this was the right thing to do. The right time, and the right thing to do.'[22]

The programme has been immensely robust and successful, and continues to be popular. It supplements traditional wellness offerings with unique initiatives such as the Headspace app to support mindfulness and meditation, hand-selected TED Talks, curated resources for stress and anxiety (rather than sending people to sort through the Employee Assistance

Programme resources), an original podcast series, and an online learning platform that pulls it all together. Employees love it.

To develop the programme, HPE analysed loads of data to spot trends in what conditions needed to be addressed in their population. They also assembled a behavioural health council consisting of some of the thought leaders of their vendor partners in the behavioural health space. 'We had a charter, basically. We asked, "What are we trying to achieve here and what should our goals be?"' Stark explains. 'We really relied on the behavioural health council to help us formulate that for our initial US rollout.'

One interesting tack they took was the launch of an original podcast series called *Straight Talk for Real Life*. Stark explains the general premise:

> 'The idea was to introduce experts in their topics externally to really focus in on the different components of behavioural health. We led with anxiety and stress, but we have sleep episodes, we have episodes about movement.'

Their first ten episodes surpassed 18,000 listens. Episodes included hot topics such as 'Addiction: What You Need to Know' and 'Meditation: Could It Work for You Like It's Worked for Millions?' They also have a survey tool connected to the podcast if an employee accesses it through the internal wellness portal. This allows employees to submit topics of interest and tell HPE what they would like to hear about. HPE evaluates the feedback monthly, and it guides decisions about the content for future episodes.

As the support your people are looking for moves beyond traditional employee assistance programmes, insights such as the ones HPE took the time to gather are key to any mental health and wellbeing initiatives you develop. For example, an increasing number of companies are offering 'mental health' days, although critics of this concept believe that people have always taken these days (they just call in sick under the guise of a headache or a stomach ache), so these may not be as effective because people may still feel a lack of permission.

What if we reframed it? Studies suggest framing health decisions in terms of either gains or losses changes people's perception of them. In one famous study, people were more likely to recommend an operation when it was framed as 'ninety of a hundred will come out alive' vs 'ten out of a hundred will die'.[23] What if we applied that general concept to how we named these days off – perhaps a less formal, more positive name could encourage uptake? Often, if an employee takes a mental health day, it's likely because they are just, for lack of a better term, 'not feeling it'. Employers can call these mental health days something with more levity that rings truer (and more positive) for employees. For example, you could call it a 'I'm just not feeling it day' or a 'I'll try again tomorrow day'.

Greenhalgh does have a word of caution on this approach:

'We have a concern about people taking odd days off anyway. Factoring that in across the whole business, I don't think it would discourage those that do it anyway, but it might encourage those who don't do it to start doing it. It could also legitimize the symptom instead of trying to find out what the cause is and helping people with the cause. Our aim is to encourage healthy wellbeing and create an environment conducive to good health.'

Intervention #2: Increase connection and feelings of community

We spoke with Paul Gerrard, Campaign and Public Affairs Director for Co-op, a beloved UK food and insurance provider, who led their famous Co-op Loneliness Campaign. When asked why they identified loneliness as an issue to tackle, the short answer is: they didn't. 'The members told us to,' he says.[24] When reflecting on why the campaign was a success, he identified two keys that can be used both in campaigns, as well as to bolster the business case for funds to focus on mental health.

First, they busted common myths about *who* was lonely. This was important (and effective) because it helped identify those who may need help, such as new mums or someone recently divorced, and showed 'people like me' examples to those who might otherwise have been overlooked.

Second, they commissioned research that looked into the economic impact of lost productivity (a whopping £2.5 billion each year).[25] It's numbers like this that help make the business case to company leaders who demand a hard return-on-investment for wellbeing programmes.

Wrapping it up: Applying what you've learned at work

Once we abandon the idea that our employees make rational decisions about health and come to terms with the fact that we are all somewhat flawed decision-makers, employers can use their privileged position to help employees make better choices. We've covered the conflict between want and should, and how our perceptions of time influence decision. We've looked at how you should always ask yourself if the action you want employees to take involves a trade-off between a want and a should, or instant gratification and a future benefit. We've also looked at how to take that theory and apply it in practical ways. Let's review.

Five motivation and mindset barriers to good health choices

1. People choose the instant hit.

2. We think 'future us' will make better choices.

3. We think of 'future us' as a different person.

4. Poor employer incentive models.

5. A scarcity mindset.

Six workplace interventions to help employees make healthier choices

1. Guard against future temptation.

2. Find the 'today' hook.

3. Pair the fun with the 'not so fun'.

4. Influence the environment.

5. Try implementation intentions.

6. Use commitment contracts.

Two workplace interventions to battle loneliness

1. Understand and monitor what support your employees want and expect.

2. Increase connection and feelings of community.

Exercises and resources

- Would you rather…?

- First steps towards a health campaign goal at work

EIGHT

Safety

When it comes to workplace safety, no news is good news. That's because when all works as it should, the negative incidents that create headlines simply do not occur. You'll never see 'eighty-eight days since company X's last incident!' being widely reported (although if companies were smart, they'd share those statistics internally and we will explain why later in this chapter). Occupational and workplace safety teams work incredibly hard to live up to safety standards and maintain safe places of work, but sometimes things go wrong. When they do go wrong, it's often front-page news.

For example, a famous and beloved American brand of canned food captured headlines in 2012 for a horrific onsite safety incident. A worker at the facility was loading pallets of tuna into one of the 32-foot ovens at the company's main plant when a co-worker, mistakenly thinking his colleague had stepped out to the restroom, turned it up to 270 °F. You don't need us to tell you how this story ended. In 2015, the company settled the case for around $6m – which, at the time, was the largest pay-out in a safety workplace violation death the state where the incident occurred had ever seen.[1]

It is not just criminal charges or the number of fatalities at work that businesses should be concerned with, though the numbers are sobering. The Bureau of Labor Statistics in the US reported 5,250 on-the-job fatalities in 2018,[2] and while the number of deaths in a similar period in UK is decidedly smaller at 147,[3] every business owner would argue that even one death due to a workplace safety mishap is one death too many. Non-fatal safety hazards at work are everywhere as well, which means companies and employees need to be ever vigilant. Safety accidents have a high cost to businesses in terms of productivity. For the 2018/2019 reporting period, 28.2 million working days were lost in UK due to safety incidents.[4]

The other area of safety that can generate negative headlines if handled poorly is psychological safety. Increasingly, as mental health takes a more prominent role in wellbeing strategies and conversations, the definition of safety at work is expanding to include psychological safety. For example, the ride-sharing company Uber was thrust into the spotlight in 2017 when engineer Susan Fowler penned a blog post titled 'Reflecting On One Very, Very Strange Year at Uber'.[5]

In it, she detailed a workplace where women were marginalized, excluded and sexually harassed.

> **Psychological safety** is the ability to show your true self without fear of negative consequences on how others view you or your career.

It's of strategic importance to have teams operate in an inclusive environment where everyone is treated fairly and respectfully and can contribute fully. For someone to contribute fully, they need to first feel psychologically safe. While psychological safety can be harder to achieve in some work cultures than others, it's an ongoing challenge for all businesses.

Both workplace physical safety and psychological safety are serious workplace topics. This chapter will examine both and make the distinction between the two. When we talk about physical safety, we are talking about understanding when, why and how physical accidents occur in some lines of work. This work is usually in the remit of an occupational safety team or a workplace safety team. When we talk about psychological safety, it's about creating cultures where people feel safe. This work usually falls in the remit of both the diversity and inclusion (D&I) team and health and safety teams.

In this chapter, we will explore:

- Why physical and psychological safety must be at the forefront of any wellbeing strategy

- Seven reasons why physical safety incidents happen at work

- Unintended consequences of physical safety interventions

- Lessons from the Covid-19 pandemic

- Understanding psychological safety

- Four ways that a psychologically safe workplace benefits business

- Measuring and increasing psychological safety

- Four tips for increasing psychological safety at work

- Eight workplace interventions to build safer places of work

Why physical and psychological safety must be at the forefront of any wellbeing strategy

First and foremost, it keeps people alive – much more than any subsidy for a gym membership or healthy food offered in the cafeteria ever could. The shocking and improbable events are the ones that make headlines, but they're not the deadliest. An example is how firefighters are most likely to die not from fighting fires, but from not wearing their seatbelts on the way to the fire.

Rosanne Bonanno, founder of RoBo Communications, has carried out important work on road safety with the United Nations (UN) in conjunction with Fleet Forum, a not-for-profit that provides support to the aid and development of commercial transport sectors in low- and middle-income countries in the areas of road safety, cost efficiency and environmental impact. The road safety lessons are quite applicable to workplace physical safety and are shared throughout this chapter. In our interview, Bonanno explains how it's the mundane events rather than the sensationalized, reported ones that companies must control:

> 'It might surprise some to know that road
> crashes are the leading cause of death and
> serious injury to humanitarian staff around the
> world... Road crashes, in fact, kill more UN
> staff than terrorism. This is a really big deal
> for UN organizations, as well as NGOs. That's
> why they can't afford to ignore it.'[6]

Psychological safety in the workplace keeps people alive, too. How many headlines have you seen of people feeling harassed at work or worked to the state of exhaustion by a callous manager, and then suffering poor mental health consequences that, in some cases, lead to them taking drastic actions? The widely reported suicides at Foxconn in 2010 spring to mind as an obvious example.[7] Another egregious example comes from French telecommunications giant Orange, whose CEO is now in jail for creating policies deliberately designed to lead to an atmosphere of fear so that employees would quit. What these policies did instead was lead to the suicides of thirty-five employees.[8] There are so many untold stories, and these are the ones that we hope to prevent from occurring in the first place.

Seven reasons why physical safety incidents happen at work

We can look to behavioural science to help us unpack several key reasons why most safety incidents happen at work. When you understand these reasons, you'll be better equipped to spot the gaps in your own physical safety procedures, guidelines and ways of working. These reasons are:

1. Poorly designed default systems

2. Misaligned incentives

3. Complicated instructions

4. Lack of organizational commitment

5. Fatigue

6. Routine

7. Trade-offs between safety and speed

Reason #1: Poorly designed default systems

We tend to go with whichever default options we are presented with because it's simply easier. Why forge your own path through a warehouse or worksite when one is clearly marked for you? Defaults just work. If they are not designed well, the fact that they work can become problematic – sometimes extremely problematic. When user interfaces are poorly designed, they can be deadly in some circumstances.

The excellent podcast *Cautionary Tales* by Tim Harford recounts true stories of mistakes and what we should learn from them. When he appeared as a guest in another popular podcast, *99% Invisible*, he shared a light-hearted story about the 2016 Oscar fiasco where *La La Land* was mistakenly announced as the winner of the prestigious Best Picture award, when the true winner was *Moonlight*.[9] There, a poorly designed system gave us all a laugh. In the same episode, he recounted the tale of a poorly designed safety system that could have had much more dire (and far-reaching) consequences. What event in American history was his reference point? The nuclear accident in 1979 at Three Mile Island.

During the first few minutes of the accident, over *one hundred* alarms went off. A system like that made it impossible to discern the critical alarms from the less important alarms that were (literally and metaphorically) just noise, but it wasn't just the alarm system at fault. The control panels were unnecessarily complicated with lights, switches and instructions going every which way. There was a special inquiry ordered by the Nuclear Regulatory Commission[10] to review the accident. They concluded that while a multitude of factors was to blame (including lack of training for, and absence of, a description in the written emergency procedures for the event that started off the disastrous chain of subsequent events), poorly designed systems had also had adverse effects. For example, the high-pressure injection pumps used in Three Mile Island had a design flaw. They could mix up normal and emergency reactions by other systems, so when the operators saw these come to life, it didn't necessarily indicate that something was wrong.

Reason # 2: Misaligned incentives

Every company will have different policies regarding safety – and may even incentivize safe behaviour through the form of an external reward. While it's great to provide an additional form of extrinsic motivation, organizations must be careful that the 'reward' doesn't have unintended consequences. In the aid and development sector, financial incentives designed to encourage better, safer driving actually fostered an atmosphere where the opposite happened. Bonanno says:

> 'We discovered that in some organizations, road crashes were simply not being reported. While there could be a number of reasons to explain why, part of the problem was that

drivers were inadvertently incentivized not to report them. In some cases, they were penalized for reporting a road crash that they'd had (by missing out on a potential bonus, for example), or they didn't report a road crash because they feared that it would lead to the loss of their job, or perhaps worse, that they would be on the hook for the cost of any damage associated with the road crash.'

But it is only in the systematic reporting of road crashes, and the subsequent thorough investigation of those crashes, that companies will be able to identify and actively address existing safety gaps. Bonanno continues:

'Effective workplace road safety policies should aim to create an environment where drivers, and, frankly, employees at all levels feel encouraged to report crashes and even near-miss situations. The organizational safety culture should focus not on attributing blame or doling out punishment in the event of a road crash, but on learning from these crashes, uncovering their root causes and implementing sustainable interventions.'

While this example was about road safety, the idea of misaligned incentives can apply to any safety challenge in the workplace. It's good practice to review what you're incentivizing and ensure it doesn't come with unintended consequences.

Reason #3: Complicated instructions

Compliance teams and technical writers responsible for creating manuals leave nothing to chance and often use lengthy and overly technical prose in the smallest font imaginable. While important, these complex instructions can also be cognitively taxing, leading people to miss critical information or steps.

In communications, one of the most common pieces of advice you see and hear is to 'keep things simple'. Simplicity has a critical role to play in helping people to understand instructions, because simplicity enhances cognitive fluency. Put simply: it makes information go down easier.

Reason #4: Lack of organizational commitment

Let's carry on with road safety as an example. Globally, more than 1.3 million people die in road crashes every year, and even more suffer serious injuries. Today, road crashes rank among the top causes of death in low- and middle-income countries.[11] While many organizations recognize that road safety management is important, particularly those that operate large fleets and employ multiple drivers, too often the commitment to make safety a sustained priority simply isn't there.

The reasons for not addressing road safety are varied, says Bonanno, but, ultimately, it comes down to a prioritization of finite resources. Some organizations believe that road safety is a driver's responsibility, and the problem will be addressed with more comprehensive driver training. That is, until it becomes evident that the cause of their road crashes is more deeply rooted in cultural or organizational issues. Bonanno says:

'Organizations often are not aware of the root causes of their road crashes because they don't consistently report and analyse those crashes. Not knowing the root cause makes it difficult for organizations to identify interventions that will correct the problem in a sustainable way. And not correcting the problem… well, that results in continued damage to their vehicles and other property, and sadly, continued injuries and even death to their drivers or to road users who live in the communities that those same organizations seek to serve.'

The true tragedy in that scenario is that serious road crashes are entirely preventable, she continues. Through her work with Fleet Forum, she has learned that one way to prevent serious road crashes from occurring is to commit to creating a positive safety culture which is not just a policy or programme, but a way of thinking and behaving that permeates the organization at every level. An organization with a positive safety culture is characterized by high levels of employee trust and empowerment. Employees all agree that safety is important and safety management systems work effectively.

(If you need assistance creating the change that overcomes lack of organizational commitment, refer to the lessons from Chapter 2.)

Reason #5: Fatigue

Exhaustion (physical, emotional and environmental) impairs our ability to perform. Think about this in your own life: how much harder is it for you to make decisions before your first cup of coffee or after a bad night's sleep? It is likely no coincidence that some of the most serious workplace safety incidents have occurred between midnight and 6am (eg Three Mile Island, the Exxon Valdez oil spill and the nuclear meltdown at Chernobyl).

EasyJet, the budget European airliner, has taken great strides in mitigating fatigue risk by developing a Human Factors Monitoring Program (HFMP).[12] This programme looks at the interaction between fatigue, scheduling and human error with the end goal of creating a new roster that reduces pilot fatigue. When they trialled the new schedule suggested by the HFMP, 91% of pilots agreed they felt less tired on it.

Reason #6: Routine

Have you ever driven home from work and parked your car only to realize that you don't remember how you got there? You might start asking yourself questions to make sure you drove home in a safe manner. Were those traffic lights all green? Did you blow through a stop sign? Did you slow down in that school zone near your house? The answer to those questions is probably yes. The reason you can't recall for sure is because you were on autopilot. It was routine.

This occurrence of forgetting chunks of time is related to how we form memories. If there is less new information to process, then our perception of time changes. If driving home is a routine task, it feels like you've arrived in the blink of an eye. While routine may be fine for your commute, it can be disastrous for onsite safety. It only takes one alteration in an input to the routine for an accident to happen, and if you're on autopilot, you might not 'wake up' fast enough to react.

Reason #7: Trade-offs between safety and speed

Sometimes, the default is to view speed and safety as a trade-off. For example, some might be tempted to take a few calculated risks to get something done faster under the guise of efficiency. If that trade-off keeps rewarding someone without any downside, then they don't have much incentive to change their behaviour to a new one that puts safety first. This is a gamble. It's really just a matter of time until one day, that calculated risk *doesn't* pay off and you have a safety incident on your hands.

Unintended consequences of physical safety interventions

The aim of any safety device or procedure is undoubtedly to increase safety, but there can be unintended consequences. When you focus on a single aspect of a problem, you can sometimes miss the impact that your 'solution' has on the entire system. This can introduce new hazards and new sources of potential failures. Behavioural scientists like to call these 'spillover effects'.

> Like 'ripples on a pond' after one skips a stone, a **spillover effect** is the subsequent effect of an action that was taken as a result of an initial intervention – because no behaviour sits in a vacuum.[13]

A perfect example of a negative spillover effect is the trouble the UN ran into with the lack of reporting of road crashes. By incentivizing those who didn't have any road crashes, it created the effect of people under-reporting (or not reporting at all) because they did not want to miss out on the reward. These spillover effects are a crucial – and often overlooked – consideration for those responsible for safety in organizations. Ask yourself what the impact of the second, third, fourth (and so on, and so forth) steps is.

EXERCISE: FORECASTING SPILLOVER EFFECTS

A hypothetical scenario planning exercise can be an effective way to forecast spillover. First try and predict the four most likely outcomes of an action. Now do the same for the four actions you've predicted. This will help you to start building a picture of what could happen.

Spillover effects can also be positive – which means that the next action a person takes furthers the original goal. An example of this would be going for a run because you had a healthy lunch: the run furthers the original goal of looking after yourself. This is called a *promoting* spillover. Unfortunately, spillovers can also work in the opposite direction. For example, you then indulge in a piece of delicious chocolate cake because you went for that run. 'Hey, I earned it,' you think. This would be called a *permitting* or *purging* spillover effect (or in simpler terms, a negative spillover effect). This is the one most concerning in the workplace.

Let's tell a story to bring this concept to life, as it's incredibly important. Every time a feature is added to prevent a problem, you know what else is added? Complexity. That complexity could have a negative consequence, ie the negative spillover. A famous example of this is demonstrated by none other than Galileo. He recounts a tale in *Two New Sciences* about support beams for marble columns. When a third support beam was added in the middle of the columns (because three would clearly be better than two), much to everyone's surprise, the columns eventually cracked right in the spot where the additional beam was added.

The key takeaway here is: when you add a new safety feature or procedure to anything you do at work, consider the unintended consequences. Remember that new features add new complexity and could create a negative spillover effect.

Lessons from the Covid-19 pandemic

Let's hope a global pandemic is a once-in-a-lifetime occurrence for most of us. When the virus emerged, businesses were forced to adapt quickly. For the first time since the 1918 Spanish flu, employers had to add a new element to their traditional safety plans: stopping the spread of a viral disease. One-way systems, face masks, quotas for how many people could be in the office at a time and environmental changes such as plexiglass screens, temperature checks and more became standard.

Covid-19 was also a clear and present threat to psychological safety. Extreme amounts of background stress, uncertainty and a sense of disorientation with a world that no longer looked or operated as it once did hugely impacted workplace interactions. Businesses that talked openly about this shared fear were better able to lessen it. Like any burden, sharing the load suddenly makes it feels lighter.

Regardless of what threat emerges next, the lessons we can learn from teams deemed successful in navigating the crisis can be applied to future safety challenges. The most successful teams took several key actions when Covid-19 emerged. Understanding what those actions were will set you up for success, regardless of the nature of the next new crises.

What did those teams who successfully navigated Covid-19 do?

- They didn't delay in addressing the fact that there was a crisis and lost no precious time in co-ordinating a response.

- Their responses to the crisis were informed by facts and insights.

- They understood that pivoting (in terms of strategy, ways of working, and the work itself) was crucial to business success.

- They applied laser-like focus – not on the final destination, but on the first step, and then the second, and then the third, etc. They were specific on the 'here and now' actions.

- They encouraged colleagues to focus their energy on what they could control (their day-to-day work) rather than on the multitude of things they couldn't (lockdowns, restrictions, healthcare, R-rates).

- They looked for, and successfully spotted, the opportunities and restructured their efforts in pursuit of them.

- They didn't pretend to have all the answers and talked honestly about what they did not know. This brutal honesty and shared vulnerability generated trust.

- They made it OK to not be OK – creating safe spaces to talk about less than positive feelings – and their leaders role modelled this effectively.

In a nutshell: they adapted. Companies that courageously and honestly put themselves under a microscope to uncover and learn the hard lessons, and then made a conscious effort to take those lessons forward, will be much better positioned to weather the next storm.

Understanding psychological safety

Let's shift our focus to psychological safety. We'll take a closer look on what it is and how it benefits businesses. We'll also look at how to measure and increase it. First, let's talk about what psychological safety does (and doesn't) feel like at work.

Our brains are trained to scan the environment for individuals or situations that we view as a threat to our physical or emotional wellbeing. For example, think about how your body reacts when you see a hooded figure on an isolated road at night. Your heart starts to beat faster. You become hyper-alert. Maybe you even freeze. When we spot someone who we perceive as a threat to us, the classic 'flight or fight' response kicks in.

This is problematic, because while you probably don't want all-out brawls in the workplace cafeteria, you also don't want employees choosing to flee confrontation rather than speaking up, as this will allow bullies to thrive. A psychologically unsafe place to work can create a similar response in employees to the hooded, shadowy figure. No one wants to work in a place where brilliant jerks thrive at the expense of a gentler majority.

A lack of psychological safety is problematic for everyday, general workplace interactions. When we are in flight mode, it's harder to listen or ask questions – quintessential activities for high-functioning workplaces. Another business perspective is that you want to create an environment where people feel they can speak up when things aren't working as well as they could.

What does it look like when psychological safety is breached in the real world? This story is from a leading D&I practitioner who has led in-house D&I efforts in multiple sectors:

> 'We had a CEO who, while he wasn't *quite* an autocrat, he was not well liked. The 49th floor was where the executive team sat, and everyone was afraid to go there because they didn't want to cross paths with him. But me being me, I said, "Let's break the norm and remove the fear. In fact, we'll turn part of this floor into an open zone, with collaboration spaces, pool tables, mini breakout rooms, and more." This was all done to make sure other people feel safe.'[14]

Reflect on this story for a moment. Can you imagine working at a place where there was an entire floor that people felt too scared to go to? On the flipside, what does psychological safety look like when it is done well? In short, a psychologically safe environment is one where people feel safe to speak up, offer ideas and ask questions. It's a place where people can bring their whole selves to work, without fear of repercussions. It's an environment where people self-correct more often because they are less afraid of any consequences that come from making (and owning up to) a mistake. It's a place where innovation flows because teams are harnessing the power of diverse ideas.

New international standards for psychological health

Psychological safety is so important that the first global standard for practical workplace guidance on managing psychological health in the workplace has been developed. Launched in the summer of 2021, ISO 45003 supports the UN sustainable development goals. Developed by the British Standards Institution, it's full of practical training and insights for businesses to implement.[15]

There are three key elements for those in charge of psychological safety workplace efforts to consider:

- Understand how a psychologically safe workplace benefits your business, because at some point you may have to build a business case for resources.

- Learn how to measure psychological safety, because what gets measured gets improved.

- Increase psychological safety at work – it's an ongoing process that can be continually improved, not a 'one and done' activity.

Four ways that a psychologically safe workplace benefits business

Employees in psychologically safe workplaces perform better on just about every key performance indicator (KPI). When Google looked into what made some teams more successful than others, they didn't find any correlation with some of the usual suspects (eg hobbies, education or general background). What they *did* eventually find was that psychological safety was the key factor that successful teams had in common. *The New York Times* produced an excellent story detailing Google's efforts to study team effectiveness, nicknamed 'Project Aristotle'.[16] In it, they described the line of questioning and elimination researchers used before coming across their revolutionary finding that psychological safety is the key component. In essence, 'who is on the team matters less than how the team members interact, structure their work, and view their contributions.'[17]

It's not just improvements in the typical performance KPIs that psychologically safe workplaces benefit from. Their businesses also enjoy four distinct elements that foster innovation, spot problems before they occur and encourage wider sharing of original ideas:

1. You're more likely to spot the cracks.

2. It encourages learning and growing.

3. It enables better decision-making.

4. People are more likely to take risks.

Let's look at these four ways in more detail.

Way #1: You're more likely to spot the cracks

When things aren't working as they should, businesses need to know. Your people will be the first to spot those cracks, but they need to feel like they can bring that constructive feedback to the right person's attention without fear of repercussion. If people don't speak up, you won't get that valuable insight. Bonanno's recounting of the road safety issues in the UN illustrates this:

> 'You know, there's probably many examples
> where drivers or other employees could have said
> things or come forward with things if they were
> in a culture where they felt comfortable to do so.'

People being reticent to speak up in a room or the same vocal few dominating with their viewpoints could be a warning sign of a psychologically unsafe team dynamic that needs to be addressed.

Way #2: It encourages learning and growing

Workers in inclusive teams are also more likely to receive regular career development. One needs to be motivated to provide help to someone else, and this type of pro-social motivation, or 'helping behaviour', is linked to inclusive environments.[18]

Way #3: It enables better decision-making

Inclusive teams are more pro-socially motivated.[19] That means they engage in workplace behaviours that are deliberately aimed to benefit others, which can lead to a more harmonious work environment and a greater willingness to collaborate. When teams work together collaboratively, they often make better decisions and have better outcomes – simple as that.

People are also more likely to harness diverse ideas from their teammates in a psychologically safe environment. Part of the generation of these diverse ideas can be credited to a form of diversity that is increasingly getting attention: neurodiversity.

Neurodiversity is the viewpoint that neurological differences (such as autism) are normal variations in how the brain functions, rather than divergent.

While leaders of the neurodiversity movement are careful to point out that conditions such as autism bring both advantages and disadvantages, neurodiversity can enable better decision-making by bringing novel ideas and perspectives to the table.

Way #4: People are more likely to take risks

Let's go back to Sarah Spooner, who we heard from in earlier chapters. She says:

> 'I don't sit within my own boundaries. If I
> see something that I think needs fixing, I'll
> go and poke around in it, even if it belongs to
> someone else. I feel like I come from a position
> of relative safety in the organization, in that
> I can be disruptive and I know I'm not going
> to get sacked for it because the organization
> welcomes it.'

That attitude takes courage and confidence, which a psychologically safe environment helps create.

Measuring and increasing psychological safety

What gets measured, gets improved. Organizations can – and should – measure psychological safety. A leader in this space is Elsevier, which is part of RELX Group. Elsevier is an information and analytics company specializing in science, technology and medicine. It should be of no surprise that a company such as Elsevier utilizes the latest in science to advance its own internal goals. Elsevier partnered with Harvard University to implement psychological safety across all their teams via an employee-to-employee facilitated learning approach. Their executive leadership team (ELT) went first and participated in an initial psychological safety assessment in 2019. Sure enough, they found that they had room to improve and put in the work to do so. When it came time to remeasure their team's psychological safety score, they ended up with the second highest score at Elsevier.

The work with the ELT was a great start, but they still had more work to do. Adam Travis, former Global Head of Inclusion and Diversity at Elsevier, describes where he realized that, while Elsevier's heart and strategy were in the right place, they could further improve as a company:

'What got me was when we were piloting an "Equality Ally" program, which is essentially where you need to step in and say something if someone inadvertently shares a thought which might be negatively construed by another. We ran training in Amsterdam on how to be an Equality Ally and what it means. I asked at the end of the training, "How many of you feel that you could step in with psychological safety?" Of the colleagues who attended the pilot, I was surprised that a relatively small percentage of those in attendance felt they could "step in". That made me hit pause. I wondered what was happening. That's led us on this journey for a year, and I've honestly never seen such a transformation.'[20]

An important point of clarification here is that this training was not unconscious bias training. As we unpacked in Chapter 3, unconscious bias training is great for raising awareness, but not so great for creating lasting change.

The simplicity of the programme belies the hard work that went into developing it, but in a nutshell, Elsevier has trained facilitators who help measure psychological safety within a designated group or team. (We'll talk about how to specifically measure psychological safety later in the next section.) They then review the survey results and primary recommendations within a team. With a facilitator, they select a small number of recommended steps to work on. The facilitator re-administers the survey three to six months later to remeasure and recalibrate.

Measuring psychological safety

Again, we look to Elsevier for guidance here, who partnered with Harvard professor Amy Edmondson to adapt her psychological safety measurement strategy – bringing it out of academia and into practice. Edmondson is a pioneer in the psychological safety space, having first identified the concept of psychological safety in work in teams in 1999. Elsevier adapted the key questions as part of their measurement strategy. Typically, we find questions and models developed in academia somewhat unpractical for deployment in organizations, but these questions are quite easy to deploy via a measurement tool such as Qualtrics or SurveyMonkey. The statements are measured on a scale of 1 to 5, with 1 being 'strongly disagree' and 5 being 'strongly agree'. The statements are:

1. If I make a mistake in my team, it is held against me.

2. Members of my team are able to bring up problems and tough issues.

3. It is difficult to ask other members of my team for help.

4. It is safe to take a risk in my team.

5. People in my team sometimes reject others for being different.

6. Working with members of my team, my unique skills and talents are valued and utilized.

7. No one on my team would deliberately act in a way that undermines my efforts.

These questions are illuminating for teams and leaders. When Elsevier went through this process, it helped them to focus their strategy. Travis explains the thinking of how they took these questions (which are in the public domain) and turned them into meaningful insights. They later turned those insights into action. He says:

> 'Behind it, it's all about when is it safe, and when is it unsafe? When is an overarching report safe or not? What are the questions that mean more than others [to determine that]? And what are the scores that trigger non-psychological safety?'

That's where the magic for individual teams happens. It's in identifying which questions illuminate the pressing issues in your particular organization. The answer will be different for everyone. For Travis, it was the final question around deliberate undermining. He says:

> 'I got most stuck on question seven. You're going into true perceived safety issues and, potentially, toxicity. Everything happens at question seven, and I struggled the most around that. So, how will I give suggestions? How would I build further psychological safety for all colleagues?'

Four tips for increasing psychological safety at work

Here are four tips for increasing psychological safety at work:

1. Show what healthy conflict looks like.

2. Create a zero-tolerance policy for bullying and harassment.

3. Help managers and leaders show up authentically.

4. Acknowledge (rather than punish) failure.

Let's look at each in more detail.

Tip #1: Show what healthy conflict looks like

Psychological safety isn't about being nice. It's about feeling like you can have necessary difficult conversations and that these interactions will be in a productive and judgement-free zone. Engaging in civil debate is healthy. It shows that people within teams can hold conflicting viewpoints; and that's OK.

A key part of healthy conflict is also making sure people feel heard. To do this, listen carefully to make sure you are really hearing what everyone has to say. Thank people for speaking up and for sharing their viewpoint. If their feedback is productive, act on it (and then report back to them that you did just that).

Tip #2: Create a zero-tolerance policy for bullying and harassment

Workplace bullying looks a little different than school-yard bullying. At work, bullying can take the forms of exclusion, verbal insults, humiliation, threats to job security and more. It's more common than you might think. The UK Statistics Authority's 2018 Corporate Report found that 12% of people surveyed had been bullied in the last year.[21]

There's lots of widely available guidance on how to create a zero-tolerance bullying policy, but here's the point we feel strongest about. Hold people accountable for their behaviour. Teams shouldn't make room for brilliant people on the team who treat everyone else horribly.

Tip #3: Help managers and leaders show up authentically

Sometimes, our managers and leaders think they have to have all the answers. If you are in a management or leadership role, it's OK to show humility and vulnerability. Be comfortable with acknowledging that you don't always have the right answers or make the right decisions. This shows your team that you're also human, and makes you more approachable. When you're more approachable, people will feel more comfortable speaking up.

Tip #4: Acknowledge (rather than punish) failure

Thomas Edison viewed things that didn't work out not as failures, but simply as lessons. We can learn a lot from what didn't work well. That's a big part of why we run post-mortem sessions at the conclusion of a project – to acknowledge what went well and what could have been done differently. A post-mortem or post-implementation review (PIR) session is a more formal version of a project debrief. Cultures and teams who understand how and why something failed or was problematic are fundamental to being successful going forward. They are better positioned for future wins; but post-mortems are only successful in cultures of psychological safety where team members can talk frankly about what occurred.

Eight workplace interventions to build safer places of work

Systemic safety can only be achieved if your people know that safety is a top priority and understand that they have an active role to play regardless of their position within the company. Workplace safety guidelines can sometimes be seen as restrictive, so you need to shift mindsets from, 'Why are these rules here?' to, 'This is one way the company shows it cares for me.' When it comes to psychological safety, we recognize that it can be scary for people in some organizations to talk about. Much like it has taken time for mental health to be part of the ongoing and accepted conversation, companies are undergoing a shift where psychological safety is now increasingly openly addressed.

In the past, increasing workplace physical safety meant addressing the last link in the chain. It meant taking a hard look at the immediate thing, that 'next to last' step that went wrong, but as Jim Hall, former chairman of the United States National Transportation Safety Board says, 'The proximate cause is not the probable cause.'[22] That is why understanding the conditions under which physical safety accidents occur (conditions such as fatigue, complicated manuals and routine that this chapter has already discussed) matters. Thankfully, through the lens of understanding why physical safety accidents happen, there are many proactive actions companies and safety teams can take to prevent them.

The same holds true for psychological safety. Understanding what it is, seeing examples of it *not* occurring in the real world, and getting practical tips on both how to measure and increase it in your organization is invaluable. It gives you a leg up on the competition in creating a workplace where people feel it is safe to be their true selves and contribute fully.

Here are eight workplace interventions to build safer places of work:

1. Review your current physical safety training procedures.

2. Make unsafe stuff harder to do, with good defaults.

3. Utilize counterfactual thinking.

4. Make it a streak.

5. Crowdsource physical and psychological safety ideas from employees.

6. Draw attention to the hazardous with salient reminders.

7. Create a psychological safety behaviour guide for managers.

8. Make your safety strategy known to the business.

Intervention #1: Review your current physical safety training procedures

Let's take another trip back to our favourite fictional office, Dunder Mifflin. In the third season episode, aptly titled 'Safety Training', we are treated to hilarious blunder after hilarious blunder in how not to conduct safety drills and how not to run safety trainings. 'We do safety training every year, or after an accident. We've never made it a full year,' Darryl says with a sigh.

We start with a visit to the warehouse, where warehouse manager Darryl begins to relay the 'dos and don'ts' of operating forklifts. He reminds everyone that only those with the proper licence are allowed to drive them. He then asks Michael, the general manager (and someone decidedly *not* equipped to drive the forklift), if he should get behind the wheel. 'I can, and I have,' Michael replies. 'No, no, no!' exclaims Darryl. It rapidly declines from there.

We then move up to the office staff training. Considerably drier, it covers issues like computer eye strain and carpal tunnel syndrome. This prompts Michael to ask when they are going to get to the dangerous stuff like computers exploding. No one leaves the training with valuable, memorable information that might actually have a chance at preventing accidents.

Could this episode have been filmed at your office? Look at both your current safety training procedures *and* your safety manuals. When was the last time they were reviewed for the optimal user experience? Are they dry as a bone and overly technical? Are your safety manuals eighty pages long? If so, can you put the most salient points into a summary or a checklist? Don't make employees do the work of figuring out safety procedures. If you do go the checklist route, put the key points first and last. This will make it easier for employees to remember them.

Intervention #2: Make unsafe stuff harder to do, with good defaults

When officials in England and Wales reduced the maximum number of pills allowed in a paracetamol pack, deaths from paracetamol overdoses fell 43% over the timeframe of the study (1998 to 2009). Liver transplants due to paracetamol-induced hepatotoxicity fell 61%. Why? The reduction in pack size meant slightly more effort was required to access the large number of pills required to inflict such bodily harm.[23] This is a prime example of increasing safety behaviours by making the unsafe stuff harder to do.

Imagine that you are trying to get construction workers to put their tools back where they belong. They never do, and you're tired of it. You could place lots of reminders around sites, or you could paint tool-shaped lines on the walls with hooks. This should make people more likely to put the right thing back in the right place.

Onsite walkabouts can be helpful in spotting some of these unsafe behaviours at work and in identifying where you can make something that is unsafe harder to do.

Intervention #3: Utilize counterfactual thinking

Humans are great at imagining how things could have turned out differently if just *one* thing had or hadn't happened. Think of it as having a case of the 'would've, could've, should'ves'. Hypothesizing alternate endings has a name: counterfactual thinking. For example, pretend you missed your bus by one minute on a morning you were already running late. A common reaction to this scenario would be to tell yourself that if you'd just spent less time looking for your coat or hadn't fumbled for your keys while locking the door, you would have caught the bus.

> **Counterfactual thinking** is the tendency to create possible alternatives to events that have already occurred.

Counterfactual thinking does not always have to be a look backwards; it can also look forwards. In this instance, you imagine a scenario that *could* occur. A common form of counterfactual thinking appears in messages you see warning people of the dangers of texting and driving or walking while not paying attention to the road.

Transport for London took a particularly hard-hitting approach, utilizing counterfactual thinking to encourage people to pay attention when travelling, in their 'Stop. Think. Live.' campaign. In one billboard, a picture of a dead teen lying on the road with ear-buds was accompanied by the text: 'My friend heard the track. He didn't hear the van. Stop. Think. Live.' In the workplace, this could be replaced with messaging like: 'My daddy never came home from work,' with the supporting message that accidents at work affect your loved ones, too.

Intervention #4: Make it a streak

Loss aversion (the idea that we hate to lose something we already have more than we enjoy gaining something we don't) can play a unique role in safety practices. Calling attention to the number of days that it has been since your last safety incident has the side-effect of creating a streak. Nobody wants to break a streak once it has started. Think about this in your own life. How many days have you exercised in a row, or avoided coffee, or made sure to start your day with a smoothie? Once that streak gets started, we become attached to it and will work hard to avoid losing it. Shouting this number from the rooftops and updating it daily will create a streak and people will work harder to not be the person to break it.

Want to make announcing that streak even more effective? Employ a little friendly competition, with a boost by utilizing social norms. You could report the number of safety incidents in your safety managers' departments or on their teams, and tell them if that number is higher or lower than the company average.

Intervention #5: Crowdsource physical and psychological safety ideas from employees

Often, the best ideas on how to make safer workplaces come from those doing the work. They have first-hand experience of their close calls and the circumstances that caused them. Additionally, employees are more likely to be engaged in safety solutions when they are part of the solution-creating process. Go ahead and ask your people for ideas. You'd be surprised what they come up with.

Intervention #6: Draw attention to the hazardous with salient reminders

Our brains are wired to pay attention to things that stand out. There are many ways you can do this, and we've previously covered how novelty captures attention, but there is another technique you can use to grab attention about hazardous activities or places: you can use the colour red. The colour red not only captures our attention, but it also triggers our risk-aversion tendencies.[24] This means we pay much more careful attention and give a lot more focus to the task at hand when the colour red is employed. If you've ever wondered why the majority of warning signs, stop signs, and stop lights are red – now you know.

Another creative way to draw attention to the hazardous is to make it culturally relevant. In one clever experiment, people found that adding a series of gold coin stickers (a symbol of good fortune) to the floor of a Chinese garment factory reduced the amount of waste thrown on the floor by 20%. They limited waste because employees didn't want to cover up the signs of good fortune. This had an impact on workplace safety because waste on the floor (rather than in the bins) was a common cause of workplaces slips and falls.[25]

You could also employ humour. West Coast Express, a Canadian train commuter railway serving British Columbia, used a brilliantly simple, yet funny sign to keep people off the tracks. What did the sign say? 'Stay off the tracks. They are only for trains. If you can read this, you're not a train.'[26]

You could also go high-tech. In Hong Kong, there are some construction sites that use location-based data to warn workers when they are approaching hazards. The construction site is created in virtual reality, and as the worker moves through the *real* site, their helmet tracker sends data back to the virtual site which can then 'speak up' to warn them of impending danger.[27]

Intervention #7: Create a psychological safety behaviour guide for managers

Elsevier knew that a key component of psychologically safe teams would be in the hands of line managers. They also knew it would not be fair or effective to simply educate line managers in a 'one and done' workshop fashion and then expect them to be able to guide those behaviours in their teams, so they created a psychological safety behaviour guide for managers.

The guide included actionable insights for key areas of psychological safety such as reaction to mistakes, dealing with issues, taking risks and mutual respect. What might one of these actions look like? Let's look at the idea of taking risks. If that's to be encouraged, then employees need to know that (so tell them directly), but they also need to *see* it or picture it in action. One of the actions in Elsevier's psychological safety behaviour guide suggested rewarding those who experiment, and gave the example of Ratan Tata who, as chairman of Tata, created a prize for 'Best Failed Idea'.[28]

Travis has some guidance for those developing a similar guide in their own organizations. 'Our role is not to be psychologists. It's to give guidance.' As with many benefits that companies communicate about – health and financial benefits quickly jump to mind – disclaimers are key in protecting your company. The disclaimer language Elsevier currently uses for psychological safety is:

> 'If significant issues are raised, outlets to report concerns/violations of RELX's Code of Ethics and Business Conduct of Ethics and Business Conduct include managers, HR, company lawyers, Compliance Committee members and the Integrity Line.'[29]

Intervention #8: Make your safety strategy known to the business

Employees can't be expected to follow the rules and help live out your safety strategy in the business if they don't know about the strategy. This was something the UN did extraordinarily well when it officially launched its first ever UN-wide road safety strategy. The strategy was actually a detailed road safety management approach that spells out how the UN will reduce its global road crash rates and carbon emissions. It represented an important milestone: it was the first time in the history of the UN that each of its agencies contributed to, and committed to, a collective road safety approach. Hence, the occasion deserved some fanfare. The UN launched the strategy with an interactive event, held at UN headquarters in New York City and at World Health Organization (WHO) headquarters in Geneva, Switzerland, to ensure that employees knew about the new strategy and felt engaged to play an active part in its road safety efforts. Bonanno says:

'The idea behind the event was to demonstrate solidarity and top-level commitment to road safety, so we actively tried to get as many UN leaders as possible to attend the event and address why road safety was so critically important. We also featured employees from the field and several well-known external speakers, such as actress and UNDP Goodwill Ambassador, Michelle Yeoh, to share compelling personal stories of loss or challenges they faced due to road crashes. As we know, that kind of emotional storytelling is what really hits home with people. We created custom-produced films, event marketing and social media materials and we featured immersive road safety activities for employees to engage in on the day of the launch to reinforce the collective responsibility of tackling road safety.'

You may not have to launch your strategy via a big event, but you can employ some of the tactics of the UN launch event in your own communication planning – videos, vocal leaders, compelling testimonials and immersive experiences.

Wrapping it up: Applying what you've learned at work

The safety of employees – both physically and psychologically – is a serious responsibility for companies. Those tasked with the responsibility do not take it lightly. When you understand the root causes behind why physical safety accidents happen at work, such as fatigue, misaligned incentives and routine, you're better positioned to put policies and communications in place that help mitigate them. With psychological safety, it is critical for business performance and overall wellbeing that you get this right.

Seven reasons why physical safety incidents happen at work

1. Poorly designed default systems

2. Misaligned incentives

3. Complicated instructions

4. Lack of organizational commitment

5. Fatigue

6. Routine

7. Trade-offs between safety and speed

Four ways that a psychologically safe workplace benefits business

1. You're more likely to spot the cracks.

2. It encourages learning and growing.

3. It enables better decision-making.

4. People are more likely to take risks.

Four tips for increasing psychological safety at work

1. Show what healthy conflict looks like.

2. Create a zero-tolerance policy for bullying and harassment.

3. Help managers and leaders show up authentically.

4. Acknowledge (rather than punish) failure.

Eight workplace interventions to build safer places of work

1. Review your current physical safety training procedures.

2. Make unsafe stuff harder to do with good defaults.

3. Utilize counterfactual thinking.

4. Make it a streak.

5. Crowdsource physical and psychological safety ideas from employees.

6. Draw attention to the hazardous with salient reminders.

7. Create a psychological safety behaviour guide for managers.

8. Make your safety strategy known to the business.

NINE

Financial Wellness

K ohler remembers a key finding from a financial hackathon she helped to run in 2014. Hosted by Goldman Sachs in the heart of Wall Street, representatives from Intuit, Comcast, FedEx, State Street Global Advisors and more dove into the pressing financial wellness issues facing their people at the time. One discovery from the session stood out in particular: financial wellness, in large part, had nothing to do with how much money someone did or didn't make. Josh Newmister, who currently designs and leads all financial wellness programmes for Facebook in North America, participated in that event while he was the global retirement manager at Intuit. 'For all intents and purposes, salary and compensation are not going to have any effect on financial wellbeing. None,'[1] he says bluntly.

There's this idea that if we make a lot of money, our finances will naturally be in tip-top shape. We'll experience no money issues whatsoever and live happily ever after. It's a nice belief, but also patently false. This belief is a core driver of why so many people struggle to get on their feet financially. There are many famous examples of billionaires declaring bankruptcy due to mismanagement of funds. Equally, there are many examples of people with modest incomes dying as secret millionaires because they saved prudently and invested modestly.

That's not to say that there isn't a large part of the population who need to earn more to get on their feet. The US Census Bureau's 2018 report on income and poverty identified the official poverty rate in America as 11.8%.[2] This means over one in ten people are not earning enough to get by. Investing in retirement is likely the last thing on this group's mind. The point is that often the narrative around financial wellness is that if we just focus on having enough money saved for the future, then everything will be fine. Long-term wealth management, while important (and it will be addressed in this chapter), is not the only money issue we should care about.

Financial wellness is about making sure that people can make ends meet. It's about striving to create a world where one bad piece of luck doesn't financially ruin someone. A 2020 study in the US by PwC revealed that over 60% of Gen Z and almost 40% of Millennials have less than $1,000 saved to deal with emergency expenses.[3] Financial wellness works towards solving issues like that.

In this chapter, we will explore:

- What does being financially well look like?

- Eight reasons why being smart with money is challenging

- Critical money issues keeping people up at night

- Ten workplace interventions to boost financial wellness

What does being financially well look like?

Does having more money make you happier? That's the standard assumption. There has been quite a bit of academic debate on this front. In the 1970s, economist Richard Easterlin first proposed the 'Easterlin Paradox'.[4] The paradox stated that, over time, a country's happiness did not increase as its income increased. Ergo, more money *does not* make one happier.

Over time, the lack of connection between income and happiness has been somewhat debunked. The prevailing viewpoint is that having a higher income generally leads to higher life satisfaction, but not necessarily higher sustained happiness levels. If we take that concept further and assume that having loads more money *doesn't* make you ridiculously happier on a day-to-day basis, that begs a larger question: what is the goal of being financially well all about – and what does it mean?

Defining what being financially well means in your organization

Taking financial wellness seriously (and by seriously we mean seeing companies actually make a plan around it) is somewhat recent. As little as five years ago, employers were talking about financial wellness, but their efforts didn't extend beyond promoting the counselling and educational services from their 401(k) or pension provider. There was a lot of lip service and good intentions, but unfortunately, little action.

That's starting to change. While a survey by Aon Global in 2018 found that just 14% of companies had a financial wellbeing strategy in place, 75% of them intended to have a strategy in place by 2021.[5] Clearly business leaders know that they must have a financial wellbeing strategy, but does the strategy reflect the company's unique definition of financial wellbeing?

Companies must ask themselves what financial wellness looks like for their people, and, more importantly, how that manifests within different segments of the employee population. Some people live pay cheque to pay cheque (regardless of income). Others could be in a much more comfortable financial state and are focused on wealth management.

Demographics such as women (especially women of colour) also require different tools and levels of support. For example, the Financial Health Network US Financial Health Pulse 2020 Trends Report[6] found that women's finances were disproportionally negatively impacted by the Covid-19 pandemic.

We asked several of our interviewees for this book what financial wellness means to them. Here is the perspective of Ennie Lim, President and CEO of employee financial wellness product, HoneyBee:

> 'I think financial wellness is not comprised of one factor, but multiple. It's questions like, "Do you have enough cash to cover an emergency? Do you have a financial safety net? (Of course, most Americans do not.) Do you spend less than your income? Do you pay your bills on time? Are you able to manage debt? Do you have a good credit score? Do you have insurance?" These are all simple questions, but when you take all these factors into consideration and works towards them, that's what enables you to be resilient and pursue future opportunities.'[7]

Will Sandbrook, Executive Director of Nest Insight, the behavioural research unit of UK pension scheme Nest, has this to say:

> 'There's a standing definition of financial wellbeing that the Money and Pensions Service uses that just works really well. They

say financial wellbeing is about feeling secure and in control. It's knowing you can pay the bills today, can deal with the unexpected, and are on track for a healthy financial future. In short: being confident and empowered. The reason I think this works well is because it combines the practical, rational components of actually having enough money in short-term savings and long-term savings, but also the emotional and psychological components of wellbeing.'[8]

Eight reasons why being smart with money is challenging

Before we jump into solution mode, let's once again start with examining the core problem we have in front of us. When HR and IC teams understand the nuanced (and not-so-nuanced) ways in which saving more and spending less is so hard for people, they can start creating solutions and building safeguards that boost people's financial wellbeing. These are the eight key reasons people struggle with money:

1. Spending money feels good.

2. People are uncomfortable talking about money.

3. Scarcity.

4. Money is emotional.

5. Financial planning is complex.

6. Predatory products and advice.

7. Procrastination.

8. We think we have more time than we do.

Let's look at each in turn. When you understand the barriers preventing people from being good with money, you can design more effective policies and campaigns to help boost your employees' financial wellness.

Reason #1: Spending money feels good

As introduced in Chapter 7, people want to do what feels good in the moment – not necessarily what sets them up for long-term success. This tendency, as it turns out, is just as responsible for poor financial decisions as it is for poor health decisions. That's also why the most demotivating retirement savings message people can use (but unfortunately commonly do) is 'save for the future'. That message essentially asks someone to do something that they don't want to (save) for a time that means nothing to them (the future). Overcoming this tendency requires an extraordinary amount of self-control; and self-control ebbs and flows. When it ebbs, we may be more likely to spend, spend and spend some more.

Reason #2: People are uncomfortable talking about money

Lim reflects on this taboo:

> 'Money is just a topic that our culture doesn't allow people to talk about. People love talking about literally anything else. More than two in three people would rather talk about their weight than talk about money. People tend to suffer in shame and in silence.'

Sandbrook agrees:

> 'I think there is a significant element of shame and embarrassment. People don't like talking about their money worries because they fear judgement about that, particularly from their employer. When we say talking to your employer, we really mean talking to your manager – the person you see every day. People are concerned about sounding like they are asking for more, or sounding like they are complaining about whether their income is sufficient.'

Newmister feels this uncomfortableness is especially prevalent in his segment of the market – the highly-paid tech employees of Facebook: 'For my people, financial wellbeing will still have a stigma associated with it that prevents employers from doing anything with it.' The taboo can also go the other way, where employers don't want to touch financial wellness with a ten-foot pole. Newmister says:

> 'Many employers think that to help, they have to give more money or increase the 401(k) match and it's going to create a sense of entitlement, but it's not. This is no different than any other wellbeing initiative. I would argue that it's just as important, if not more important, than the other wellbeing programs at work.'

This is where a company culture of openness can help break the taboo of money at work. Lim explains that new hires to her company know right from the start that HoneyBee is a place where people can talk about money:

> 'During the hiring process, I talk with candidates about what I went through after my divorce. My credit was wrecked, I couldn't get approved for a new apartment, and I contemplated sleeping in my car. I was relieved that I was able to move back with my parents, but it was a few years before I was back on my feet. I then ask new candidates about a financial setback they might have had and how they overcame it. Starting with my own story creates a safe space where candidates feel comfortable talking about money, and that ripples into the rest of the organization.'

Lim is a leader of her business and sets the example. Likewise, leaders in organizations must get more comfortable talking about money. This will signal to their people that the conversation about money should be, and needs to be, happening. Heidi Johnson, Director of Behavioral Economics for the Financial Health Network,[9] one of America's most trusted financial resources for business leaders and policy makers, has a nuanced take on this taboo. She relates it to social normative behaviour. She says, 'Norms around money management aren't really visible. Consumption is visible; but someone declining to buy something because it's not in their budget isn't visible.'

Reason #3: Scarcity

The excellent book *Scarcity: Why having too little means so much*[10] by Sendhil Mullainathan and Eldar Shafir explores the multitude of ways that being poor in some resource – be it time, money, food, energy, etc – impacts our decision-making. When something is scarce, it can create a tunnel vision of sorts and we become absorbed by it. For example, in their book, they share a study which found that hungry people recognized the word 'cake' faster than those who were well fed. In the world of money, this could mean that people who are so focused on it will go to great lengths to procure more of it – even at the cost of turning to predatory products such as payday loans to make ends meet. It also means we prioritize the urgent over the important. Scarcity also reduces our mental bandwidth; and when we have less bandwidth, it's harder to make good decisions. Finally, scarcity reduces slack. If someone has less money, they have less slack – and therefore fewer options when it comes to their money.

Johnson reflects on the more traditional view of scarcity. She says, 'We are dealing with problems of scarcity with people trying to cover everyday financial needs, and close that gap between their income coming in and their expenses going out.' This leads to people turning to short-term solutions that are not in their long-term interest. She also notes that there is a lack of empathy between those at companies making financial programme decisions, and those who need them:

> 'Something that we see quite a bit of is a misunderstanding of the scarcity mindset challenges, and I think that's so important to highlight. It's hard to put yourself in the mindset of someone who is really facing those constraints and to understand that it's the scarcity mindset impairing their decisions, not a lack of information or education. It's just what happens to the human brain under those conditions.'

Reason #4: Money is emotional

'Money is a highly emotional issue.' That was one of the first statements Newmister made when we spoke, and he's absolutely right. We posit that the emotional attachment occurs because money, at the end of the day, is about security. About freedom. About your ability to not worry about where your next meal is going to come from.

Sandbrook highlights the emotional side of money when he talks about the challenges the self-employed face. While this group may not be the immediate concern of HR and IC teams, there is likely to be some portion of the employee population who join after being self-employed – and they will bring their money issues with them:

> 'The emotional impact of tying up large sums
> of money in a retirement account is really
> difficult for this group when their income can
> be volatile. If you have a bad month, the idea
> of locking your money away and not being
> able to get it out again until you're fifty-five (in
> the UK) is a particularly strong barrier.'

It's also psychologically painful to do what feels like giving up money, even though someone is not *technically* giving up money. Rather, they are saving it for their future selves – but we know by now how ungratifying that is. Johnson says:

> 'I think there is a big reticence for people to
> use their savings. People would much rather
> borrow than spend down their savings.
> It's really painful – there's a sense of loss
> aversion going on there. I also think there is

a morality issue going on. A lot of people feel uncomfortable taking on debt when it would benefit them because it feels wrong. I've seen some people have an attitude toward debt that is, "I don't take debt on." It's really black and white because those are the easiest rules to follow; but then it adds in a layer of morality that complicates decision-making.'

Reason #5: Financial planning is complex

Basic financial skills such as budgeting, saving, investing, etc, are not taught in school. Let's say someone does master the basics of budgeting and saving; they then face the more challenging questions of how to make the money work harder with multiple investment vehicles and tax-sheltered accounts. 'There's so much information online. You get extremely overwhelmed,' says Lim. Sandbrook agrees:

'There's a massive conflation between financial capability and financial wellbeing. People persuade themselves that if they do enough things to enhance financial capability, then that's the job done. There is piles and piles and piles of evidence that shows education alone won't change behaviour.'

Facebook has a great way of bringing this to light and helping people take the first step. They made the complex simple by identifying eight key helping statements from qualitative research they conducted in 2018. One of these helping statements is, 'Make me feel less dumb.' That may sound a little silly, but fear of feeling dumb or doubting one's ability to understand something is a large barrier to action. When things feel so big and challenging, it can be hard to take the first step. Newmister says:

> 'This was a big shocker to our leadership team. They thought because we have a large body of engineers who are crazy intelligent, that they would clearly know how to manage their finances. The reality is that it was the engineers who were articulating that issues like this were holding them back.'

The larger, philosophical question is whether the onus should be on people to learn something complex and make even more complex decisions. In response, let's take health care as an example. It's too important and difficult not to regulate, so we do. We don't leave it to the masses to figure out how to diagnose and treat their ailments. One could argue the health of one's finances falls into the same category.

Reason #6: Predatory products and advice

'Payday' loans and short-term loans with extraordinarily high interest rates make it almost impossible for those living from pay cheque to pay cheque to get ahead. Here's what happens. Someone barely making ends meet has a bill they can't pay, so what do they do? They go to their friendly neighbourhood cash lender to get an advance, knowing they have to pay it back in full (plus interest). According to the Consumer Financial Protection Bureau, a typical two-week payday loan has an interest rate of between $10 and $30 for each $100 borrowed.[11] Johnson notes that predatory products are still widely in existence, and a contributing factor to some not being able to pull themselves out of debt. She says:

> 'At the Financial Health Network, we see it as an incredibly important part of our mission to make sure the marketplace is offering solutions that set people up for success to pursue opportunities, rather than dragging them down.'

Let's also not overlook the role poor financial advice plays. Together with poor financial literacy, this throws a double punch at people's efforts to make sound financial decisions. *Last Week Tonight with John Oliver* did an excellent episode highlighting the minefield that is saving for retirement,[12] and called attention to the fact that the Financial Industry Regulatory Authority specifically warns people to 'be aware that Financial Adviser, Financial Consultant, Financial Planner, Investment Consultant or Wealth Manager are generic terms or job titles, and may be used by investment professionals who may not hold any specific credential.'[13] Yikes. What's more, these advisers make money on fees and commissions, so may not necessarily have their clients' best interest at heart. Brnic Van Wyk, Head of Asset and Liability Management at Australian pension fund QSuper, has an equally passionate view on the dark side of financial advisors:

> 'For this financial advice to work for buyers, it's got to be good. I've yet to come across an advisor that can give me a metric to prove their advice is actually good. And then, of course, that advice has to be implemented and reviewed. And again, I've yet to come across an advisor that meets with his client once a year to say, "Hey, remember that advice I gave you last year? Let's see how it went."'[14]

Reason #7: Procrastination

You don't need us to dive into why people procrastinate from a behavioural science standpoint. All of us have enough first-hand experience with procrastination to understand the reasons why we do it. *There will be time tomorrow. I don't feel like it. It's not as important as whatever I'm doing at the moment. If I just ignore it, maybe it will go away.* We mistakenly assume that whatever we will be doing later will not be as important as what we are doing now, so we just... don't take any action.

Even more disastrous is a misguided belief that you will probably make more money in the future, so it's OK to spend wantonly today. 'I think a lot of times, people in general hold this idea that, "When I make more money, I can do this,"' says Lim. She goes on to give an example:

> 'I have one specific employee; she's like twenty-two or twenty-three. She kind of roughly said here and there that she has debt. But every time I ask her why she hasn't taken advantage of the coaching we offer, her response is, "When I make more money, I'll talk to a coach."'

Procrastination also does something quite devious. In addition to waylaying our best-laid plans, it encourages inertia. Researchers William Samuelson and Richard Zeckhauser dubbed this tendency to just go with the flow *status quo bias*.[15]

> **Status quo bias** is a preference for the current state. It's viewed as a baseline reference point, and any change from that baseline can feel emotional.

Newmister partnered with an external financial research institute to conduct comprehensive research into what Facebook employees wanted support on when it came to their finances. He found that over 90% of employees had a strong motivation to do something about their finances – but weren't. He says, 'A lot of people had these goals, but there was a huge gap between the priority of the goal and then people actually doing something about it. The classic intention-action gap.'

The longer we do nothing about our finances, the easier it is to continue thinking, 'I'll do it tomorrow.' Tomorrow will be here before we know it; and many people won't have enough money saved up when it arrives.

Reason #8: We think we have more time than we do

Closely related to procrastination is the belief that we can start saving for retirement later and still be alright. We can view the barriers of procrastination and thinking we have more time than we do as best friends. In certain cases, some people *can* start saving later and end up alright, but most of us need to harness the power of the time value of money if we hope to have enough to support us when we're ready to stop working.

> **Time value of money** is the idea that, due to the potential that your money has to earn more, the money you have now is worth more than the same sum would be in the future.

Of course, a large part of that growth is compound interest – which needs time to do its magic. This isn't a maths or economics book, so we're not going to fill it with examples of how compound savings and interest works. (You're welcome.) Just know that's the concept at work when you see or hear ads about how someone who starts saving $100 each month at age twenty will have a bazillion more than someone who starts saving $100 each month at age thirty-five.

Not enough time is problematic. Too much time can be problematic as well. If someone misjudges how long they need their money to last (eg living for thirty years after retirement instead of fifteen years), you can see how that would get them into trouble. As the spoof commercial about retirement in the aforementioned *John Oliver* episode quips – the last step in a sound retirement plan is: 'Don't forget to die!'

Critical money issues keeping people up at night

First, there is likely a difference between what employers think their employees are stressed about when it comes to money – and what they're actually stressed about. Lim is more emphatic on the subject:

'There is definitely a difference between the two, and I'll start with the employee first. 89% of HoneyBee's users are people of colour, women or both. Our data shows that the emergency funds are most often used to cover basic necessities like gas and food. Covid-19 has caused one in six Americans to rely on a food bank. Now, health care is a big one, and, of course, rent. Employers, however, they don't see everything. The data they see is employees borrowing against their retirement and assume employees don't understand the importance of retirement savings. Employees living pay cheque to pay cheque do not have the disposable income to cover an essential car repair and thus tapping into their retirement savings is their best option. Without additional context, employers bring in retirement specialists to talk to their workforce rather than addressing the real issue. Employers should be conducting surveys, asking their employees directly about their financial health and providing the right tools, which is why giving your employees access to emergency funds and financial coaching are the first steps towards a financially healthier workforce.'

Sandbrook calls our attention to the large volume of work done by a team of academics looking at leakage in the US retirement system:[16]

'So much leakage out of the system in the US is evidence that there's an actual problem, which is, people lacking any other kind of place to go when they suffer some kind of financial emergency. If you lack short-term financial resilience, that's the biggest single indicator of debt... If you have a problem with debt, that undermines your overall earnings capacity, and undermines your health.'

Sandbrook also didn't mince any words about the biggest stressor, and it's one we agree with:

> 'I think the number one stressor when it comes to money is income. I don't think we should let ourselves off the hook for that. A lot of people just don't have enough money to go on and do all the things we tell them are good, rational things to do with your money.'

Being aware that money is a concern, and that having 401(k) reps talk to your people about the importance of retirement is not addressing the real issues; is there anything employers can do? Luckily, the answer is yes.

Ten workplace interventions to boost financial wellness

First and foremost, you need to have a financial wellness strategy. We could write a complete book just on how to develop one, so it is difficult to give the time and space in *this* book on how to do that, but the general principles of pulling together a solid strategy apply. For example, defining what financial wellness means in your business; understanding the financial landscape (working, economic and personal life); creating clear goals that connect to the larger business goals; defining your audience; getting feedback and information from your audience on what they need;

and then plugging the gaps through the right programmes and solid communication.

Once that strategy is in place, we advocate for simplicity, simplicity and more simplicity. As we've stressed throughout this book, people won't do hard things – even if it is in their best interest. They *especially* won't do hard things when it comes to money. The question for HR leaders is therefore: how do we make the right behaviours easier, and the wrong behaviours harder? There are ten workplace interventions that can be used to boost financial wellness:

1. Default the good money behaviours.

2. Use the power of mental accounting.

3. Leverage data for more personalized support.

4. Break down big numbers.

5. Show people what they're missing out on.

6. Connect to the future.

7. Enhance your benefits package.

8. Communicate throughout the year.

9. Try implementation intentions.

10. Create a financial wellness brand.

Let's look at each in more detail.

Intervention #1: Default the good money behaviours

Put savings and other desirable money behaviours on autopilot. One of the first examples of this in the workplace is the oft-cited and oft-referenced Save More Tomorrow programme.[17] Conceived by economists Richard Thaler and Shlomo Benartzi, Save More Tomorrow is a programme that lets employees commit in the present to increasing their retirement savings rate each time they receive a raise. This helps them overcome the desire to spend more when they have it later on. After all, if you never see it, you never miss it.

Ask any behavioural economist or individual with an interest in behavioural finance, and this study is often the first one that comes to mind some twenty years later (Save More Tomorrow was first implemented in 1998). Why does this intervention have so much staying power and get so much more airtime than other recent interventions in the space? Sandbrook has an interesting explanation:

'The size of the treatment effects you get in behavioural interventions is often significant, but quite small; but with a couple of these canonical interventions that people keep coming back to (auto-enrolment and Save More Tomorrow), the effect sizes were massive. When the UK introduced mandatory auto-enrolment to workplace pensions, the

> participation rate went from 50% to 90%. So
> now, because interventions we look at tend to
> look a lot weaker by comparison, people keep
> coming back to these original interventions.
> Maybe that's why people still talk about Save
> More Tomorrow.'

Contributions to, and enrolment in, retirement accounts are not the only thing employers can default. Employers can default contributions to other important components of financial wellbeing, such as an emergency savings account. One nifty player in this space, DoubleNet Pay, does exactly that. (DoubleNet Pay has since been acquired by Purchasing Power.) The product helps employees reach their financial goals by automatically diverting their pay cheque into specific accounts for savings, bills and spending. Essentially, people have to pay themselves first rather than receiving their entire pay cheque and then having to do the work (and have the self-control) to divert the funds into the respective accounts. It makes spending harder to do.

A similar approach was taken by the Nest Insight team in the UK, as Sandbrook explains. They called it 'sidecar savings':

> 'We got interested in this idea of a two-account
> model, where instead of saving all your money
> in your pension, you also use the power of
> mental accounting to get people to make a
> "set it and forget it" contribution to a savings
> account. The goal is to preserve the value of

the retirement account while also managing this short-term emergency savings issue. Once the emergency pot is sufficiently full, those additional contributions roll over into the retirement account, so it also serves as a pre-commitment device to increase pension contributions later.'

Nest has since built that into a product concept with several partners. It's too early to tell the results, but it is a promising idea. There is also an increasing number of apps that default your savings by rounding up your purchases to the next dollar into a savings account. Employers can bring attention to such apps in their financial wellness communications.

If defaults are part of your programme, be conscious of the danger if that pesky status quo bias creeps into the picture. Americans' employer 401(k) account balances often stagnate because their contribution rates remain unchanged. Employees' contributions default into the account at a savings rate of 3% and these are never increased – even when their income rises or their finances reach stability.

Intervention #2: Use the power of mental accounting

The idea of mental accounting (also developed by Thaler) explains how people treat money differently based on factors such as what they intend to use the money for. While the value of a dollar is exactly that

– a dollar – our minds don't always work in absolute values. It's why it's emotionally easier to spend money with a credit card than it is to spend money with cash; even though the monetary outlay is the same, we're not physically handing over dollar bills. Another way we view money in relative values vs absolute values is with labelling.

These labels, or earmarking money for particular purposes, have been shown to be especially effective in helping lower-income households save more money. While not substantially different than good old-fashioned budgeting, there is something about labelling something such as 'my new kitchen fund' that makes it more compelling and easier to stick with. It acts as a pre-commitment contract of sorts. If you want to make the act of saving even more compelling, add a picture. In one study in rural India, when participants were given their weekly wages in partitioned envelopes and one envelope was earmarked for their children and included the children's pictures, people saved more.[18]

A good challenge for employees then, is the earmark challenge. Have them create a savings pot in their vehicle of choice – in their bank, on their phone app, even an envelope under a mattress – and have them label it with a financial goal of theirs. Chances are, they will meet their savings goal quicker.

Intervention #3: Leverage data for more personalized support

Sandbrook says:

> 'I think data science is going to play a large role in addressing financial wellbeing. There are some very small, but quite interesting, things being done. There's a pension fund in Australia who have moved towards personalizing the default investment strategies based on what they know about their members.'

We asked the Australian pension fund Sandbrook referenced, QSuper, how that strategy was working out for them. Van Wyk says:

> 'We've known we have a pension problem, but nobody's been doing anything different to solve it. We are very proud that we started something. We are not suggesting that this is how it should be done, or that this should be a template for anybody else. There was no textbook we could copy, but we're very proud of the fact that at least we tried something new.'

What did they do? They leveraged data to create novel default investment strategies for participants. It wasn't just birth date and desired retirement date. It was much smarter than that. Van Wyk continues:

'The first person I employed was a PhD statistician. At the time, we were the same as pretty much any other fund, with most in an asset allocation of 60% stocks and 40% bonds; that makes the trustees and directors happy. Then our board of trustees took a hard look at things after the 2009 financial crisis and basically came to the conclusion that a "one size fits all" investment strategy is indefensible.'

With 600,000 members, QSuper decided that if they were going to invest money on these members' behalf, they'd better know what their members looked like, how much money they had, what they did, etc. 'We looked at everything we could get our hands on,' says Van Wyk. That included when people accessed their money, inferences about salary, why contributions stopped, life expectancy, current account balances and more. Did this plan to maximize returns work? According to Van Wyk, that's the wrong question to ask. 'We don't have an objective of maximizing returns. We have an objective of managing risk,' he says.

Intervention #4: Break down big numbers

Researchers Benartzi, Hershfield and Shu did great work in showing how transforming a big number that feels unattainable to something much smaller increases savings behaviour. They found that people were almost four times more likely to participate in a programme to save money when they changed the savings goal from a big number to a smaller one.[19] For example, $150 a month can seem like a stretch to many. Broken down into its daily equivalent of $5, that same amount suddenly seems much more attainable. It's much less painful to give up $5 than $150. That's why it works, and why it could be a way to help motivate employees to save more.

Now, one note here is that if you use this technique to get enrolment in a programme or encourage a sustained action (vs a one-time action), this same study found much larger drop-off rates among those who signed up to participate under the daily framing of $5 vs the monthly framing of $150, so be sure to follow up with your people regularly.

This concept can also be used to help break down the amount someone needs to have when they retire. Telling someone they will need $1m to be comfortable? Forget it. If you can break that down into smaller, more tangible figures and goals, it makes it easier for people to grasp the full extent of the challenge ahead – and how to start working on it.

Intervention #5: Show people what they're missing out on

Ever missed a big sale and silently berated yourself for it, lamenting the potential money lost? If so, you're in good company. In general, we don't like to miss out on things we could have had. We can harness this highly effective loss-framing in retirement communications. Kohler remembers one of the first times she tried this tactic in retirement communications, when she managed benefits communications for luxury retailer Nordstrom, Inc.:

> 'It was time for our annual Meet the 401(k) Match campaign, and our hired consultancy wanted to run the same campaign as they had in previous years. We were lucky if we could update the colours, but the 401(k) manager at the time had just finished reading *Predictably Irrational* by Dan Ariely, and him and I decided to play around with this idea of loss aversion. We performed personalized calculations on how much money people had left on the table by not meeting the company matching contribution. Sure enough, we had about 50% more people than the year before sign up to increase their 401(k) contributions.'

Johnson says:

> 'With communications, employers could really trigger the endowment effect a lot more by framing benefits as things you have and that you can opt out of – even if the enrolment requires an affirmative opt in. This change-frames it as losing the benefit.'

There's something to be said for letting people know what they've missed out on; but can it be demotivating?

That's what Nest Insight decided to find out by funding work by PhD student Emma Stockdale. In this study, participants received a fictional letter from ten years ago, informing them about the opportunity to increase their retirement contributions by £50 to live more comfortably in retirement. Next, some participants received a letter with retrospective framing. This letter told them that ten years ago it would have only been £50 but would now be £215 to achieve the same wealth. The group that got the retrospective framing were less likely to increase their contributions. Our conclusion is that loss-framing can be effective, but keep the frames relatively short. You don't want to highlight such a large loss that making it back up feels demotivating. That could lead to inaction.

Intervention #6: Connect to the future

One promising idea in the field to help overcome our instinct to put our 'present self' needs over that of our 'future self' needs is with finding a new way to connect to the idea of future you. As discussed in Chapter 7, we think of 'future us' as a different person, but if we could close that gap by enhancing the sense of emotional connection felt between our current and future selves, would it change behaviour? Several studies indicate that the answer is yes.

How connected we feel to our future self is partially determined by whether we see the core traits that make up our identity as fixed or as changing. If we feel they are ever-changing, we feel less connected to our future self – and thus more likely to make choices that aren't in our own long-term best interest.[20] If we can increase feelings of connectedness, however, then that may motivate people to make better choices.

How do we help people feel closer and more connected to their future selves? One tactic is *episodic future thinking*, which asks people to essentially imagine the future – with a twist. People are asked to imagine *positive* future events. No asking people to imagine themselves old and poor living on the streets and begging for change as a tactic to get people to take retirement savings seriously. We're not fear-mongers. Rather, have them imagine something positive that's coming up in their life. The prompt needs to be something personal to the individual; asking them to imagine sailing the French Riviera won't produce the same results. Episodic future thinking works because it tackles one of the main causes of poor financial decision-making: spending money feels good. Researchers have found that engaging in episodic future thinking does decrease time-discounting rates – meaning that people who practised this form of imagining the future could wait longer for better things to come their way.[21]

Intervention #7: Enhance your benefits package

What products do you currently offer? There are far more options to consider than just free financial counselling offered by an Employee Assistance Programme.

Many companies also offer unique ways to lessen the burden, such as:

- Retirement planning services

- Tuition reimbursement

- Child and elder care support

- Student debt assistance

Another programme to consider is an emergency savings fund. As we mentioned previously, according to PwC's 9th Annual Employee Financial Wellness Survey, over 60% of Gen Z and almost 40% of Millennials have less than $1,000 saved to deal with an emergency expense. Lim's HoneyBee Financial Wellness coverage does just that:

> 'I took a big risk. I shifted our business to the same way employers look at medical, dental and vision coverage. We provide the first-ever rainy-day coverage. You pay a premium like you would for medical, vision or dental insurance, and your entire workforce is covered with rainy-day funds at zero-percent interest anytime, regardless of your credit. I wanted to move us away from being a traditional lender to helping employees get a financial safety net.'

Lim's product is unique in the market and plugs a noticeable gap. Evaluating the counselling tools, budget trackers, financial apps, stand-alone products, etc, that HR teams get inundated with requests to share demos for is exhausting; but by asking just a few simple questions, HR teams can more quickly evaluate what products might be right for their financial well-being strategy.

Johnson also has an inside view on what companies and products are new on the market and is particularly interested in liquidity solutions:

> 'I think there are some interesting products out on the market right now, and one company our Financial Solutions Lab has invested in is a company called Even. This provides access to your earned wages in advance of receiving your pay cheque. It's the money you already earned, but instead of having to wait for the pay cheque to hit your bank account, you can access it right away.'

A product like that could reduce dependence on controversial credit products such as payday loans.

Johnson also advocates taking a deeper insight than most when evaluating benefit packages and products:

> 'We've done some research that found that employers often rely on a limited set of data to make these decisions. They might focus on how many people are participating in the retirement plan, or what health insurance claims look like, but they're not necessarily getting that pulse on what the true financial needs of their employees are.'

EXERCISE: FINANCIAL WELLNESS SERVICE EVALUATION CHECKLIST

First, inventory what products you currently offer. An important consideration here is quality and ease of use. Just because your 401(k) provider offers free budgeting tools, are they easy to use? Can people find them or are they buried seven pages deep within the provider's website? Second, double-check any preconceived notions of what employees do and do not want.

Lim explains the tact HoneyBee takes when employers question the product's value:

'What we highly recommend is sending over a very simple survey that you can just pass along to your employees. Then you will know, anonymously, what your employees would like to have. And they're always surprised by the results.'

Once your inventory is complete, these are the questions to ask about the product or service:

- Is it redundant to something you already have?
- If so, does it perform a critical function better than your current platform?
- Does it fill a need in your audience where there is currently a gap?
- Is there something a current vendor provides that can be used?
- How does the vendor plan to communicate with your employees?
- Is it user-friendly?
- Does the product align with your company values?

- Does the product have a track record?
- Is it easy to bring on board and integrate with your existing systems?

Note: Many financial tech start-ups fail to take this last point into consideration as they are founded by people who have never worked in-house and seen just how antiquated some of the systems are and how hard it is for HR to get IT to prioritize their needs.

If nothing on the market meets your bespoke needs, don't be afraid to create something yourself. Facebook did just this. Newmister says:

> 'We looked at seventeen financial wellbeing platforms, seven financial counselling platforms, seven financial providers, four blogging communications, two benefits navigation sites and about six parallel channels. We found some were doing things well, some were during things poorly – but none of them were getting a score meaningful enough that we could plug and play them into our ecosystem and they would have an immediate benefit. Then there were many providers that had no proven track record. So, we built our own.'

Intervention #8: Communicate throughout the year

Regularly remind your people of the financial support offered by the company – not just once a year when a financial-themed day or week like 'America Saves Week' comes around. Many HR and IC teams have a regular cadence of wellness communications and they should have the same cadence around financial wellness. Campaigns can be around savings, debt management, retirement, purchasing your first house and more. Campaigns should also share personal stories as a way to bring down the barrier of talking about finances.

You have to be inventive. As many of you know, engagement in this area (well, all areas) is difficult. As Lim says, 'Who wants to sit around and play on a budgeting app?' Communications can also be tailored for what people care about. Kohler once designed a financial wellness email series for a prominent global data storage company that spoon-fed relevant content throughout the year. Those who signed up could choose between different tracks based on their interests. Tracks included 'Money Basics for Any Stage of Life', 'Mid-Life Planning' and 'Transitioning from Work to Your Next Journey'.

Part of communicating throughout the year means making sure you have a cohesive message. Companies employ so many vendors with a plethora of offerings that it makes it hard for employees to know where to go for what. Playing the part of air-traffic controller if you're in IC (or listening to your IC team if you're in HR) can help get financial wellness messages out in an accessible and non-overwhelming manner.

Intervention #9: Try implementation intentions

We talked about implementation intentions in Chapter 7, but their magic works for an array of challenges – including helping people to reach their money goals. In your next financial wellness campaign, include a way or a prompt for employees to make their money implementation intentions. Implementation intentions could include things such as:

- When I get my next raise, I'll increase my savings rate by 5%.

- If I spend money on something frivolous, I won't buy (insert guilty treat of choice).

- On X day, I will open my investment account with X provider.

Intervention #10: Create a financial wellness brand

You've done the work. You have a strategy. You have the right vendors in place to support the programmes your people want. What's more, you have a communication plan around financial wellness to get all this great stuff into the hands of employees. Now you need an identity to bring it all together. That's where a financial wellness brand can come into play. Newmister says:

'After we had done all of the research into what our people wanted, we wanted to anchor it. I don't necessarily mean a financial wellbeing brand. However, with this financial initiative we were doing, we were partnering with so many people and collaborating with our people to create whatever it was we were going to create. We wanted to have a brand behind that. Literally within a week, we figured out a name, logo, and collateral.'

Part of this collateral include branded t-shirts, one of which Newmister wore for his interview:

'The shirts were actually in high demand. The brand was key in creating a community; and that community was one of the biggest motivators for people to turn up to our events when we went across the country to launch our new financial wellness support.'

The point is – you need a wrapper to make all the messages around financial wellbeing easily recognizable as you start to build your community.

Wrapping it up: Applying what you've learned at work

Financial security enables so many other positive behaviours. We know it's difficult, but with a different and more scientific lens to the work you do in the space, you can make it easier for your people to get on their feet, buy that house, save for the future – or whatever it is that their goals may be.

Eight reasons why being smart with money is challenging

1. Spending money feels good.
2. People are uncomfortable talking about money.
3. Scarcity.
4. Money is emotional.
5. Financial planning is complex.
6. Predatory products and advice.
7. Procrastination.
8. We think we have more time than we do.

Ten workplace interventions to boost financial wellness

1. Default the good money behaviours.
2. Use the power of mental accounting.
3. Leverage data for more personalized support.
4. Break down big numbers.
5. Show people what they're missing out on.

6. Connect to the future.

7. Enhance your benefits package.

8. Communicate throughout the year.

9. Try implementation intentions.

10. Create a financial wellness brand.

Exercises and resources

- Financial wellness service evaluation checklist

Even Better If:
Our Closing Thoughts

That's about all, folks. If you've read the book, in part or in its entirety, we hope you enjoyed and learned from it. If you tend to flick straight to the ending and haven't started it yet... go on and read the book; we think it's great and we're proud of it.

As this book is about learning, growing and becoming even better, we thought we should sum up what we learned and what we're even better at as a result of almost eighteen months of book gestation and birthing.

We learned that careers spanning a collective sixty-nine years accumulate a *lot* of knowledge, opinion and perspective. Taking time to reflect, prioritize and curate your beliefs around what's most important (and what you think about that important stuff) is hugely beneficial – personally and professionally.

Perhaps try it yourself, maybe on a smaller scale, in relation to your own career and experience. We all know so much, but the process of properly arranging it in the mind helps you access it far more easily when you need it.

We learned that almost all business and interpersonal successes and failures are due to communication skills (or the lack thereof). Communication is the master skill and super-power of all humans, whether in the boardroom, contact centre, on the shop floor or at the kitchen table. Improve your ability to communicate and you improve your likelihood to reach business goals, lead others effectively, smash your personal targets and perform as part of a team. Never stop honing your communication skills.

Our questioning and listening skills were so important (and got even better) during the dozens of interviews we conducted for this book, and in building the rapport we needed to glean such fascinating insights and perspectives from our contributors. We also needed to lean on our communication skills as a threesome of authors all juggling day jobs and personal lives through lockdown to get this book nailed, without ever once losing our shit with each other.

People are complex, unpredictable and hugely diverse, so founding much of the book in behavioural science was a winner. Understanding why people do what they do is critical when you're attempting to get them to do something differently or do different things. The better you can understand those you lead, work and live with, the more successful you will be – in everything.

We learned that writing a book is difficult, satisfying and enlightening. It taught us about business, about topics in which we already thought we were experts and about how hundreds of other amazing professionals approach their worlds of work. It taught us about ourselves and each other, and something of the legacy we want to leave in our professional lives.

We intended for this book not to be a 'business book' kind of business book. We wanted to write something practical, crisp and refreshing. We hope that having read it, you keep it on your desk or nearby bookshelf and refer back to it and the exercises regularly. Please tell us if you think we have or haven't achieved it; we'd love to hear from you.

Finally, thank you to all the people who gave of their time, perspectives, insights, experience and expertise in helping us turn this literary pipe-dream into reality.

Thank you, reader, for being part of *Even Better If*.

Notes

Chapter One

1 Helen Willetts, Director of Internal Communications, BT, interviewed July 2020

2 PE Tetlock, L Skitka and R Boettger (1989) 'Social and cognitive strategies of coping with accountability: Conformity, complexity, and bolstering', *Journal of Personality and Social Psychology*, 57, 632–641

3 Andrea Mattis, Global Internal Communications Manager, Collinson, interviewed December 2020

4 Shanna Wendt, various VP-level roles, interviewed January 2021

5 Jesper Ambrosius, Head of LEGO Workplace Experience, interviewed February 2021

6   A Maslow (1970) *Motivation and Personality* (New York: Harper & Row)

7   R Thornton (2020) *2020 World Changers* (scarlettabbott), https://scarlettabbott.co.uk/topic/2020-world-changers-report, accessed 7 August 2021

8   P Juneja (no date) 'Charles Handy model of organization culture' (Management Study Guide), www.managementstudyguide.com/charles-handy-model.htm, accessed 15 July 2021

9   Gillian McGill, Global Director of Internal Communication, Aviva, interviewed June 2020

10 Jon Hawkins, Global Internal Communications Lead, Aviva, interviewed June 2020

11 Andy Wales, Chief Digital Impact and Sustainability Officer, BT, interviewed August 2020

12 Maxine Goff, Head of Employee Engagement Communications, BT, interviewed July 2020

13 Research was conducted by a large financial services firm in 2017 with a sample of approximately 300 of their employees (unpublished)

14 M Alagaraja and B Shuck (2015) 'Exploring organizational alignment-employee engagement linkages and impact on individual performance: A conceptual model', *Human Resource Development Review*, 14(1), 17–37

15 R Quinn and A Thakor (2018) 'Creating a purpose-driven organization', *Harvard Business*

Review, https://hbr.org/2018/07/creating-a-purpose-driven-organization, accessed 16 July 2021

16 P Dolan and D Kahneman (2015) *Happiness by Design: Finding pleasure and purpose in everyday life* (London: Penguin Books)

Chapter Two

1 Sarah Burbedge, Head of Change, BBC, interviewed January 2021

2 P Brickman, D Coates and R Janoff Bulman (1978) 'Lottery winners and accident victims: Is happiness relative?', *Journal of Personality and Social Psychology*, 36(8), 917–927

3 JL Huang et al (2014) 'Personality and adaptive performance at work: A meta-analytic investigation', *Journal of Applied Psychology*, 99(1), 162–179

4 M Sainato (2020) 'Walt Disney layoffs leave thousands of workers in an awful lot of pain', *The Guardian*, www.theguardian.com/film/2020/dec/02/walt-disney-layoffs-workers-struggle, accessed 27 June 2021

5 B Chesky (2020) 'A message from cofounder and CEO Brian Chesky' (Airbnb), https://news.airbnb.com/a-message-from-co-founder-and-ceo-brian-chesky, accessed 7 August 2021

6 Claire Holt, Global Communications Director, Capgemini, interviewed October 2020

7   Jane Hanson, Chief People Officer, Nationwide
    Building Society, interviewed November 2020
8   Anonymous, interviewed June 2020
9   Martha Férez, Head of Change for Non-Financial
    Risk, Deutsche Bank, interviewed December
    2020
10 Marina Gonzalez, Director of People Experience
    Design, Rivian, interviewed December 2020
11 Survey carried out by scarlettabbott
    (unpublished)
12 C Heath and D Heath (2011) *Switch: How to
    change things when change is hard* (London:
    Random House Business)

Chapter Three

1   Russell Norton, Head of Client Experience,
    scarlettabbott, interviewed December 2020
2   Nadia Younes, Chief Diversity Officer,
    interviewed January 2021
3   Grace Lordan, Associate Professor of
    Behavioural Science, London School of
    Economics, interviewed January 2021
4   L Kohler (2021) 'Deloitte's new equity
    imperative report gives businesses roadmap for
    action', *Forbes* – edited with approvement from
    Deloitte
5   C Goldin and C Rouse (2000) 'Orchestrating
    impartiality: The impact of "blind" auditions
    on female musicians', *The American Economic*

Review, https://pubs.aeaweb.org/doi/ pdfplus/10.1257/aer.90.4.715, accessed 7 August 2021

6 HR DataHub (2020) *Ethnicity Pay Gap Report*, www.hrdatahub.com, accessed 7 August 2021

Chapter Four

1 Hayley Macdougall, former Global Head of Talent for the International Manager (IM) Programme, HSBC, interviewed February 2021

2 Sir Stephen O'Brien, Chair of Barts Health NHS Trust, interviewed August 2020

3 Sarah Spooner, Head of Customer Experience, Vodafone, interviewed September 2020

4 Aileen O'Toole, Chief People Officer, Prosus Group and Naspers, interviewed September 2020

5 J Bezos (2017) '2016 letter to shareholders' (Amazon), www.aboutamazon.com/news/ company-news/2016-letter-to-shareholders, accessed 27 July 2021

6 Ibid

7 Richard Kimber, founder, Daisee, interviewed September 2020

8 Jeremy Petty, MD, scarlettabbott, interviewed January 2021

9 Chris Brindley MBE, Chair of the Board, Rugby League World Cup 2021, interviewed December 2020

10 Jason Wilcox, Academy Director, Manchester City FC, interviewed September 2020

Chapter Five

1 J Boehm (no date) 'Unequally distributed psychological assets: Are there social disparities in optimism, life satisfaction, and positive affect?', *PLoS One*, 10(2), E0118066

2 D Drachman, A DeCarufel and CA Insko (1977) 'The extra credit effect in interpersonal attraction', *Journal of Experimental Social Psychology*, https://e5c29080-75f7-4a11-93bb-b7a79a06c9b1.filesusr.com/ugd/8c461c_47674 d578bcb4600b3767bc8e3a64744.pdf, accessed 26 July 2021

3 MF Scheier, CS Carver and MW Bridges (1994) 'Distinguishing optimism from neuroticism (and trait anxiety, self-mastery, and self-esteem): A re-evaluation of the Life Orientation Test', *Journal of Personality and Social Psychology*, 67, 1063–1078

4 CS Carver (no date) 'LOT-R (Life Orientation Test-Revised)', University of Miami, Department of Psychology, https://local.psy.miami.edu/people/faculty/ccarver/availbale-self-report-instruments/lot-r

5 N Celestine (2021) 'What is the Life Orientation Test and How To Use It? (LOT-R)', PositivePsychology.com, https://positivepsychology.com/life-orientation-test-revised

6 Dr Laura Taylor, urgent care doctor, NHS,
   interviewed April 2021

Chapter Six

1 D Sheff (1985) 'Playboy interview: Steven
   Jobs', *Playboy*, https://web.archive.org/
   web/20120322025837/http://www.playboy.
   com/magazine/playboy-interview-steve-jobs,
   accessed 27 July 2021
2 H Blodget (2009) 'Mark Zuckerberg on
   innovation', *Insider*, www.businessinsider.com/
   mark-zuckerberg-innovation-2009-10, accessed
   27 July 2021
3 J Estrin (2015) 'Kodak's first digital moment',
   The New York Times, https://lens.blogs.nytimes.
   com/2015/08/12/kodaks-first-digital-moment,
   accessed 27 July 2021
4 Verona Frankish, former MD of lettings, Purple
   Bricks, interviewed April 2021
5 TFL (2016) 'All London black cabs to take
   cards and contactless payments from Monday'
   (Transport for London), https://tfl.gov.uk/info-
   for/media/press-releases/2016/october/all-
   london-black-cabs-to-take-cards-and-contactless-
   payments-from-mond, accessed 27 July 2021
6 J Bezos (2017) '2016 letter to shareholders'
   (Amazon), www.aboutamazon.com/news/
   company-news/2016-letter-to-shareholders,
   accessed 27 July 2021

7   Ibid

8   Tom Lowe, co-founder, Fourpure Brewing Co.,
     interviewed April 2021

9   R Arthur (2019) '"Probably not the best beer in
     the world – so we've changed it": Carlsberg
     challenges drinkers to reappraise its beer',
     Beverage Daily, www.beveragedaily.com/
     Article/2019/04/16/Probably-not-the-best-
     beer-in-the-world-Carlsberg-challenges-
     drinkers-to-reappraise-its-beer, accessed 27 July
     2021

10 D Spajic (2020) 'How many iPhones have been
     sold worldwide? – iPhone sales analyzed',
     Kommando Tech, https://kommandotech.com/
     statistics/how-many-iphones-have-been-sold-
     worldwide, accessed 27 July 2021

11 A Grant (2021) 'Persuading the unpersuadable',
     Harvard Business Review, https://hbr.
     org/2021/03/persuading-the-unpersuadable,
     accessed 27 July 2021

12 Institute of Directors (2018) 'What is the role of
     the non-executive director?' (IOD), www.iod.
     com/news/news/articles/What-is-the-role-
     of-the-NonExecutive-Director, accessed 27 July
     2021

13 J Bezos (2017) '2016 letter to shareholders'
     (Amazon), www.aboutamazon.com/news/
     company-news/2016-letter-to-shareholders,
     accessed 27 July 2021

14   Response Source (2021) 'Research reveals email dominates business communication but poor processes kill productivity and frustrate employees' (Response Source), https://pressreleases.responsesource.com/news/100633/research-reveals-email-dominates-business-communication-but-poor-processes-kill, accessed 28 July 2021

15   E Bradner (2015) 'Carly Fiorina: Oprah, Steve Jobs got fired too', *CNN Politics*, https://edition.cnn.com/2015/08/09/politics/carly-fiorina-fired-oprah-jobs-disney-bloomberg/index.html, accessed 28 July 2021

Part Three

1   D Ariely (2009) *Predictably Irrational: The hidden forces that shape our decisions* (New York: Harper, first edition)

Chapter Seven

1   D Fujiwara et al (2020) *The Wellbeing Costs of COVID-19 in the UK* (London: Simetrica-Jacobs and the London School of Economics and Political Science), www.jacobs.com/sites/default/files/2020-05/jacobs-wellbeing-costs-of-covid-19-uk.pdf, accessed 28 July 2021

2   I Papanicolas, LR Woskie and AK Jha (2018)
    'Health care spending in the United States and
    other high-income countries', *JAMA*, 319(10),
    https://pubmed.ncbi.nlm.nih.gov/29536101,
    accessed 28 July 2021

3   Dr Richard Caddis, Chief Medical Officer, BT,
    interviewed December 2020

4   G Loewenstein (1996) 'Out of control: Visceral
    influences on behavior', *Organizational Behavior
    and Human Decision Processes*, 65, 272–292

5   S DellaVigna and U Malmendier (2006) 'Paying
    not to go to the gym', *American Economic
    Review*, 96(3), 694–719, www.researchgate.net/
    publication/4720318_Paying_Not_to_Go_to_
    the_Gym, accessed 28 July 2021

6   David Lynch Foundation (2014) 'Bob Roth
    interviews Jerry Seinfeld on "Success Without
    Stress"', Sirisu XM Indie radio show, www.
    youtube.com/watch?v=IeRdy6LrOAI, accessed
    28 July 2021

7   K Volpp et al (2011) 'Redesigning employee
    health incentives: Lessons from behavioural
    economics', *The New England Journal of Medicine*,
    365, 388–390

8   Nate Randall, founder and president, Ursa
    Major Consulting, interviewed January 2020

9   Lori Golden, Abilities Strategy Leader, Ernst &
    Young, interviewed May 2020

10 R U OK?, Australian suicide prevention charity,
    www.ruok.org.au

11 Bruce Greenhalgh, Global Health and Wellbeing Clinical Lead, BT, interviewed December 2020

12 'Ulysses contracts' and the idea of advanced directives also have a connection with commitment contracts. Kirsten Bell's 2015 piece, 'Thwarting the diseased will: Ulysses contracts, the self and addiction' presents a nice overview of the history and applications of the Ulysses contract: https://pubmed.ncbi.nlm.nih.gov/25374370

13 K Milkman, JA Minson and KGM Volpp (2013) 'Holding the hunger games hostage at the gym: An evaluation of temptation bundling', *Management Science*, www.ncbi.nlm.nih.gov/pmc/articles/PMC4381662, accessed 28 July 2021

14 B Dahlberg (2018) 'Cornell food researcher's downfall raises larger questions for science' (NPR), www.npr.org/sections/thesalt/2018/09/26/651849441/cornell-food-researchers-downfall-raises-larger-questions-for-science, accessed 28 July 2021

15 B Wansink and A Hanks (2013) 'Slim by design: Serving healthy foods first in buffet lines improves overall meal selection, *PLoS One*, 8(10), https://journals.plos.org/plosone/article?id=10.1371/journal.pone.0077055, accessed 16 September 2021

16 J Black (2020) 'How Google got its employees to eat their vegetables', *OneZero*, https://onezero.medium.com/how-google-got-its-employees-to-eat-their-vegetables-a2206820d90d, accessed

28 July 2021 (an excellent in-depth overview of Google's cafeteria and food choices, if you're looking for additional ideas)

17 P Gollwitzer (1999) 'Implementation intentions: Strong effects of simple plans', *American Psychologist*, 54(7), 493–503

18 K Milkman et al (2011) 'Using implementation intentions prompts to enhance influenza vaccination rates', *Proceedings of the National Academy of Sciences of the United States of America*, 108(26), 10415–10420

19 Jo Cox Loneliness Commission (2017) *Combatting Loneliness One Conversation at a Time*, www. ageuk.org.uk/globalassets/age-uk/documents/ reports-and-publications/reports-and-briefings/active-communities/rb_dec17_jocox_ commission_finalreport.pdf, accessed 29 July 2021

20 V Murthy (2017) 'Work and the loneliness epidemic: Reducing isolation at work is good for business', *Harvard Business Review*, https:// hbr.org/cover-story/2017/09/work-and-the-loneliness-epidemic, accessed 29 July 2021

21 A great read on all the myriad ways loneliness directly impacts performance at work can be found in H Ozcelik's paper 'Work loneliness and employee performance', https://journals.aom. org/doi/pdf/10.5465/ambpp.2011.65869714, accessed 29 July 2021

22 Allison Stark, Global Wellness Programme
    Manager, HPE, interviewed June 2020

23 A Tvserky and D Kahneman (1981) 'The framing
    of decisions and the psychology of choice',
    Science, 211(4481), 453–458

24 Paul Gerrard, Campaign and Public Affairs
    Director, Co-op, re-use of his interview from
    2020 scarlettabbott *World Changers* report

25 Co-op (2017) 'Loneliness epidemic costs UK
    businesses £2.5 billion a year' (Co-op), www.
    co-operative.coop/media/news-releases/
    loneliness-epidemic-costs-uk-businesses-gbp2-5-
    billion-a-year, accessed 29 July 2021

Chapter Eight

1 Associated Press (2015) 'Bumble Bee Foods
   settles for $6m in death of worker cooked with
   tuna', *The Guardian*, www.theguardian.com/
   us-news/2015/aug/12/bumble-bee-foods-
   settlement-man-cooked-death-tuna, accessed 27
   July 2021

2 Bureau of Labor Statistics (2020) 'National
   census of fatal occupational injuries in 2018'
   (Bureau of Labor Statistics), www.bls.gov/news.
   release/pdf/cfoi.pdf, accessed 29 July 2021

3 Health and Safety Executive (2019) *Health and
   safety at work: Summary statistics for Great Britain
   2019*, (HSE), www.hse.gov.uk/statistics/overall/
   hssh1819.pdf, accessed 29 July 2021

4   Ibid

5   S Fowler (2017) 'Reflecting on one very, very strange year at Uber' (blog post), www.susanjfowler.com/blog/2017/2/19/reflecting-on-one-very-strange-year-at-uber, accessed 27 July 2021

6   Rosanne Bonanno, founder, RoBo Communications, interviewed October 2020

7   B Merchant (2017) 'Life and death in Apple's forbidden city', *The Guardian*, www.theguardian.com/technology/2017/jun/18/foxconn-life-death-forbidden-city-longhua-suicide-apple-iphone-brian-merchant-one-device-extract, accessed 19 August 2021

8   J Kelly (2019) 'French CEO sent to prison after his policies resulted in the suicides of 35 employees', *Forbes*, www.forbes.com/sites/jackkelly/2019/12/23/french-ceo-sent-to-prison-after-his-policies-resulted-in-the-suicides-of-35-employees, accessed 29 July 2021

9   R Mars (2019) 'Episode 379: Cautionary tales', *99% Invisible* (podcast), https://99percentinvisible.org/episode/cautionary-tales/transcript, accessed 29 July 2021

10 US Department of Energy Office of Scientific and Technical Information (1979) *Three Mile Island: A report to the commissioners and to the public*, Volume I (OSTI), www.osti.gov/biblio/5395798-three-mile-island-report-commissioners-public-volume, accessed 29 July 2021

11   WHO (2020) 'The top 10 causes of death', www. who.int/en/news-room/fact-sheets/detail/the-top-10-causes-of-death, accessed 29 July 2021

12   S Stewart et al (2006) 'An integrated system for managing fatigue risk within a low cost carrier' (59th Annual International Air Safety Seminar), www.clockworkresearch.com/wp-content/uploads/2017/10/An-integrated-system-for-managing-fatigue-within-a-LCC_IASS-Paris-2006.pdf, accessed 29 July 2021

13   P Dolan and MM Galizzi (2015) 'Like ripples on a pond: Behavioral spillovers and their implications for research and policy', *Journal of Economic Psychology*, 47, 1–16, www.sciencedirect.com/science/article/pii/S0167487014001068, accessed 29 July 2021

14   Anonymous, interviewed September 2020

15   ISO (2021) *ISO 45003:2021: Occupational Health and Safety Management: Psychological health and safety at work: Guidelines for managing psychosocial risks* (ISO), www.iso.org/standard/64283.html, accessed 29 July 2021

16   C Duhigg (2016) 'What Google learned from its quest to build the perfect team', *The New York Times*, www.nytimes.com/2016/02/28/magazine/what-google-learned-from-its-quest-to-build-the-perfect-team.html, accessed 29 July 2021

17   Ibid

18 P Nelissen et al (2017) 'Lending a helping hand at work: A multilevel investigation of prosocial motivation, inclusive climate and inclusive behavior', *Journal of Occupational Rehabilitation*, 27(3), 467–476

19 Ibid

20 Adam Travis, Global Head of Inclusion and Diversity at Elsevier, interviewed September 2020

21 UK Statistics Authority (2018) *UK Statistics Authority (Corporate Report)*, https://uksa.statisticsauthority.gov.uk/wp-content/uploads/2019/01/UKSA-UK-Statistics-Authority-Corporate-Report-2018.pdf, accessed 29 July 2021

22 G Eiff (1988) 'Moving toward an organizational safety culture', *Journal of Aerospace*, 107, section 1, 1311

23 K Hawton et al (2013) 'Long term effect of reduced pack sizes of paracetamol on poisoning and deaths and liver transplant activity in England and Wales: Interrupted time series analyses', *BMJ*, 346, f403

24 R Mehta and RJ Zhu (2009) 'Blue or red? Exploring the effect of color on cognitive task performances', *Science*, 323(5918), 1226–1229

25 SJ Wu and EL Paluck (2021) 'Designing nudges for the context: Golden coin decals nudge workplace behavior in China', *Organizational Behavior and Human Decision Processes*, 163,

43–50, www.sciencedirect.com/science/article/ abs/pii/S0749597818305119, accessed 19 August 2021

26 SafetySign.com (2016) 'If you can read, you're not a train – funny sign Friday', www. safetysign.com/blog/if-you-can-read-youre- not-a-train-funny-sign-friday, accessed 29 July 2021

27 H Li et al (2015) 'Proactive behavior-based safety management for construction safety improvement', *Safety Science*, 75, 107–117

28 R McGrath (2011) 'Failure is a gold mine for India's Tata', *Harvard Business Review*, https:// hbr.org/2011/04/failure-is-a-gold-mine-for-ind. html, accessed 5 August 2021

29 Used with permission from Adam Travis, Global Head of Inclusion and Diversity at Elsevier, August 2021

Chapter Nine

1 Josh Newmister, designer and leader of the financial wellness programmes for Facebook in North America, interviewed December 2020

2 US Census Bureau (2018) 'Income and poverty in the United States', www.census.gov/library/ publications/2019/demo/p60-266.html, accessed 28 July 2021

3   PwC (2020) '9th annual employee financial wellness survey', www.pwc.com / us / en / industries / private-company-services / library / financial-well-being-retirement-survey.html, accessed 28 July 2021

4   R Easterlin (1974) 'Does economic growth improve the human lot?', In P David and M Reder (Eds) *Nations and Households in Economic Growth: Essays in honour of Moses Abramovitz* (New York: Academic)

5   Aon Global (2018) 'Financial wellbeing study', www.aon.com / getmedia / 36b54779-b657-4735-b10e-16e6b410440b / Aon_Financial-Wellbeing-Study.aspx, accessed 28 July 2021

6   T Garon et al (2020) *US Financial Health Pulse 2020 Trends Report* (Financial Health Network), https:/ / s3.amazonaws.com / cfsi-innovation-files-2018 / wp-content / uploads / 2020 / 10 / 26135 655 / 2020PulseTrendsReport-Final-1016201.pdf, accessed 7 August 2021

7   Ennie Lim, President and CEO, HoneyBee, interviewed October 2020

8   Will Sandbrook, Executive Director, Nest Insight, interviewed November 2020

9   Heidi Johnson, Director of Behavioural Economics, Financial Health Network, interviewed November 2020

10 S Mullainathan and E Shafir (2013) *Scarcity: Why having too little means so much* (New York: MacMillan USA)

11 Consumer Financial Protection Bureau (2017) 'What are the costs and fees for a payday loan?', www.consumerfinance.gov/ask-cfpb/what-are-the-costs-and-fees-for-a-payday-loan-en-1589, accessed 29 July 2021

12 J Oliver (2016) 'Episode 74: Retirement Plans', *Last Week Tonight with John Oliver* (TV programme), www.hbo.com/last-week-tonight-with-john-oliver/2016/15-june-12-2016, accessed 7 August 2021

13 This and other FINRA rules can be found online at www.finra.org/investors/professional-designations/pd-rules-and-resources

14 Brnic Van Wyk, Head of Asset and Liability Management, QSuper, interviewed November 2020

15 W Samuelson and R Zeckhauser (1988) 'Status quo bias in decision making', *Journal of Risk and Uncertainty*, 1(1), 7–59

16 John Beshears, James J Choi, David Laibson and Brigitte C Madrian have published numerous works that serve as a great resource in this area

17 RH Thaler and S Benartzi (2004) 'Save More Tomorrow™: Using behavioral economics to increase employee saving', *The Journal of Political Economy*, 112(S1), S164–S187

18 D Soman and A Cheema (2011) 'Earmarking and partitioning: Increasing saving by low-income households', *Journal of Marketing Research*, 48(SPL), S14–S22

19 H Hershfield et al (2020) 'Temporal reframing and participation in a savings program: A field experiment', *Marketing Science*, 39(6), 1039–1051

20 DM Bartels and O Urminsky (2011) 'On intertemporal selfishness: How the perceived instability of identity underlies impatient consumption', *Journal of Consumer Research*, 38(1), 182–198

21 J Peters and C Büchel (2010) 'Episodic future thinking reduces reward delay discounting through an enhancement of prefrontal-mediotemporal interactions', *Neuron*, 66(1), 138–148

Acknowledgements

Rachel

I've had a book bubbling within for a good decade, but it took Lindsay Kohler joining my consultancy to light the touchpaper. So, firstly, thanks LK for your endless energy, optimism and grit. You were the rocket fuel behind this endeavour. I don't think I would have managed it without you.

Thanks also to my coach, friend and co-author Charlie Sampson, who inspires me with his knowledge and expertise, and makes me laugh when I least feel like it.

I'm grateful and thankful to my scarlettabbott team for their wisdom, wit and expertise, and for making sure the good ship SA was powering on when I was busy writing. Thanks Jez and JA. Thanks also to Andy Payne, my former workmate, who told me to write a book about business and leadership. I did, AP!

Thanks also to the countless experts we interviewed for *Even Better If*. They gave of their time, experience and insights so generously and brought our book to life with brilliant stories, opinions and anecdotes.

Finally, thank you, Mum. You made me believe I could do anything. Seems, with the right partners, I can.

Enjoy the book. It's been a blast writing it.

Lindsay

I always knew I'd write a book someday; I just thought (hoped) that it would be the next great American novel. Imagine my surprise that the first book out of the gates is a business book, but contributions to the community vary; if I can't entertain you with fiction, I hope to empower you with science!

First and foremost, a huge thank you to Rachel Thornton who, when we sat down one day over coffee, didn't blink an eye when I said, 'How about we write a book?' Most would've responded with hesitance, or worse, they would've thought I was crazy. Rachel? She went all in, and then pulled in her longtime friend, Charlie Sampson, to round out our book. It's been a delight co-authoring this book with you both.

I have a huge thank you to give to all of our contributors, but especially Adam Travis from Elsevier and Rosanne Bonanno from RoBo Communications. Their expertise heavily guided our chapter on Safety (a previous weak spot of mine) and the resulting content is much richer for it. I also have a special thank you for Josh Newmister from Facebook. Facebook is doing really innovative things in the financial well-being space; and I'm delighted he was so willing to share their knowledge with us.

It turns out, writing a book is the easy part. Getting it out into the world and into the hands of you fine people is exceedingly more difficult. To that end, I'd like to thank scarlettabbott's marketing manager, Kate Went, for making sure we didn't just post this on Amazon on launch day and hope for the best.

I also want to thank two former colleagues of mine from my first job at Nordstrom, Inc. Kathy Bell and Chadd Thomas were the first people to introduce me to behavioural science, and the first to let me experiment with it in the employee engagement space. Without them, I might never have been inspired by what was, at the time, an emerging field. I've since found so much inspiration to apply academic insights to our HR and internal communication world and I hope the work is better for it.

I think this is the part where I'm supposed to thank my family for putting up with me while I wrote a book, but as they live on the other side of the world and were spared dealing with the occasional fallouts of the creative process, I'll instead say thank you for always reinforcing the fact that at the end of the day, I'm a damn good writer. That gave me the confidence to even think I could write a book you would all want to read.

Thank you all for coming along with us on this journey. I hope it's been inspirational and insightful.

Charlie

Many people talk about writing a book, but few do. I would still fall into the former category if it weren't for Lindsay Kohler. You made this book happen LK, and always with a smile on your face. Thank you.

To my other co-conspirator, Rachel Thornton, whom I am proud to call both a client and a friend. You epitomize inspiring leadership and have taught me so much.

Thank you always to my amazing family, especially my wife Hayley, for all your advice, support, and most of all, your patience!

I am indebted to all those who gave up their time to contribute to this book; it is your expertise and insight that really matter the most. And to all the extraordinary people and organizations I've worked with over the years, who have challenged and shaped my approach to leadership development. I have yet to work with a great business leader who was not, first of all, a great human being; because leading is as much about who you are as what you do. You allow me to have the best job in the world, and it's your fault I ever wanted to write this book in the first place.

It requires tremendous courage to lead and inspire others to want to be better, and so this book is dedicated to my beautiful brother Tom – the bravest man I have ever known.

Never stop trying to be better.

The Authors

Rachel Thornton

As well as heading one of Europe's leading employee engagement consultancies, Rachel Thornton is an in-demand facilitator, executive coach and strategic advisor. A gifted big-picture thinker, she works with the C-suite of major brands to accelerate thinking on strategy, leadership and high performance. With a twenty-seven-year career spanning journalism, in-house and consultancy roles, Rachel has a unique, challenging and fresh perspective on how communication and engagement can positively impact business performance.

🌐 www.scarlettabbott.co.uk

Lindsay Kohler

Lindsay Kohler is an applied behavioural scientist who holds an MSc in Behavioural Science from the London School of Economics and Political Science and specializes in employee engagement. She is a *Forbes* contributor, and her writing also appears in a wide variety of industry publications, including *Harvard Business Review*, *Workforce*, *HRDirector*, *CorpComms Magazine* and more.

🌐 www.lindsayannkohlerwrites.com

Charlie Sampson

An acclaimed expert in the field of leadership development, Charlie learned his trade as the Head of Executive Development for Orange in the UK and then later as the Head of Talent at HSBC EMEA. Charlie has since worked with scores of individuals and teams across the globe, helping deliver significant improvements in performance and results. Charlie is the co-founder and MD of two further organizations that are dedicated to enhancing leadership attitude, ability and culture: The Business Coaching Academy and Leading Energy Profile.

⊕ www.thebcacademy.com

Printed in Great Britain
by Amazon

71700888R00251